1001 DESIGNS FOR WHITTLING AND WOODCARVING

E. J. TANGERMAN

BONANZA BOOKS · NEW YORK

To Molly, who for almost half a century has
understood and pardoned my chips and dust,
absent-mindedness, elation or irritability, tinted my
productions, rendered advice when asked, and faced
uncomplaining the endless problems that beset the
helpmates of whittlers and woodcarvers—and through
her to those helpmates, as well as to those carvers
who have read and used my books—and told me so.
They have taught me more than I can ever teach
them.

This edition is published by Bonanza Books,
distributed by Crown Publishers, Inc.,
by arrangement with McGraw-Hill Book Company.
      d   e   f   g   h
BONANZA 1979 EDITION
Manufactured in the United States of America

Library of Congress Cataloging in Publication Data

Tangerman, Elmer John, 1907-
    1001 designs for whittling and woodcarving.

    Includes index.
    1. Wood-carving. 2. Design, Decorative. I. Title.
TT199.7.T37 1979   736'.4   79-17880
ISBN 0-517-29408-7

Also written by E. J. Tangerman
THE MODERN BOOK OF WHITTLING AND WOODCARVING
HORIZONS REGAINED
THE WOODCARVING MERIT BADGE
DESIGN AND FIGURE CARVING
THINGS TO DO WITH A POCKET KNIFE
WHITTLING AND WOODCARVING

CONTENTS

Let Me Say at the Outset . . .   1

Christmas Ornaments for Fun or Profit
Silhouettes Are the Key to Success   2

Molds for Butter and Cookies
Intaglio Designs Are Easy Exercises   5

Chip Carving: Ancient and
International
Interest Is Reviving in This Craft   8

Instruments and Other Noisemakers
Percussion, Reed, Wind and String   12

You Can Whittle Toys
Some Old, Some New, Some Exotic   16

Stage Properties Can Be Whittled
How to Help Your Local Theater   25

Twenty Transportation Silhouettes
Nostalgic Outlines for Decoration   26

How to Solve Knotty Problems
Sometimes the Knots Can Be Carved   29

Weathervanes, Wind Toys and Signs
From Our Past, Simple but Graphic   32

Love Spoons from Wales and
Elsewhere
Scandinavia, Germany, Mexico, Spain   38

The Carved Spanish Colonial Door
Traditional Revival Makes These
Modern   43

A Whale of a Carving Project
Seagoing Mammals Provide Designs   44

A Tropical Fish Mobile
Whittling and Balancing Sixteen Woods   46

With Animals, the Silhouette is the
Key
Low-relief, Applique, Intarsia   51

Primitive—And Crude
Cuna (San Blas) Indians Carve for Utility   54

Primitive—But Not Crude
Indian Carvings Are Strong, Original   57

African Animals—Typical & Atypical
Great Diversity Characterizes Tribal
Designs   60

Misinterpretations Can Be Fun
Make Several Pieces from One Blank   63

Some Selected Small Animals
Detail Suits Size and Shape   66

Common Animals Uncommonly
Carved
A Gallimaufry of Fauna and Ideas   68

The Descent from Ararat
Animals in Low Relief—How They Grew   72

Contrast in Bird Carving
No Feathers vs. Almost Every One   74

Cuckoo Clocks Are a Tradition
Design Elements Standardized   77

Questions I Wish You Hadn't Asked   79

A Potpourri of Panels about People
Carvers Preserve National Traditions   80

Pierced Carving in Japan
Intricate Panels Typify a Traditional
Craft   81

Don't Forget Multipart Assemblies
Sometimes the Background Holds Parts
Together   84

Possible—A Carved Jigsaw Puzzle
Animal Panel and Furniture Blocks   87

Escher Adapted to Wood and 3-D
Intaglio and Intarsia Reinforce Low
Relief   88

Just for the Fun of It
Fifty Pieces to Carve for Pure Pleasure   94

Simplicity Builds Strength, Cuts Time
Salvadorenos Show How to Cut Corners   98

A King-Sized Chess Set
Large Pieces Help the Audience   101

Try a Mayan Motif Panel
Powerful and Different Designs from
Central America   104

Panels Can Be Challenging   109

Indians, Idols and Images
Each Culture Has Its Traditional Carved
Figures   110

Sundials—And How to Carve Them
Each Must Be Calculated for Place and
Time   115

How Much Detail Is Necessary?
Animals, Faces and a Temple Provide
Examples   122

A Face Can Be Your Fortune
How to Carve the Features   126

A Comparison of Faces and Figures
Commercial Examples Show Skill   131

Stylizing Can Strengthen Figures
Some Widely Varied Examples Make the
Point   134

Stylizing Old and New
A Study in Nonportraiture   137

Selected Figures from Central America
Native Designs Show Strength—And a
Difference   138

An Introduction to African Figures
Fewer Fetishes, More Figures, as
Tourism Takes Its Toll   144

Small Figures from the Alps
From Switzerland and Germany   150

Carvings Inspired by Folk Tales
Three Answers to "Where Do You Get
Ideas?"   154

The Pied Piper of Mittenwald
Three Panels in Tandem, and How They
Grew   157

Panels Designed from Transparencies
Projecting to Scale Provides Easy
Patterns   161

The Whimsies of Winnie Baker
Silhouette Panels Need No Titles   162

Variety Characterizes Michael
DeNike
He Carves Many Materials   164

Emil Janel's "Little People"
Why and How He Makes Them   166

How to Make Your Own Designs
Modify, Adapt or Innovate—But Try   170

So You've Been Asked to Teach
Some Hints for the Neophyte Instructor   176

Books Helpful to the Carver and
Teacher   177

A Basic Instruction Sheet for the Knife
Selection, Use and Care   180

Pointers on Sharpening and Mallets
A Roundup of Suggestions   183

Every One a Masterpiece
Five Examples of "Technical Acrobatics"
from Museums   186

Index   187

✳ Let Me Say at the Outset . . .

"With chiselled touch/The stone unhewn and cold/Becomes a living mold./The more the marble wastes/The more the statue grows." Thus wrote a poet four hundred years ago. He was also a scientist, architect and engineer, but even better known as a painter and sculptor. He was a genius—and probably the greatest artist that ever lived, Leonardo da Vinci (1452–1519). He frequently said that sculpture was the highest of the arts.

Second only to Leonardo was Michelangelo Buonarroti (1475–1564), also architect, engineer, scientist, painter and sculptor, who said, "Sculpture is the queen of the arts; the others are but handmaidens. It creates; the others merely imitate."

Longfellow, writing of Michelangelo, echoes this opinion: "Sculpture is more than painting. It is greater to raise the dead to life than to create phantoms that seem to live." Similar sentiments have been echoed by many authors. Karin Michaelis, in *Little Troll*, describes her visit to Ivan Mestrovich: ". . . the small and slender sculptor of giant heroic figures. I had seen many of his works in European museums. But when he took me around to his studio, I was surprised to see woodcarvings, in addition to the marble, clay and bronze figures I had expected. He told me in his soft, pleasant voice, that he loved to work in wood best of all. Since Donatello, I have never seen faces carved in wood with such vitality, so much humanity, and such power."

Richard Llewellyn, in *How Green Was My Valley*, writes: "I found little joy in working with iron, for it had no will of its own. A pump on the bellows, a heat blown pale, and out comes your iron like a slave, ready to be hit in any shape you please. In wood, you must work with care, and respect, and love. For wood has soul and spirit, and is not at the mercy of triflers. One slip of your chisel in carelessness or ignorance, one shave too many with your plane, and your work is ruined, and fit only for burning."

We who carve wood obviously have a rich heritage. It is an achievement to produce something of beauty and strength in wood, and more of an achievement to create something new and different. But many of us are impatient; because we come to woodcarving with known manual skill, we expect to become instant sculptors. This is usually not to be. Even Leonardo and Michelangelo spent years in study and practice before they achieved acclaim. So did Riemenschneider, Gibbons, Durer and the other greats. First they copied and learned.

This is my purpose here: to provide such help as I can to anyone interested in shaping wood into objects of beauty. I have, in previous books, detailed the fundamentals as well as I know how; it is my intention here to provide more ideas, more designs, more starting points. In the interest of providing additional examples, I have avoided step-by-step detailing on most, limiting my explanations to those steps or procedures that I feel may be different or require especial care and attention or skill. Most of the designs are new; some, however, are old and hallowed but not readily available. As in earlier books, I am not devoting myself to masterpieces "for inspiration" (and little else, as far as most of us are concerned). Instead, I will concentrate on smaller works of people all over the world who may be more gifted or inspired than we but in many cases are no better craftsmen. My search has been for ideas, not for talent; for source material, not for unattainable ideals.

As in *The Modern Book of Whittling and Woodcarving* (1973), most of the drawings are half-sized patterns, with at least two views for in-the-round pieces. They can be enlarged easily by photostat or the method of squares (see page 90). They are grouped, as far as feasible, by subject, difficulty and technique; the examples become more difficult—at least in my opinion—as you go.

So: for those of you who are impatient with the sameness of our mass-produced world, and want to express yourself, here are ideas from all over the earth, with my sincere and admiring thanks to those artists, named and unnamed, who created them. Turn the page, and you're on your own. Good luck, and happy carving!

✳ Christmas Ornaments for Fun or Profit:

Silhouettes Are the Key to Success

Christmas decorations are excellent exercises for tyro whittlers and can be first-class problems for the skilled woodcarver, depending upon the design and the detail. For at least a two-month period every year, newspapers and magazines are filled with potential patterns. People decorate for Christmas more than for any other holiday, so your products can be given as presents or sold with considerable ease. (I know several carvers whose Christmas trees have *only* whittled ornaments.) A mere silhouette, painted, is perfectly acceptable, and minor crudeness in design or execution is considered "primitive" and hence allowable.

The designs I have drawn here are less familiar ones, many of them from foreign countries, but they have the characteristic that they can be done as simple two-dimensional silhouettes, as low-relief carvings, or as fully in-the-round designs in most cases, and the amount of detail can suit your own desire or skill. And they are not shapes that will be found in the usual store displays or whacked out in plastics—at least at the time this is written.

While Germans produce all sorts of decorations for Christmas trees, other nations tend to stress the Nativity and thus produce a great many designs of the three Magi, the Holy

These ornaments are whittled from thin white pine and painted in bright colors. They can also be surface-carved or chip-carved, if preferred, to improve shadow effects, but they are logical subjects for painting so they can stand out against any background. The group at upper left includes two figures not sketched, a foreshortened owl and a jester made from shavings. The owl is a design different from most and can be made in the round and finished with curled-chip indication of the feathers, or with gouge cuts. It will also make a good desk ornament, if set on a base. The human figure is *not* Santa Claus, but a Magus wearing a crown and a long robe. He carries conventionalized fruit rather than frankincense or myrrh in the usual elaborate casket or jar.

Can be shavings

Family and the like. In the panel of drawings, the two silhouettes at upper left and the group at center right illustrate this. They come from the Philippines and were originally done in transparent capiz shell bound in brass, but they can be made of wood just as readily. Other forms of the three Magi are the modern group at center, the panel at lower right and the traditional form at left center, all from Mexico, as are the three angel patterns at center left and the tree with star at lower left. These were made in both tinplate and wood, painted. The angel with trumpet at lower right is an American Colonial design, now also appearing in Mexico, and the twin angels at the bottom can be extended to as long a decorative strip as you like, with color variations to suit your fancy. The angel just above the twins is very interesting; it is made from thin veneers or shavings, the body being a cone, and the wings and arms shaped pieces, all glued around a whittled head that can be detailed or just a painted ball.

The miscellaneous group at upper right are South European in origin and decoration, and can be used as Christmas tree ornaments, window decorations, parts of a mobile, or as pendants from light fixtures and the like. In their original form, most were thin wood, painted on both sides, but the unicorn and two of the birds were cloth and were triangular in cross-section—and were made in Taiwan. I have included them here both because of their unique design and to suggest the triangular

shape, thicker at the bottom, as an interesting variation on flat silhouettes. The three elaborate enameled birds at left bottom are carved in various shapes in Mexico and Guatemala and decorated in multiple colors, and the buck near them is a familiar Christmas ornament in Scandinavia. All are in-the-round in the original form and are made in various materials—and the buck was woven in straw!

Familiar figures also make good subjects—witness the snowman (and snowwoman) at bottom and the hobby-horse at bottom right. There are also a number of bell forms, the standard one (shown in a group of four as a decoration), the ball-shaped ones once so common for sleighbells, and the Swiss cowbell (lower left). The latter one was commonly carved from wood, so it had a deeper tone than conventional bells. It makes a complicated hollowing problem if carved in-the-round unless you make it in halves and assemble by gluing. All these figures, incidentally, should be suspended by a single thread; I prefer nylon filament glued into a tiny drilled hole. In some cases, I have indicated the approximate balance point with a small arrow; it will vary with your whittling, of course.

All these figures can be laid out easily on thin wood and sawed to shape, then cleaned up and painted, or they can be carved from a flat piece or a block. I would suggest painting them with colors, so they will be readily visible and contribute their share to the holiday cheer.

Left—These 5-in. angels were made by Donald M. Fenner, Herkimer, N.Y., of 1½-in. white pine. The head is rounded with the hair carved like a Dutch-bobbed wig, high on the forehead. The face is longer than normal and concaved slightly to accent the lips. Eyes and mouth are painted on. The song sheet is veneer. Below—Mexican painted birds and an older Russian "Father Frost," who nowadays begins to resemble our Santa Claus.

✳ Molds for Butter and Cookies:

Intaglio Designs Are Easy Exercises

In these days of oleomargarine and fast-food service, of TV dinners, vitamins, weight and cholesterol consciousness, it is surprising to find the good old-fashioned butter and cookie molds still extant. They are relics of the days of formal food; all northern European countries produced and used them: Germany (remember the pictures pressed into *Springerle*?), Denmark, Sweden, Norway, England, Wales. And, from these sources, we in America also used them, particularly among the people of English origin along the East Coast and the Pennsylvania Dutch. Nowadays, you'll find the cookie press or roller in "old-fashioned country stores" and the butter molds in gift shops (or in the luggage of travelers returning from Scandinavia; these molds are to be looked at more than used.)

Both cookie and butter molds have a peculiarity: They are usually carved in intaglio so the product has a raised design rather than an inset one. For the carver, this offers an interesting variation from the usual raised design, and patterns range from the very simple to the very complex, so some can be chosen to meet any level of skill. Some can be carved with the knife alone; others go much better with gouges and a veiner or V-tool. In every case, however, it is essential to have sloping sides on the design and a smooth finish. Many of the designs are symbolic or reminiscent of an area, but others feature coats of arms, family crests, elaborate flower or animal patterns and chip-carved variations. The best of them all are the simplest, particularly for the cookie molds, because the cookie itself is porous and does not hold detail too well.

I have drawn a number of designs from various countries and of varying degrees of complexity, as well as the more elaborate forms of butter press. Some consideration must, of course, be given to final form of the stamp before the design is laid out on wood. Cookie stamps fall into five basic forms:

1. A single stamp of some regular geometric shape, possibly enclosed by a sleeve which retains and sizes the butter pressed into the mold and can be slipped back to release the finished pat.
2. A large disk, to form the top of a large block.
3. A four-sided box with a top, all hinged together, and which produces butter cubes with designs on the five visible sides.
4. A four-sided hinged "fence" with a design in each panel, which can be closed and locked with a pin, and a top carrying a design also which fits over the closed fence.
5. Two mating plates having opposite halves of a figure which has its own silhouette, rather than a pat shape.

Most of these are made from pine or basswood, so must not be wetted, or the wood swells and makes difficulties with the fitting. (The trick is to have the butter hard enough to press in and not to stick.) The commonest is the first.

Cookie molds, on the other hand, are much more simple, because they are usually used to press the design into the hot surface of the cookie as it comes from the oven, or to press the design into the raised cookie just before it goes into the oven. Thus the simplest form of cookie stamp is just that: a block or disk, usually larger than a butter stamp, with a handle for convenience. For multiple impres-

Two cookie molds and a butter mold. That at far right is for butter pats, with sleeve, in the traditional pineapple design. The center mold, of the same design, is to press on hot ginger cookies and is about 2½ in. in diameter, of pine. The cross-hatched pattern was made not by veiner cuts, but by individual indentations. This and the left-hand mold I made for the local historical society; the left-hand one impresses its name and the shape of the peninsula on cookies over 3 in. in diameter. It is of primavera.

ENGLAND   Butter stamps

ENGLAND   Typical butter prints, made in pairs as at left, produced shaped pats

Dowel indexes in pin on mating half

SWEDEN
Two 4-part butter presses (Härjedalen)

4 faces of 1 mold

SCANDINAVIA (Three types of mold)

Separate top fits V-groove

Groove fits over adjacent side(s)

Design below

Central motif sunken, then grooved

Note: Two molds at left make blocks, that below makes pats

Mold held closed by reed strap

Staple hinge

Groove interlocks

Lock pin

Dowel

Gouge chamfers

Whittled chamfers

Turned elements

"PENNSYLVANIA DUTCH"

Center unit intaglio

Gouge work, except for rim

Toothed

Toothed

CSSC

Sunken area
Veiner lines
Chip-carve

2 flutes
Raised triangles
Veiner pattern

ENGLAND   ALSACE   ENGLAND   SICILY

WALES

ENGLAND

Intaglio face

Chip-carved
Veiner lines

6

sions, the patterns may be cut into a wood panel divided into squares which can also divide a cookie block into appropriate squares; or a rolling pin, which has the designs worked into its surface so it can be rolled over a sheet of dough or cake.

In making any design, the secret is to preserve an adequate slope on the sides of each cut so the butter or cookie will not stick in the channels. The greater the slope, the easier the parting and the less distinct the design, so a happy medium must be found. Gouge cuts, unless made with a very deep-sweep gouge, are naturally sloped on the side walls, as are V-tool cuts. But veiner cuts must not be too deep, and knife cuts must be clean-walled and without corner and bottom slivers.

This all assumes, of course, that the carvings are to be used. If the designs are made instead as decorations for a box, tray, or other object—even a ring—the sidewalls can be vertical. But, if the carving is to be used as a pattern for gingerbread men or similar figures to be converted into metal molds, due allowance must again be made for "draw." In this case, however, the pattern will usually be carved in relief, so the slope or draw allowances on vertical surfaces must be reversed. (There was a time when it was quite fashionable to have your own molds of brass or cast iron for gingerbread and cakes, or of nickel-silver for chocolate—all made from carved wooden patterns. Now, such molds for gingerbread can be purchased at places like Wil-

liamsburg, but usually they are hung on the kitchen wall rather than used.)

For patterns, and for cookie molds, a harder wood like maple or cherry will work better than pine. This is also true of butter molds made with a sleeve; apparently the denser wood has less tendency to stick. Also, in the case of the sleeved mold for butter, it is quite usual to turn the elements in a wood lathe, so that the design must be carved in end grain. This offers no particular problem, if you keep your tools sharp; in fact, it reduces the likelihood of slivers and vertical lines, since the end grain tends to break out slightly at the surface.

The same designs and principles can be applied to molds for other purposes—for jellies, aspics and other foods, plaster, plastics, soap, rubber. In such cases it is better to finish the interior with a smooth and impervious coating to prevent sticking. These intaglio designs can be made also in better woods, like mahogany or walnut, to be finished by varnishing and waxing and hung as decorations. In this case, of course, it is unnecessary to provide "draw" or slope on the sides and designs can be deeper; thus sharper shadows can be obtained.

These five-part molds produce butter blocks with designs on all four sides and top. They are compared here for size with a mold for pats. The mold below is a complex fitting and hinging job, which I've found better for display than for use.

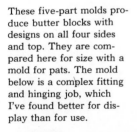

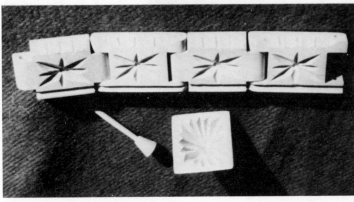

❋ Chip Carving: Ancient and International:

Interest Is Reviving in This Simple Craft

Chip carving seems to have been a spontaneous expression of man's desire to express his appreciation of utilitarian objects by decorating them. It antedates more formal carving and seems to have been developed independently in many areas. It has been familiar for a thousand years or so in Europe, particularly in Holland, Germany and Scandinavia; it was in fact called "Friesland" or "Friesian" carving because of its prevalence in that area of the Netherlands. The Pennsylvania Dutch brought it to the United States, as they did its companion, so-called "tramp carving." Russian peasants used it on their mangle boards a hundred years ago at least. And Captain Cook saw it in the South Pacific in areas where the white man had never been before.

Chip carving is essentially geometric and based on a triangle with a deeper cut apex. It is a form of surface decoration—so the triangles can be arranged in patterns, given more elongated shapes, made arcuate, converted into and interspersed with special shapes or even worked into quite sophisticated pictures. But in every case, the form is essentially a variation of the triangle and the individual cut is a V-groove of some sort. Loose use of the term by some antique hounds for other kinds of peasant carving or folk art is in error, just as is calling it tramp carving, of which I will show an example later.

In many respects, chip carving is like rug weaving; it is an exercise in patience because it consists of the repetition of basically the same forms. It must be sharp and neat and without corner splinters, so tools must be kept sharp and must be carefully handled, and grain direction must be kept constantly in mind. Chisels can be used, of course, but on most woods a stiff-bladed knife is faster and easier. Any blade with a point can be used, but if a great deal of surface is to be covered, it is advisable to buy or make two special blades like those sketched. They can be ground from

The pipe rack below, 3½ × 7 × 17½ in., was made as a combined stage property and chip-carving piece. On it, I combined a number of basic designs, plus an eagle and the elaborate compartment lid. The canoe at far left is African, shows chip carving combined with squares cut through a dark finish on light wood.

Skew Splitting

CHIP-CARVING KNIVES — IN USE

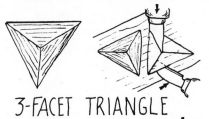

3-FACET TRIANGLE

CURVED or ARCUATE FIGURE
Requires movement of skew

↑SIMPLE-TRIANGLE PATTERNS   3-FACET↓

SIMPLE ARCUATE TRIANGLES

Based on 6-pointed star

QUARTER PATTERNS   Use as background

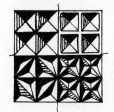
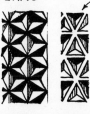
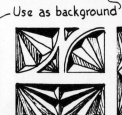

A FRAME CORNER

Background fluted or stamped

EAGLE

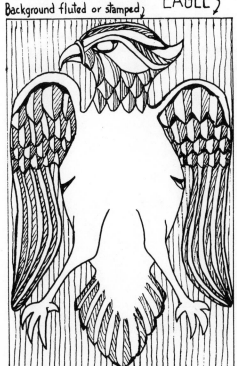

FRAME
CORNER

FIGHTING COCKS — CHIP-CARVED MOTIFS — MANDARIN HEAD

After Fred
Von Hoefer

9

old sawblades or other tempered steel and equipped with handles that leave only a short length of blade exposed. The skew-shaped blade is pushed down into the wood for $1/16$ to $1/8$ inch, with its point at the apex of the triangle to be cut, then rocked back until the edge reaches the base of the triangle. It is lifted out and reinserted at the same point, but this time aligned with the opposite side of the triangle and the cut repeated. The splitting knife is used to cut out the wedge-shaped chip thus formed. This will leave an incised triangle, deeper at the apex and reaching the surface along the base line. And so on, ad infinitum. Each triangle should take only three cuts if done properly. Only when elaborate whorls and other forms are carved is the skew-shaped blade moved along during a cut. And only when flowers or other breaks in the design are added is it necessary to use other tools, then usually only a veiner.

If the skew blade is ground with an included angle of 60 degrees, then driven vertically into the wood, it will cut a line about 30 degrees with the surface. The splitting knife can be held at this same angle, so cut triangles are uniform in depth—which is important. Chip carving should not be deep.

The second design to try is a larger triangle, about the width of the skew blade, roughly $1/2$ inch on a side. Draw from each corner a line to the center, and cut the three small triangles thus produced, inserting the skew knife at the center for each parting cut. This will produce a triangle with a depressed center. (The same technique can be used for a square or a hexagon shape.) Such triangles are the basis for a number of square designs, some of which are shown on boxes illustrated here. The third design, a rosette, is produced by drawing a circle, then dividing the circumference into 15-degree segments. Using each of the circumference points as a center in turn, and the same radius, draw arcs from the points on the circumference to the center. Every other one will be the ridge between arcuate triangles, the alternates the valleys of triangles. Draw your splitting knife along the valley lines, varying depth from nothing at the center to $1/8$ in. at the edge, then slice in at an angle from the ridge line on each side, thus removing an arcuate triangle. It requires a sharp edge and

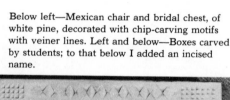

Below left—Mexican chair and bridal chest, of white pine, decorated with chip-carving motifs with veiner lines. Left and below—Boxes carved by students; to that below I added an incised name.

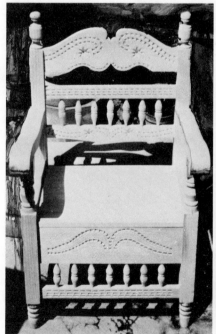

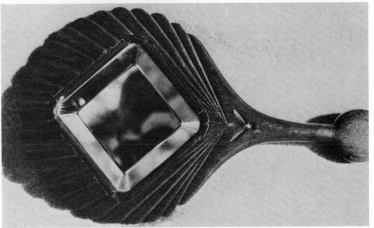

Top left—Tramp-carved picture frame, made in the late 1800s by Allen Helmer. The picture is sheet copper, by Lura Blossom. Tramp carving, reputedly done by tramps in return for hot meals, is simply stacks of thin-wood rectangles of diminishing size, each notched along the edges. This frame is more elaborate than most (he was no tramp), having light and dark sections and a combination of rectangular pyramids at the corners and elongated ones fitting the sides. Above—Walnut hand mirror, made by Frank Cole about 1920, another example of simple design and technique that works out to a dramatic piece. Left middle—A Chinese box with extremely simple surface patterns. A few lines each suggest flowers, leaves, harbor scenes with sampans. While the design takes skill, the technique is quite simple. Left—Toast tongs graduated in difficulty. The upper one is a three-piece assembly, made of tongue depressers and an end block, glued and bradded. The middle one is sections of bamboo, utilizing the greater thickness of the joint to produce the mating wedges, which are riveted together. The bottom one is one piece, of teak, and has simple decoration of flowers and vines on the sides. These can be done with chip carving and added veiner lines.

some care, because you are crossing grain, but the resulting wheel has more freedom and movement than the usual geometric pattern.

Chip carving is largely variations of these three patterns, singly or combined to fit an area. I have shown a number of the variations in the pipe rack, which I made for a Revolutionary War play in 1949, at the same time including as many chip-carving patterns as I could find space for conveniently. The basic patterns, however, have been standard for several hundred years at least—I showed as many as I could then recall in *Design and*

Figure Carving in 1939 and have repeated them here merely for convenience.

I have also included on this page several designs closely allied to chip carving, of which tramp carving is currently most in the public eye. It is an extremely simple technique—merely a series of notches around the edges of rectangles of diminishing size stacked into a pyramid. The wood was orange crates or cigar boxes (then mahogany) and the work reputedly done by tramps in return for a handout. The example I have pictured was done, however, by a solid citizen.

✳ Instruments—And Other Noisemakers:

Percussion, Reed, Wind and String

Man has, for millennia, made instruments of one kind or another from wood, some simply carved to shape, but many decorated. Some are just noisemakers to our sophisticated ears—and some, like the drum, are primarily devices for producing a rhythm rather than a variety of musical tones. The drum, perhaps the oldest of instruments, undoubtedly grew out of the observation that a hollow log, when pounded, will make a resonant sound, and some native groups still make them that way, perhaps adding a skin head so the pounding can be more subtle. Others make drums by hollowing the log, both with tools and with controlled fire—just as they make dugout canoes and caskets. While African native drums have become most familiar to us through story and our own African-derived population, hollow log drums are still used in remote areas of Central America and the South Pacific, as a means of communication as well as a source of music. A more modern variant is the wooden bell, often incorporating one or more clappers, as in Switzerland and Thailand. Another lineal derivative is the marimba, which apparently originated both in Southeast Asia and in Africa and was originally just a series of wooden bars having different tones. This same basic instrument is represented in the quite sophisticated modern marimbas in Guatemala, for example, as well as the xylophone.

Another simple instrument, again made and used all over the world, is the horn. It probably originated as an actual animal horn; we have ancient surface-carved examples. In the same family are reed pipes and flutes, as well as whistles. (The Sakai, a very primitive tribe in the Malay peninsula, and the Basques, not at all primitive, still make and play the nose flute—which to me seems a hard way to make music.) But we also have the Jewish shofar, Arab flutes, Balkan shepherd's pipes, Indian flutes, oboes, bassoons, and the Swiss alphorn, all made of wood, or largely so. Elaborately chip-carved wooden pipes are a popular Balkan tourist item, as are Arab and Indian flutes, carved with more conventional designs. The alphorn, perhaps man's largest musical instrument after the pipe organ (which once also had pipes of wood—the Bamboo Organ, outside Manila, still does), ranges from 12 to 20 feet long and is audible for more than three miles in the Alps. It is used to call cattle and to calm them in storms and at milking time, but is now disappearing; there are fewer than twenty makers left. It is made from a fir tree that has been bent naturally to the right angle by snow. This is split lengthwise, hollowed out and polished before reassembly with natural skelp, then varnished until it is waterproof. Ornamentation is usually through burned-in designs, and it has a separate whittled mouthpiece. Shaping alone takes seventy to three hundred hours. A skilled player can produce several notes—which so impressed Brahms that he took down a simple melody that he

Left—High in the mountains of northern Mexico, the Tarahumara Indians, primitive and inaccessible until recently, built a reputation for their endurance as long-distance runners and for their violins. This one, which plays quite well despite lack of varnish or soundpost, I bought for $6 late in the sixties, intending to surface-carve it. It was complete with bow and strings.

Left—Wooden temple bell from Thailand, in teak, with outside clappers. Below—Twin Balkan pipes, with chip-carved decoration.

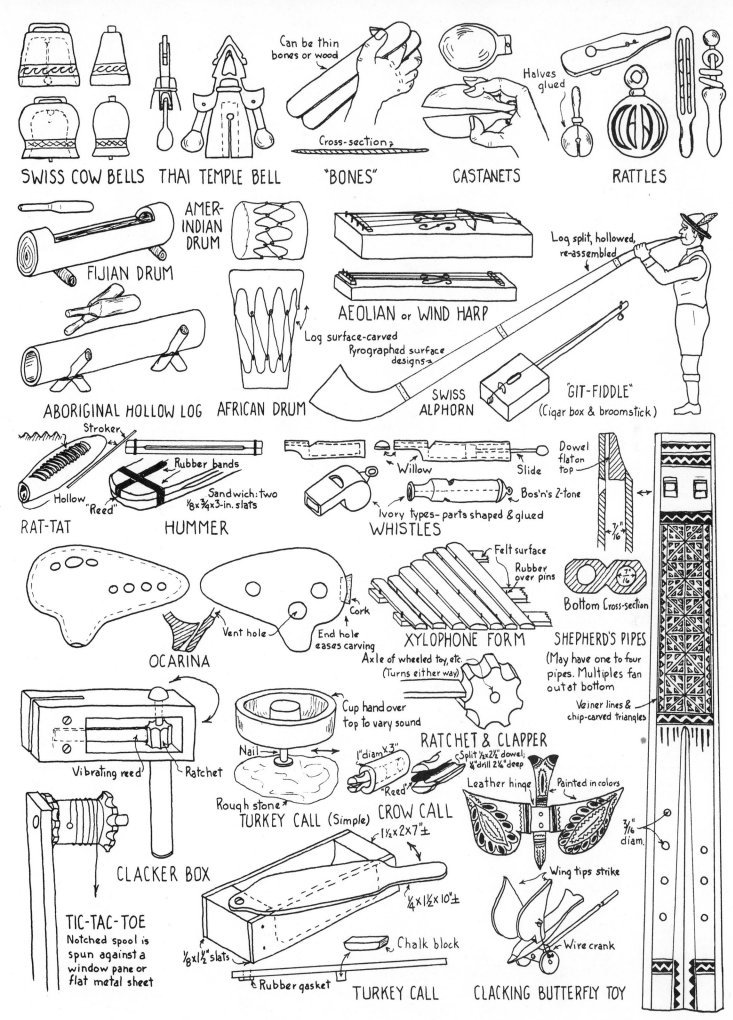

SWISS COW BELLS

THAI TEMPLE BELL

"BONES"

Can be thin bones or wood

Cross-section

CASTANETS

Halves glued

RATTLES

AMER-INDIAN DRUM

FIJIAN DRUM

ABORIGINAL HOLLOW LOG

AFRICAN DRUM

Log surface-carved Pyrographed surface designs

AEOLIAN or WIND HARP

Log split, hollowed, re-assembled

SWISS ALPHORN

"GIT-FIDDLE" (Cigar box & broomstick)

RAT-TAT

Stroker

Hollow

"Reed"

HUMMER

Rubber bands

Sandwich: two 1/8 x 3/4 x 3-in. slats

Willow

Slide

Bos'n's 2-tone

Ivory types—parts shaped & glued

WHISTLES

Dowel flat on top

7/16"

1/16"

Bottom Cross-section

OCARINA

Vent hole

End hole eases carving

Cork

Felt surface

Rubber over pins

XYLOPHONE FORM

SHEPHERD'S PIPES

(May have one to four pipes. Multiples fan out at bottom

Veiner lines & chip-carved triangles

Axle of wheeled toy, etc. (Turns either way)

CLACKER BOX

Vibrating reed

Ratchet

Cup hand over top to vary sound

Nail

Rough stone

TURKEY CALL (Simple)

1"diam×3"

"Reed"

CROW CALL

RATCHET & CLAPPER

Split 1/2 x 2 1/2 dowel; 1/4"drill 2 1/4"deep

Leather hinge

Painted in colors

3/16" diam.

Wing tips strike

Wire crank

TIC-TAC-TOE

Notched spool is spun against a window pane or flat metal sheet

1 1/2 x 2 x 7"±

1/4 x 1 1/2 x 10"±

1/8 x 1 1/2" slats

Chalk block

Rubber gasket

TURKEY CALL

CLACKING BUTTERFLY TOY

heard on Mount Rigi and incorporated it in his First Symphony. But *The New York Times* reported in mid-1975 that a senior research engineer for a plastics manufacturer in Maumee, Ohio, has produced one of fiberglass which he plays in demonstration.

In addition to the instruments and noisemakers that I have sketched or shall mention here, there are a great many which involve considerable amounts of metal. An example is the kalimba, or African thumb piano, which has reeds of hammered iron, toned to a crude scale. The wooden body is usually decorated by burning or with simple carved designs. There are also an endless number of pipes and flutes, whistles, bird calls and decoy devices, specialized for local use or made in a local tradition, some for a utilitarian purpose, some as toys for children. Among them are rattles for babies and witch doctors, some merely a ring on a rod between collars, others utilizing the ball-in-a-cage. One of the interesting variants is the rhythm device known as "bones" among blacks. They may actually be bone, but can be hard wood, whittled to the general shape of a tongue depresser, but thicker in the middle and thinned at the ends. They are held loosely between the fingers as shown, and operated by timed rapid rotary shaking of the hand. Spanish castanets are similar, but more elaborate and harder to make.

Clapping and buzzing sounds are also produced by a number of toys. An oldie is the tic-tac-toe, which we made for Halloween. It is just a notched spool that is rotated against a neighbor's window to make an unearthly clatter. The same principle becomes the ratchet and clapper, which has been incorporated in all kinds of wheeled toys. Flutes are cut in a cylinder of a hard durable wood like birch or maple, and the cylinder caused to rotate against a projecting thin vibrating reed or clapper. One virtue of the device is that it can be rotated in either direction, and the reed striking the ratchet as it slips off a tooth gives a very satisfactory clack. The Russians have produced an alternative—a butterfly on wheels which carry wire cranks to operate hinged wooden wings. The wing tips strike in each cycle, making a sound very similar to that of a ratchet.

Another familiar device in the same family is the clacker box, in which the ratchet and reed are incorporated in a block containing a long slot. The axle, a dowel, goes through the end of the box opposite the solid part, so the assembly becomes a whirligig when rotated. The block can be carved or decorated, and has a sawed slot at one end in which the reed is clamped by woodscrews. The reed can be either wood or thin metal. This is also a witch doctor's device in some remote areas, and historically was a fire alarm.

In effect a ratchet rolled out flat, the rat-tat can be made of a dried gourd or a hollow thin-walled box with notches evenly spaced along one edge. If this rack is stroked with a piece of dowel, it produces a resonating rattle.

Turkey calls also operate through vibration, but in this case, the vibration is so rapid that it becomes a buzz. The simplest is a hand-sized whittled cup with the center left in so a nail can be driven in. When the nail head is rubbed over a suitable stone, the cup resonates, and sound can be varied slightly by changing the grip or the rubbing speed. The conventional turkey call is an open box with thin slats on the sides. We made ours by hollowing out one side of a piece roughly $1\frac{1}{2} \times 2$ inches and about 7 inches long. This leaves strong ends in the box, to one of which is pivoted a paddle with a rubber gasket to insulate it from the box. The paddle has on its bottom side at about the middle a small block which is chalked to create a vibration when it rubs the sides as the paddle is moved laterally across the open side of the box. But who calls wild turkeys anymore?

All of our modern brass whistles and pipes were originally of wood or some similar material. Sailors made bosun's pipes out of turned or whittled walrus ivory, as well as the little round whistle containing a pea or pebble that traffic police use. They are more complicated to make than the familiar willow whistle (even the one incorporating a slide), but also longer lasting. A much more simple wind device is

Left—The buzzer, a Halloween toy, is made from a spool notched on the rim and put on a spindle. It is spun against a window, door panel, or other vibratory surface. Below—Ocarina of the basic shape, with end plug. Note fingerhold positions.

the hummer, which we made by cutting a tongue depressor in half. One side of each section was thinned slightly—less than $1/16$ inch—to leave a central hollow. One rubber band (a wide one) was snapped over one segment endwise, and a couple of others held the assembly together as a sandwich. Thus a portion of the first and wide band became a reed and would produce a humming sound when you blew through. The reed can also be a sturdy grass leaf or reed.

Another wind whistle is the crow call—just a wooden tube with a two-part bit in the end. This mouthpiece is a $1/2$-inch dowel, drilled most of the way up with a $1/4$-inch center hole (before it is split). The remaining solid portion is thinned to turn wedges at the outer end and a thin piece of metal (steel shim stock, for example) or plastic (a section of playing card) put in for a reed which vibrates against the tapered section when blown. The sound is not pleasant, but it does draw crows.

Balkan and Indian pipes are essentially elaborate whistles, with holes for the fingers so several notes may be played. The Indian pipe is usually a turned and drilled piece, the sound being produced by a change in hole diameter. It is carved with a floral design in low relief. The Balkan pipe, on the other hand, can handle quite elaborate tunes, because it can have as many as four different pipes cut from the same block and radiating from the mouthpiece. Traditional trim for this piece is chip carving, and it has a whistle mouthpiece made by flattening one side of a dowel section and gluing it in a drilled hole. Another instrument, now usually in pottery or plastic, is the ocarina. This is hard to hollow out unless it is split and reassembled, like the alphorn, but you can hollow it with gouges by drilling a large hole at the end which is later plugged. Hole location and size, as well as wall thickness, are critical, and have been worked out during centuries of use, and to play the "sweet potato" takes longer to learn than does the harmonica.

You may have scraps around from which you can produce a marimba of sorts. The bars should be a hard, dense wood that will resonate when struck with a wooden knocker—a 1-inch ball on the end of a $1/8$-inch dowel or withe. Bars are tuned by shortening, and are mounted on felt-covered slats so they can vibrate independently. Guatemalan Indians make big ones with gourds and carved-wood boxes below them for resonators, played by as many as three men simultaneously, but that design and construction is beyond our present scope, as are violins, dulcimers, guitars, oboes and bassoons, all rather specialized and more nearly cabinetmaking than carving. If you wish to try a stringed instrument, make a cigar box fiddle, which can be a great deal of fun for informal songfests. All you need is a wooden cigar box and a broomstick. The stick is passed through a hole in one end and fastened at the other. The top of the box may be drilled as sketched and a piece of dowel glued in under the bridge to act as a soundpost. Both bridge and tuning peg are whittled from maple or birch. The bridge, as you might assume, is like a violin bridge, a piece of $1/8 \times 3/4 \times 1 1/4$-inch wood with the grain vertical. It is rounded slightly on top and the center is whittled away at the bottom edge to leave two stubby legs that contact the top of the cigar box. Incidentally, the stem of the tuning peg should have a slight taper, as should the hole (ream it a little with file or a long-point knife at the bottom), so the peg, as it wears in, can still be pushed up to fit tightly. You can add more strings if you wish.

A very pleasant instrument—and one very little known outside of poems—is the Aeolian or wind harp. It is advisable only if your house enjoys frequent light breezes, and is designed to fit in an open window under the sash—as does an air conditioner. The box should have solid ends of a good, hard wood like maple, its length to fit the window width, its thickness 2 to 3 inches, and its width 4 to 6 inches. The sides, bottom and top are thin wood $1/8$ inch or so thick, well varnished to prevent warping under sun and dampness, before assembly. The top can have the conventional violin S-holes cut in it, flanking the center line. On one end, a block is mounted, with nails or pins to hold one end of each of the four strings, and on the other, holes are drilled for a tight fit on violin pegs or guitar pins (obtainable at a good music store). The guitar pegs require a key for tightening, so be sure you get that too. Violin or guitar strings are stretched from end to end and tuned to an enjoyable chord. Then the assembly is set in the window frame, with the window open just enough to clear it. Wind blowing through the window opening will vibrate the strings and make a continuous chord, rising and fading in volume as the wind changes. These instruments were a favorite of the otherwise austere Shakers a hundred years ago.

✳ You Can Whittle Toys:

Some Old, Some New, Some Exotic

Before TV, radio, plastics and devalued money, when I was a kid, we had to make our own entertainment between chores. Dads or uncles would produce a willow whistle or two, between *their* chores—but you were expected to produce duplicates on your own. And when neighbor kids came up with a new toy, you had to copy that as well. (If you were the eldest child, you also had the added chore of reproducing your prototypes for the younger fry.) Of course, you had your own knife, and you were instructed at what would now be considered a dangerous age in how to use hand tools, so hoops, sleds, snow shovels, tops and scooters (a 2× 4 × 30-inch board with skate wheels front and rear and a T-handle extending up from the front) were produced as needed from scraps. And enjoyed

doubly—both in the making and in the using. And cared for—because you knew the work involved in producing them. This is still the way it is in "less developed" countries, by the way. Hoops, tops, mumblety-peg and other "ancient" toys are still popular there, where canned entertainment and "boughten" toys are still thankfully rare.

In the sketches I have drawn a few of the things we made for ourselves, plus a few I wish I'd known about. They range from very simple toys like the dart, roarer and bull roarer to the quite elaborate ones like the dancer, pit sawyer and chopper. Some originated in other countries, like the jumping peg (called the "magic cricket bat" in England), the *bilboquet* (from the court of royal France), the *gazinta* (made by Eskimos from walrus ivory), and the rope climber and articulated Santa Claus (current German items).

The whip dart is perhaps the simplest of toys—or was—because it was made from a scrap of cedar shingle, nowadays hard to find. Taper the shingle toward the thicker end, and round it there to reduce the likelihood of

Below—Back-diver is a variant of the woodchopper. Wire must be stiff enough to hold weight beyond vertical; I used a coat hanger. Bottom right—Dancer also requires a coat-hanger wire for support, and a small block on the paddle to hold it rigid. Joints should be loose enough to flop. Right—Dart is thrown with a withe or dowel which is stiff enough to add spring to wrist whip. String loop catches in dart notch.

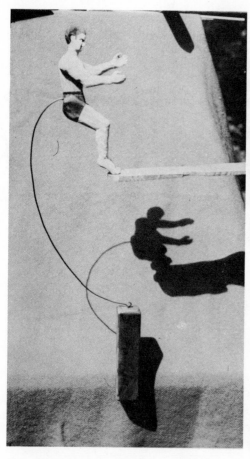

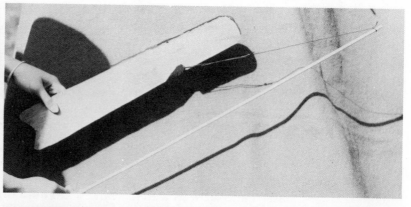

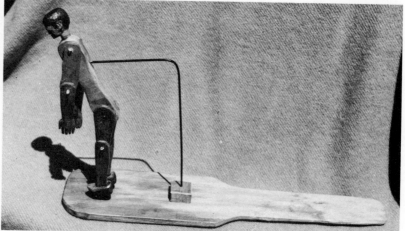

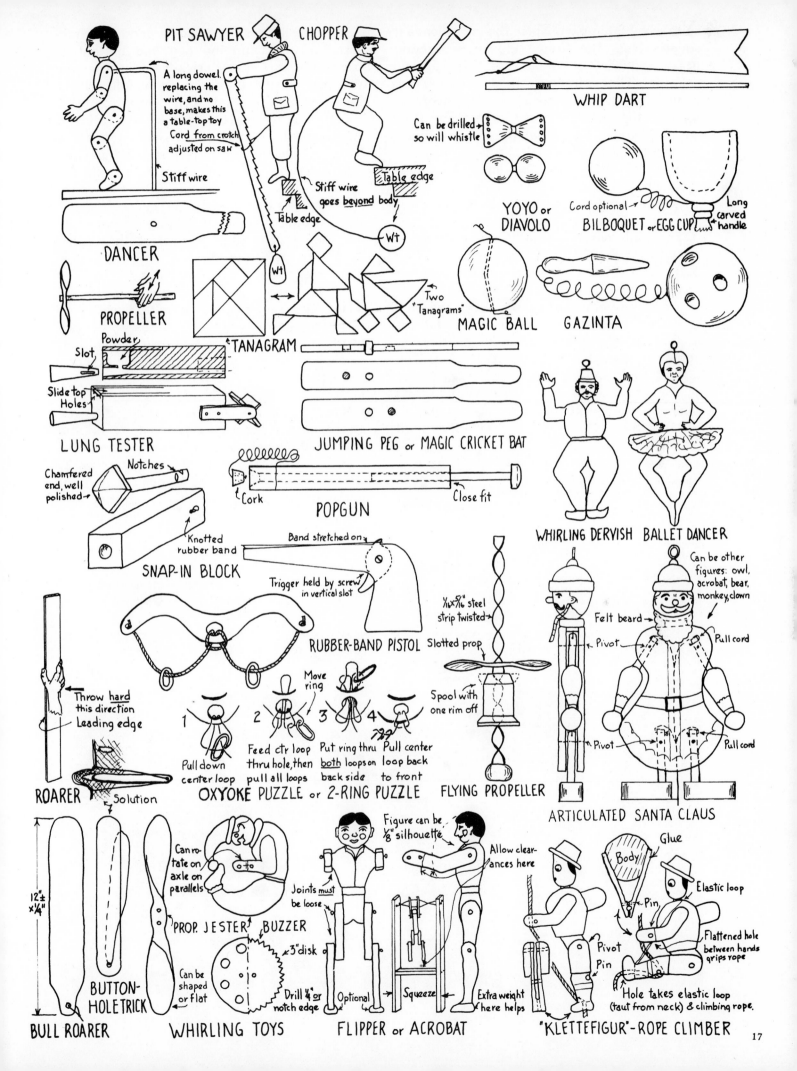

DANCER

PIT SAWYER CHOPPER

A long dowel replacing the wire, and no base, makes this a table-top toy

Cord from crotch adjusted on saw

Stiff wire

Table edge

Stiff wire goes beyond body

Table edge

Wt

Wt

WHIP DART

Can be drilled so will whistle

YOYO or DIAVOLO

Cord optional

BILBOQUET or EGG CUP

Long carved handle

PROPELLER

TANAGRAM

Two "Tanagrams"

MAGIC BALL

GAZINTA

Powder

Slot

Slide top Holes

LUNG TESTER

JUMPING PEG or MAGIC CRICKET BAT

WHIRLING DERVISH BALLET DANCER

Chamfered end, well polished

Notches

Cork

Close fit

POPGUN

Knotted rubber band

SNAP-IN BLOCK

Band stretched on

Trigger held by screw in vertical slot

RUBBER-BAND PISTOL

$\frac{1}{16}$ x $\frac{5}{16}$" steel strip twisted

Slotted prop

Spool with one rim off

FLYING PROPELLER

Can be other figures: owl, acrobat, bear, monkey, clown

Felt beard

Pivot

Pull cord

Pivot

Pull cord

ARTICULATED SANTA CLAUS

Throw hard this direction
Leading edge

ROARER

Solution

Move ring

1 Pull down center loop

2 Feed ctr loop thru hole, then pull all loops

3 Put ring thru both loops on back side

4 Pull center loop back to front

OXYOKE PUZZLE or 2-RING PUZZLE

12" ± x $\frac{1}{4}$"

BUTTON-HOLE TRICK

Can rotate on axle on parallels

PROP. JESTER BUZZER

Can be shaped or flat

3" disk

Drill $\frac{1}{4}$" or notch edge

BULL ROARER WHIRLING TOYS

Figure can be $\frac{1}{8}$" silhouette

Joints must be loose

Allow clearances here

Optional

Squeeze

Extra weight here helps

FLIPPER or ACROBAT

Glue

Body

Elastic loop

Pivot Pin

Pin

Flattened hole between hands grips rope

Hole takes elastic loop (taut from neck) & climbing rope.

"KLETTEFIGUR"-ROPE CLIMBER

17

splintering on impact. Notch the tail or leave it square. Near the front end, cut a rounded notch and sand it to be sure there are no splinters. That completes the dart, unless you want to go modern and add a wing near the front so the dart becomes a monoplane. The dart is thrown with a "whip," a 2-foot pliant withe or dowel with a short string ending in a loop on the outer end. The dart is hooked in the loop and launched by the spring in the stick plus whatever wrist action the thrower can add.

The bull roarer is simply a short-handled paddle of any $1/2 \times 3 \times 12$-inch wood. A string in the hole at one end leads to a groove at one end of a twirling stick about 18 inches long, or to a wire swivel nailed on top. When the stick is given a circular motion, the paddle follows at the end of the string, meantime rotating about its own axis to make the noise. The faster it rotates, the louder the bull. The roarer is the same idea, but is thrown by hand sidewise to make it rotate on its own axis. It can be made from a piece of a venetian blind slat or other thin wood.

Tongue depressors make a good base material for the jumping peg and buttonhole tricks. Called a magic cricket bat in England, the peg is just a miniature paddle with a handle narrow enough so it can be rotated a half turn easily between thumb and forefinger. As shown in the drawing, the bat has one through hole in which a peg is glued and two fake holes, one on each side of the paddle and on opposite sides of the peg. After the viewer sees the hole on one side, the operator says a magic word or two while waving the bat in the air, meantime turning it over so the second "hole" jumps to the opposite side of the peg. This is an easy trick to make and learn, but also fairly easy for the viewer to figure out. There are variants like a paddle with two through holes and two blind ones, so the peg can be moved from one real hole to the other, and a paddle with three spots on one side and two on the other. You can make up your own pattern.

The buttonhole trick is a piece of tongue depressor or other stick with a hole at one end and small enough to slip through a buttonhole on a man's coat. (A flat ice-cream stick works well too.) A loop of string through the hole is not quite long enough to pass over the opposite end, even when drawn taut. To put it in, you pull an edge of the victim's coat through the loop until the *free* end of the wood will enter the buttonhole, then pull the wood on through. When he tries to reverse the process, he will have problems—particularly if you put it

Below—Roarer is a $1/2 \times 2$-in. slat, held as shown, and thrown hard with a wrist twist to make it whirl on its own axis.
Right—Snap-in block, shown as two parts and ready to snap. The rubberband through the side and the notches on the pin are merely window dressing; the block is snapped in by pressure between thumb and forefinger on the tapered end. Below right—Two articulated toys from Germany, one a familiar pull-string arrangement, except that it has both front and back panels so pull strings are not exposed. It is small in size, for a tree or doorway, about 4 inches overall. The 3-inch climbers require much more elaborate fitting, to be sure the string is gripped between the hands until they are pushed up as the body straightens. Study the diagram carefully.

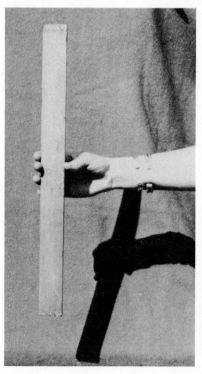

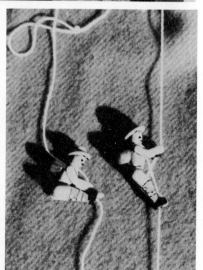

through the buttonhole in his lapel, which is hard to see with the coat on.

The tanagram is another oldie, probably Chinese in origin. It is simply a square of thin wood, cut into seven pieces as sketched. The pieces can be rearranged into dozens of little pictures; there are even books of such arrangements, I'm told. The game is to use all seven pieces in each figure.

Still another simple whittling is the propeller, which came into fashion with the airplane in the 1910s and 1920s. It can be fastened to the end of a dowel, and if properly proportioned, will lift the dowel a short distance when the dowel is whirled between the hands and released. It can also be drilled with two holes at the axis and set on headless brads on the end of the dowel so it can fly off; lifting only its own weight, it will go farther. A loop of string can be threaded through the holes as an alternate, and is twisted with the loop ends over the thumbs. A third alternative is to slot the axis so the propeller can be fed over a steel or brass strip twisted into a regular spiral. If the spiral is held in one hand and a spool beneath the prop pushed up rapidly with the other, the propeller will fly off and end a good distance. (Incidentally, watch out for the eyes when using these toys!)

Upper left—Dancing and drummer bears from U.S.S.R. Both the drummer's arms and one leg of the dancer are pivoted and have strings from back of the pivots (to make short levers) extending through holes in the board to a center weight. When the toy is swung in a horizontal circle (as in spreading grease in a frypan), the strings are pulled in turn, to move the limbs. Left—Pecking chickens from Sweden are similar actuated, pecking in turn. See sketch for details. Bottom center—A tricky hook—we called it "the impossible" in the machine shop where I first saw it—relies on the twisting movement of an ordinary pants belt to counteract its normal tendency simply to fall down. It will work only with a belt, balanced correctly in a close slot, at about 45 degrees. Outer shape is unimportant. Right—Stick horse (called "cockhorse" in England) should be adjusted to the age of the child. Upper head is perhaps too elaborate, so a simpler alternate is shown also.

Other fairly simple flat toys are the whirling dervish and ballet dancer, which can be silhouettes, low relief, or even in-the-round carvings. They are suspended from a string so that if twisted, or blown by the wind, they will rotate. The jester and the buzzer (lower left in sketches) are designed to be rotated by a twisted loop of string, as described above for the propeller. Teeth cut in the rim of the buzzer disk will make a buzzing noise, as will holes drilled through near the periphery. The jester, alternately, can be mounted on a piece of dowel so it will roll down a pair of sloped parallel bars.

Among easy three-dimensional pieces are the ox-yoke puzzle, which is explained by the diagrams, and the snap-in block. The latter is a trick, because the "snap" is imparted by

19

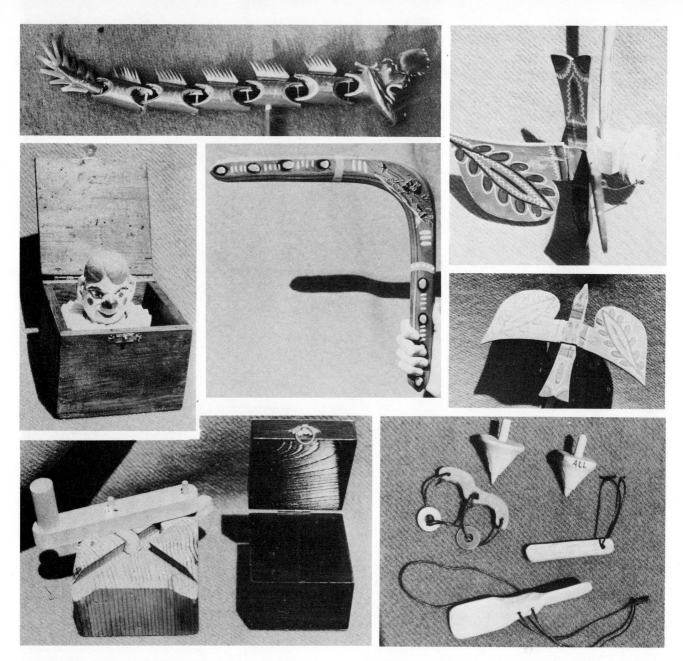

Top left—Chinese dragon, of bamboo pieces articulated, has a sinuous movement. Spines are thin wood glued on, pom-poms silk on small springs. Head is quite well carved, and the whole is enameled red with gold trim. Top right—U.S.S.R. butterfly is sketched in chapter on instruments (page 13) because wings clap together noisily when it moves. Wings and body are whittled, decorations painted. Wing hinges are leather. Center—Australian boomerang in a modern plywood version. It is thrown as shown, vertically rather than horizontally, with a sharp wrist snap and well above the horizontal. Decorations are painted. Left center—Size of this jack-in-the-box was dictated by the spring available. Head and ruff are whittled from pine and painted. Left—The zephyr grinder at left is a quite sophisticated geometric toy and somewhat of a cabinetmaker's trick. Next to it is the fly smasher or nothing box—a box in everything but insides. Right—Familiar whittled toys, including the oxyoke and buttonhole puzzles, the propeller and the tops whittled from spools.

squeezing the tapered end of the head between thumb and forefinger, so the plunger snaps into the hole. However, the end of the plunger has a notch, or even two, in apparently strategic locations, and a piece of rubberband is inserted through a small drilled hole at the inner end, so your victim thinks you are inserting the plunger and hooking the band, then drawing it back so the band will pull the plunger in. The rubberband pistol also makes use of the same device—but this time legitimately. In this instance, the band is stretched between the barrel tip and the firing pin. When the trigger is pulled, the inner end of the band slips off the pin. The only problem in making this toy is cutting a smooth-walled slot through the butt so the trigger can be inserted and held by a screw pivot.

In the same category is the lung tester, an assembly of a whittled box with a propeller (made of ice-cream sticks) pivoted on brads in arms at one end. At the other is a short mouthpiece of metal or wood, so you can blow through the block and rotate the propeller. However, the block is really a box, with a slide cover on top, into which flour or talcum powder is put. The mouthpiece has a slot which can be mated with the hole in the bottom of the powder box, and there are tiny holes under the lid through which the resulting pressure will blow powder. (Don't forget the mark on the mouthpiece, so *you* know when the slot is in line with the hole!) The routine is this: You mismate the mouthpiece and blow to rotate the propeller. Then you offer the box to the victim, but in the process, rotate the mouthpiece to align slot and hole. Tell him to blow hard—and he'll have a surprise and a powder moustache.

The popgun is simply a drilled stick with a plunger having a rounded head. A cork is fitted tightly into the opposite end, so that when the plunger end is slapped smartly with a hand the cork pops out. In these days of cork rarity, it is advisable to tie a string to the cork.

The yo-yo or diavolo (also an ancient Chinese toy) is probably familiar to you in one form or another. It is simply a pair of cones or balls connected by a neck just wide enough to take a cord. The cord is strung between two short sticks and the yo-yo rotated rapidly by moving the sticks up and down alternately. This toy should be made of fairly heavy wood and be 4 or 5 inches long for the average boy to operate. Holes drilled near the outer ends of the pyramids will add noise to the operation, which can be quite spectacular, for the yo-yo can be thrown up and recaught, caused to loop and stall, and the like. When I was a kid, we had city yo-yo championships.

The *bilboquet* and *gazinta* are essentially the same test of skill. In the case of the egg cup, the ball is tossed up from the cup, and the trick is to catch it as it falls. In the *gazinta*, the ball is swung up on its cord, and the trick is to catch it with the pin in a hole as it falls. If you miss, you're likely to get a crack on the knuckles. This takes practice and a good eye.

The magic ball is just a ball with two meeting holes drilled at slight angles so a cord passed through them will be caught when pulled tight. Thus you can control the rate of descent of the ball on the string, stop it at will, and so on.

Articulated toys take longer to make and are usually more fragile than those previously described, so are not suitable for small children. They are more in the nature of novelties, and come in endless varieties: dolls, animals, birds with flapping wings, people performing work of one kind or another. I have shown some elsewhere under wind-operated toys, as well as in earlier books.

The flipper, acrobat (also sometimes called a jumping-jack) is probably the most familiar. I've seen it recently in plastic and in kits made in West Virginia and sold in "country" stores throughout the East. (The whammy-diddle or whimmy-diddle, oxyoke puzzle, and some other devices are also available this way—taking some of the joy out of it, but making life easy for the unhandy.) The acrobat relies again on a twisted loop of string to attain rotation, as did the jester and buzzer described earlier, but in this case the loop is short and held between uprights, so by alternately squeezing and relaxing below the crossbar, you can apply and remove the tension necessary to make the loop try to unwind, carrying the acrobat with it.

In articulated toys, you must have loose joints, or the whole effect fails. It is advisable, in fact, to have almost sloppy joints, so the limbs can move very freely and in more than a plane. Even so, they will tend to catch and stick in some grotesque position or other. Articulated toys are commonly made of $1/8$- or $1/4$-inch wood, as silhouettes, to avoid the carving, but you can go as far as you like. For example, I did a little shaping of the body of my dancer and actually carved a head. Also, I used mahogany because I happened to have some around. (There *are* uses for old-fashioned cigar boxes.) Also, I secured the thighs to the body with brads, and carved 3-D shoes to add a little weight there. Knee, elbow and shoulder joints are made of wire with end loops, and the wire support is a section of coat hanger. (This can be replaced with a "springy" dowel, and the dancer will perform on a table top, if vibrated at proper height.)

The pit sawyer is the same general idea, but a bit more complicated, because the loop must be adjusted to hold the saw in position so the weight will be free to cause rocking. It is also possible to adjust saw position, then fasten the saw at the hands, thus eliminating the cord. Neither the pit sawyer nor the chopper are really articulated, by the way, because there is no movement in use; they are more properly called laminated figures. The chopper is fairly self-evident from the sketches. He can instead be an animal or bird perching on an edge, or the diver about to do a back flip, as I made him in pine. The balance wire must be stiff enough to support the weight without sagging, as you can see from the photo, and weight must be adjusted to that of the figure. I used coat-hanger wire for my figure, which is about 12 inches tall.

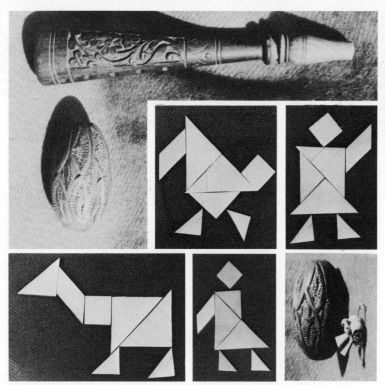

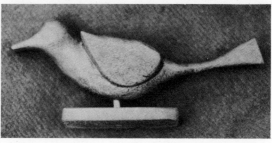

Top left—The flute and egg are of walnut, carved in India. The flute is more toy than instrument because of the difficulty of playing it; the egg is simply a pleasant shape. Shown with the egg at bottom center is a pair of lovebirds, also made in India and equipped with a safety pin so they can be worn. Top right—The "Gee" bird, with reversed wings, "flies backward to keep the wind out of his eyes." We called it the "kiki," and our explanations, one having to do with the weather and the other with eating hot peppers, are not suitable for reprinting here. Left—Four tanagram patterns of the thousands possible. The tangram is a sort of multiple puzzle in that the first trick is to assemble all seven pieces into a square, thereafter to make as many kinds of figures as time permits, in each case using all seven pieces without overlaps.

Toys drawn in the second panel are principally exotic ones, some simple and some appearing to be quite complex—like the Chinese dragon. There are included, however, several standard Americanisms like the tops made from half-spools. In the days of wooden spools and mothers who sewed, we made all sorts of wheeled vehicles out of spools—the axle hole and rim were already there—using wire or dowels for axles. The spinner, or top, required sawing a spool in half and tapering the body, as well as whittling a dowel for the stem—the hole in a spool is a bit large for a $1/4$-inch dowel. Big spools can be whittled into tops spun with a string, of course, and "killer" tops can be made by replacing the dowel point with a short section of spike. But modern kids, who don't have tops in the first place, would scarcely understand a game in which one attempts to spike an opponent's top and split it. That sort of precision takes a great deal of practice.

A spool top can be converted into the spinner for the game of Put and Take. It simply requires the cutting of four flats around the rim and lettering them as indicated in the sketches. In case you never heard of the game, it is played with buttons, beans, matchsticks, dried peas, or whatever for counters. Each player antes a "chip" to start. After that, each player spins the top in turn. If it is "Put," you ante another counter. If it is "Take," you take one. If it is "All," you take the whole pot. If it is "Nothing," you pass on the top. It is a game about as simple—and as deadly—as Chinese

fan-tan and was played for a time with a four-sided plastic top available in stationery stores. The "jet set" of the time had all sorts of variations on it, including who paid for the drinks.

An enjoyable toy, and a sort of variation on the buzzer, is the rubberband tractor. All it requires is a spool with the rims notched for traction on a rug (on a bare floor, the notches won't help) and a length of stick. A rubberband runs from the stick through the spool hole to a stub stick on the other side. The stick is wound to twist the rubberband and the piece placed on the floor; as the band unwinds, the spool is propelled across the floor, and at a fairly high speed, so be careful.

The "Gee" bird, sketched just above the rubberband tractor, is of course a gag. It is a conventional bird figure, except that the wings are carved backwards, and the tail may be vertical rather than horizontal.

The jack-in-the-box offers good practice in whittling a miniature head, but is otherwise unremarkable. I made mine with the nose at one corner, the ears at adjacent ones, of the blank, just for the novelty. I used a spring I had, but one can be made by winding music wire around a small dowel; it will expand to a larger diameter when released, and can be pulled out to the desired length—about 6 inches. The collar or ruff is a ring of $3/8$ or $1/2$-inch wood, V-notched all around to look like the folded ruff that the Elizabethans wore.

The zephyr grinder, wind grinder, smoke

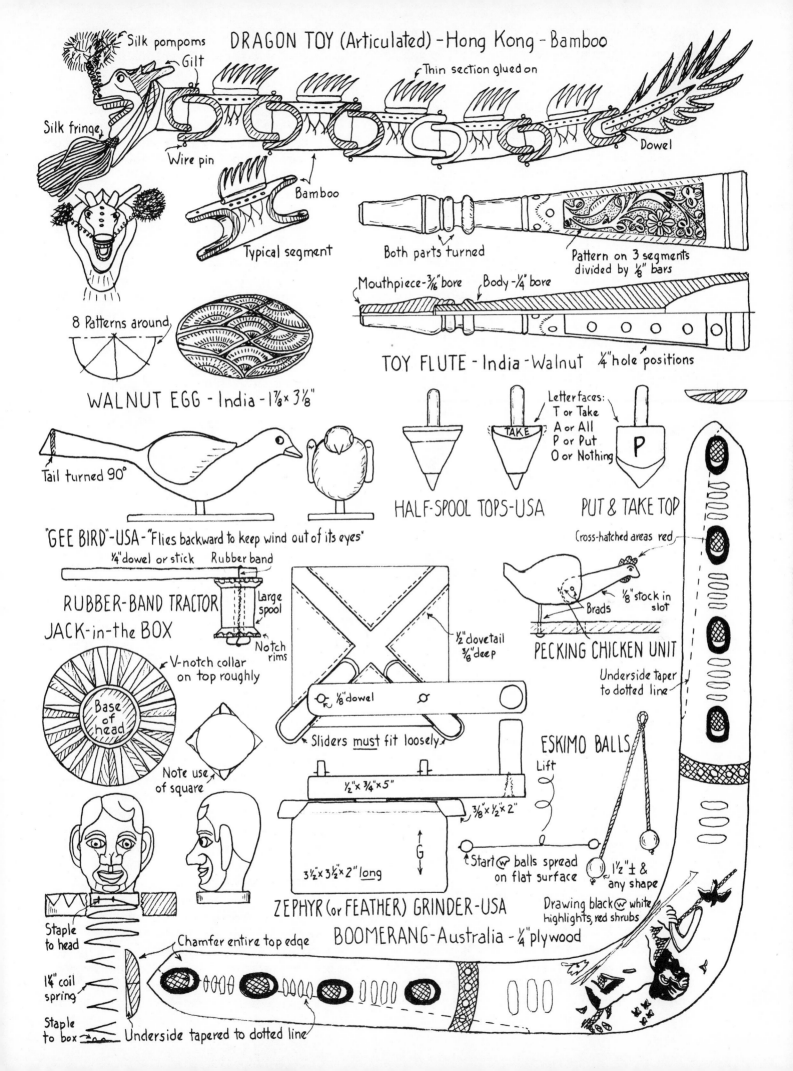

DRAGON TOY (Articulated) – Hong Kong – Bamboo

Silk pompoms
Gilt
Thin section glued on
Silk fringe
Wire pin
Dowel
Bamboo
Typical segment

Both parts turned
Pattern on 3 segments divided by ⅛" bars
Mouthpiece–³⁄₁₆" bore
Body –¼" bore
TOY FLUTE – India – Walnut
¼" hole positions

8 Patterns around
WALNUT EGG – India – 1⅞ × 3⅛"

Tail turned 90°
"GEE BIRD" – USA – "Flies backward to keep wind out of its eyes"

Letter faces:
T or Take
A or All
P or Put
O or Nothing
TAKE
P

HALF-SPOOL TOPS – USA
PUT & TAKE TOP

Cross-hatched areas red

¼" dowel or stick
Rubber band
RUBBER-BAND TRACTOR
Large spool
JACK-in-the BOX
Notch rims

V-notch collar on top roughly
Base of head

Note use of square

Staple to head
1¼" coil spring
Staple to box

½" dovetail ⅜" deep
⅛" dowel
Sliders must fit loosely
½" × ¾" × 5"
⅜" × ½" × 2"
3½" × 3½" × 2" long
ZEPHYR (or FEATHER) GRINDER – USA

Brads
⅛" stock in slot
PECKING CHICKEN UNIT

Underside taper to dotted line

ESKIMO BALLS
Lift
G
Start w balls spread on flat surface
1½" ± & any shape

Drawing black w white highlights, red shrubs
BOOMERANG – Australia – ¼" plywood

Chamfer entire top edge
Underside tapered to dotted line

grinder, or feather grinder—call it what you will—is an ancient service club gag. My cabinetmaker friend makes them by the half-dozen for awards at his Lions Club meetings. A piece of 4 × 4-inch pine or cedar post has $1/2$-inch dovetails cut across the top diagonals. Shoes or sliders 2 inches long are made to slide easily in the grooves, and drilled for center pins that extend up into a crank handle and are held there by crosspins. You turn the crank and the sliders go back and forth, but nothing else happens. The only problem is to space the dowel holes on the crank so that the sliders cannot go out the ends of the slots and to finish the assembly so the sliders move easily. A little soap makes a good lubricant if necessary.

A couple of balls on the ends of a piece of string or rope have been everything from a toy to a weapon among various peoples. The Argentine gaucho twirls these *bolas* and throws the twirling assembly at an animal's legs; the balls carry the ends around and the animal is tripped up. The Maori tribesman in New Zealand puts smaller weights on the end of a longer string and uses the assembly in a complicated dance involving whirling the balls so they pass each other without entangling. The Eskimo does somewhat the same thing, except with a shorter string and a knotted loop just off the center. The balls are spread as far as possible, then the assembly is lifted with a twisting motion to make the balls whirl, preferably in opposite directions and without entangling. *That* takes practice. We kids made the Argentine type out of the spools in the ends of a roll of butcher paper. They don't have to be balls at all—a bag of pebbles or sand, or any shape you prefer, as long as it is compact, will work if it is heavy enough to stretch whatever string you're using.

Another one-time weapon is the Australian boomerang, which I have sketched from an Australian souvenir. Note that there is a leading edge on each arm, and that it is thinned to cut the air, while the entire top surface is chamfered around the edge so it has a crude airfoil shape. The boomerang is not thrown as I thought as a kid, but is held at the end which has the underside taper outside, with the thumb running up along the taper. The other end of the boomerang extends forward, not backward as I had thought, and the weapon is thrown somewhat above the horizontal and in a vertical plane. It turns in flight so that it planes horizontally, and (one hopes) makes a complete circle if it doesn't hit what it was aimed at. Throw it hard, with a whipping motion, and you should be getting it to return in three or four tries. It can be surface-carved or painted—but be sure it flies before you put in time decorating.

Two ingenious articulated toys are the Chinese dragon and the pecking chickens. If you have access to bamboo or other tubular wood, you can make a very startling dragon, snake or alligator, depending upon the head you carve and the back decorations. The pecking chickens are usually arranged three or four around a flat board, with a string running from the back of each neck down through a hole in front of the bird body to a ball. When the assembly is rotated in a horizontal plane, the ball in its arc pulls each string in turn, so the bird heads rise and lower alternately. Bodies are, of course, rigidly pinned to the base board. The same principle can be used on many other subjects: The Russian dancing bear is just one example. Here three strings operate upper arms on the bear playing the drum and one leg of the dancer.

The Indian flute is perhaps too elaborate for a toy, but it isn't a very good musical instrument because it is too hard for a child to blow unless a reed is added. However, it makes a good project and a handsome decoration, so I have included it here. With it is a lifesized walnut egg, also not good for anything but decoration, as far as I know, but a carving project that requires some care in adapting shapes to the available area.

Several other devices seemed appropriate to include here, although some may be questioned in their status as toys. The first is the cockhorse or stick horse, simply a carved horse head on the end of a dowel or broomstick, with or without wheels at the bottom end. (It is called a "cockhorse" in England after the spare horse stabled at the foot of a hill—to help coaches over.) It can be made of good wood and have a separate bridle and be elaborately done, or it can be ultrasimple; this seems to make little difference to a child. It was only my pride that led me to adapt the horse silhouette from the knight of my oversize chess set (page 101), use mahogany, and decorate the wheels like a Sicilian cart. Then I watched a three-year-old ride it—and made a simpler pine head complete with bridle.

The sky hook, belt balancer or "impossible," as we called it, will work only with a belt. It's not too interesting to people who aren't science-minded and hence don't realize that what they're seeing is "impossible."

Stage Properties Can Be Whittled:

How to Help Your Local Theater

Stage properties—or "props"—provide endless challenges for the whittler or carver. I've made dozens of them, both of wood and of styrofoam; I've seen dozens of others. One carver in Germany has made magnificent heroic pieces for the Munich Opera from a dense foam plastic; they are finished with acrylics, so they're indistinguishable from wood or ivory.

My biggest piece was the styrofoam angel illustrated in *The Modern Book of Whittling and Woodcarving* (page 156), my most intricate is the chip-carved pipe rack (page 8). Most props, however, need not be meticulously done, because they are seen only from a distance, but they must be painted in most cases. Examples are shown. The sword and anvil at lower right were, of course, for a version of *King Arthur*—when the boy pulls the sword to prove his ancestry. The sword is transparent plastic, with designs ground in the $3/8 \times 2 \times 36$-inch blade and the edges left rough. Thus a pen flashlight concealed in the carved wooden handle projects light down the plastic when Arthur pulls the switch, and makes the roughened areas glow in dim light. The sword was thrust through a redwood anvil into a styrofoam "stone" and concealed by a breakaway two-piece styrofoam "stone" as well. At bottom left is a group including Aladdin's magic lamp, a whittled sword hilt and Captain Hook's double cigar (from *Peter Pan*). The lamp has a base made from an old faucet collar and the handle is bent heavy-duty electrical cable. The whole piece was gilded. Note the sequins and glitter pasted on sword hilts to simulate jewels.

Below and at right are two groups of very simple pieces, that at right showing the top of a fireplace andiron, made from a pedestal leg and a tennis ball, with two crosses next it—the smaller actually walnut, the other just pine and gilded—for an altar. In the group below left is an oyster cut from plywood, with folded-paper legs and paper feet. It opens on a spring hinge made from a big paper clip—(the type with the foldback wire handles—to reveal a "pearl" inside (you will recall that the Walrus and the Carpenter ate oysters in *Alice in Wonderland*). Next it is a smoke pistol, a grip with a slide on top. A kitchen match pushed through a hole in the side enters a metal pan containing smoke powder, where it is struck and ignited by a piece of sandpaper on the slide when it is moved.

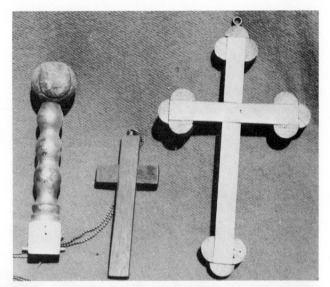

❋ 20 Transportation Silhouettes:

Nostalgic Outlines Provide Decoration—And Practice

These silhouettes date back to a time when I was interested in the almost forgotten ways of moving about, principally by horse-drawn vehicles. Most were executed in three-ply veneer, by hand, with a scrollsaw, but would go much faster on a jigsaw. They are typical of the designs now being applied to mailboxes, storm doors, mantels, set on plate rails, and the like. They can be simple silhouettes, or can be modeled slightly with low relief carving, just as you prefer. Mine were all provided with bases and finished with flat black paint, as a plate-rail series. They provide good experience with the saw, which helped in roughing out 3-D and silhouette carving blanks, and may also serve as design starters for panels. Back a century or so, a great many designs were largely scrollsaw work—the trim on window and picture frames, around doorways and windows, at eaves and peaks on Victorian houses. Typical of the more elaborate variety is the fan below, made of sandalwood slats, with the leaves carefully sawed in intricate designs that vary enough to indicate that the sawing was done singly.

PHAETON

SURREY (with the fringe on top)

HANSOM CAB

ESKIMO DOG SLED

Wire

Wire
Thread

RAIL COACH

TANDEM BICYCLE

ARGENTINE OX CART

Lead team is placed before other, as shown

SIX-HORSE STAGE COACH

Reins are heavy thread

STAGE COACH

G. WASHINGTON'S COACH

ORIGINAL FORD

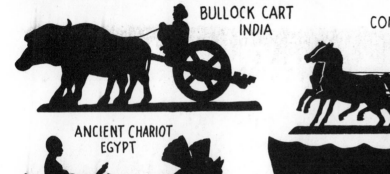

BULLOCK CART
INDIA

CONCORD COACH

ANCIENT CHARIOT
EGYPT

"PRAIRIE SCHOONER"

4-PASS. SLEIGH

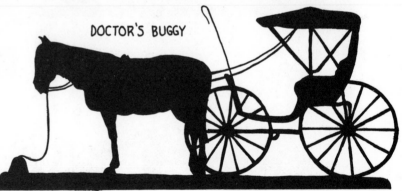

DOCTOR'S BUGGY

SICILIAN CART-ITALY

ONE-HORSE CHAISE
'ONE-HOSS SHAY"

WATER CART
MEXICO

✳ How to Solve Knotty Problems:

Sometimes the Knots Can Be Carved

There are times when otherwise good and handsome wood scraps have knots or rotted spots in unexpected places, suggesting that they are good only for firewood. But in these wood-short times, it is best to examine them rather closely before they are discarded. Don W. Lougeay, of Belleville, Illinois, had such a problem with the parts of a wild cherry log he'd gotten cut at the local sawmill to 1-, 2-, and 3-inch boards of various widths and lengths. He turned fruit compotes and candlesticks from the good portions, then had "a bunch of small pieces 1 to 2 inches thick and 3 to 4 inches long—too little to keep and too big to throw away."

A little figuring, and he began to whittle nests of scoops like those shown, suited in size for apothecary jars instead of the garish colored plastic ones available nowadays. They nest in a convenient stack and can have decorated handles—and the cherry takes an attractive color. He made a number of these sets, for wedding presents and other gifts—"and they were always well received."

Still left were bits of wood with rotten spots and knots, with good color—pink to deep red—and some very attractive figure. Don had fifteen nieces, all of whom expected handmade presents, so he remembered that ponytail hairdos are the style again and set to work designing barrettes. The results are shown here. Instead of discarding the knotty areas, he utilized the curved grain, much as the pioneers made cups and bowl from burls. Thus the finished piece has greater strength—and greater beauty—than it would have if made from good, straight-grained wood. Also, he got quite a bit of variety into both the designs and the method of holding the barrettes. Some of the latter are held by thrust-through pins that also utilize bits of curved-grain wood and lock by a quarter-turn; others by the more conventional bent wire put through a hole at one end and snapped into a slot at the other, as sketched. In fact, Don became so enthusiastic that he made several extra barrettes and sold them at prices up to $35 apiece! Not bad for scrap wood from a log that only cost $6 in the first place. (If Don's nieces had been older, he could have carved identifying collars or "gorgets" for liquor bottles—or the ladies.)

Don's major tools were six Boy Scout handicraft knives, No. 2694. They come with five blades (three straight, one right-and one left-

Three-piece candlesticks (right) and compote dish (below) were turned from best portions of cherry, nested scoops (far right) whittled from smaller clear bits, and carved with simple handle designs.

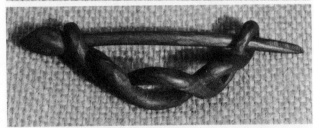

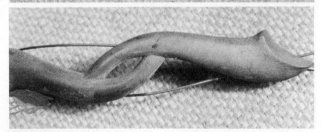

Top—Two familiar barrette shapes, made from curved wood surrounding a knot; one is twisted cords, the other heart and circle motifs. Blanks are cut so grain runs end to end. The conventionalized swallow is from a blank cut nearer the knot, hence is shorter and has greater curvature. Note the wood-pin curved catches on these three, shown more clearly in the center photo. It is also possible to use a conventional wire lock for fastening, by leaving lugs at the ends of the blank, or even by gluing them on later. The wire passes through a drilled hole, then is bent so the ends catch in a bayonet slot at the other end.

hand hook) and a handle at any Boy Scout supply store for a 1974 price of $1.25. He uses the extra handles so he doesn't have to change blades, after he has sharpened them and changed the cutting angle to suit his needs.

To fill out the panel of sketches, I have added several alternate simple—almost chip-carved—designs for scoop handles, and several suggestions for using knotty pieces of various sizes and shapes for anything from rings, cufflinks, pendants and bracelets to panels, trays and toy or table decorations.

I often run into small knots in an otherwise clear panel and usually manage to modify the design slightly so the knot becomes anything from an eye to a head or belly in the finished piece. Only when the knot interferes with the design is it necessary to cut it out and replace it—after all, knots are to be expected in wood. Rotten spots and fungous areas are a different matter: They're ugly, thus usually require immediate plugging because they're too deep or a distracting shape.

Knots are always worthy of respect, particularly for the beginning whittler or carver. Because they are harder than surrounding wood and have circular grain lines, they chip and break easily, rather than cutting, and have the tendency to take the edge off tools quickly. They are somewhat easier to carve with chisels than with the knife because the chisel edge is normally thicker and stronger, but they can cause the breakage of any kind of tool. Further, particularly in soft woods, a big knot tends to crack and/or fall out, so it's safer basically to avoid them when possible. But they do offer a curved grain structure, which Don Lougeay utilized so effectively. When encountered in in-the-round pieces, a knot can often be shaped with files more easily than with edged tools. When large knots are encountered in large pieces during carving, it is usually advisable to stop and cut out the knotty area and fill it with matching wood, although this does cause trouble in finishing unless flat paint is to be used. It is necessary to make sure the joining lines are accurate and any cracks thoroughly filled with a mixture of glue and sawdust, then to touch up the lines to correct any color variations when the finish is applied.

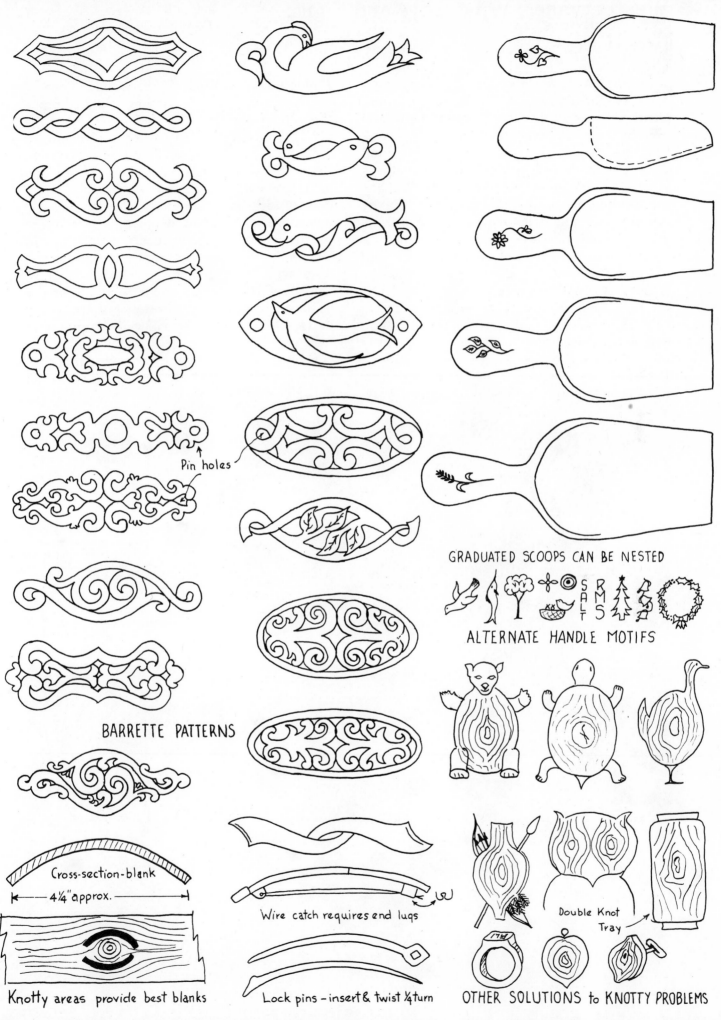

Pin holes

BARRETTE PATTERNS

GRADUATED SCOOPS CAN BE NESTED

SALT
RMS

ALTERNATE HANDLE MOTIFS

Cross-section-blank

4¼" approx.

Knotty areas provide best blanks

Wire catch requires end lugs

Lock pins - insert & twist ¼ turn

Double Knot Tray

OTHER SOLUTIONS to KNOTTY PROBLEMS

✳ Weathervanes, Wind Toys and Signs:

From Our Past, a Series of Simple but Graphic Designs

In the simpler world of long ago, man did his own weather forecasting. There was actually a weathervane on top of the Tower of the Winds built by Andronicus in Athens in 100 B.C. The vane was a bronze triton who pointed his trident in the direction of the wind. Weathervanes were common in England after William the Conqueror and in France after the Revolution. Scandinavians even had them on ships—lineal ancestors of our wind pennants on sailboats and windsocks at airports.

American vanes date back to the Pilgrim fathers. A copper cockerel was made in 1656 for the Dutch Reformed Church in Albany, N.Y. Paul Revere had a wooden codfish studded with copper nails over his coppersmithing shop in Canton, Massachusetts. Shem Drownes, born in Boston in 1683, made the famous copper grasshopper atop Faneuil Hall,

Philadelphia, in 1742. (It was a copy of one on the Royal Exchange, London.) He also made the copper weathervane and Indian atop the old Province House in Boston and a rooster atop the New Brick Church on Hanover Street, Boston (circa 1722), which are still extant. Hawthorne mentioned the copper Indian in his story, "Drowne's Wooden Image," and there was a tradition among children that the Indian would shoot his arrow each day at high noon. Drowne, incidentally, also carved trade signs, pump heads, figureheads for ships, and mantelpiece decorations. Actually, many of his designs, as well as those of others, could be weathervanes or signs or wall plaques with little or no change.

During the seventeenth and eighteenth centuries, vanes were somewhat limited in design—arrows, fish, Indians, cocks, grasshop-

All three of these weathervanes are traditional—the cod in New England seacoast towns, the horse inland (this one is in the Cooperstown, N.Y., Farmer's Museum) and the cock on church steeples (because Peter denied the Lord before the cock crowed). They may be finished naturally, as below, slightly tinted or fully colored, as at left. The cod is a good teaching project for beginners.

RUNNING HORSE (Farm areas)

ROOSTER

CODFISH (Mass. Coast)

GRASSHOPPER
1742 – On Faneuil Hall

ANGEL

SWORDFISH (Silhouette)

Modelled &
chip-carved

CSSEC

CROWING
COCK

HEN
(Silhouette)
after James Leonard

PHEASANT
(Silhouette)

VOLUNTEER
FIREMAN

DIANA

LIBERTY

MAN DRIVING PIG

INDIAN ARCHER

Whale and feather were standard weathervane shapes. These were pictured at Olde Somerville, N.J., atop restored buildings.

pers. Farmers chose their own familiar subjects: cows, horses, sheep, pigs, poultry. They put their vanes on top of their barns so they could be seen from the house. Seacoast villages had mostly sailors, seagulls, fish and whales. The rooster or cockerel—the weathercock—was very common on church steeples, a reminder of the cock that crowed the night that Peter denied the Lord. Some churches had instead Gabriel blowing his horn, a modified lyre, or in New England, the expected codfish.

Most of these vanes were copper or galvanized iron and made in factories after the midnineteenth century. However, all were preceded by wooden models or molds carved in wood, and the home craftsman made his usually of wood or of sheet metal. Tradesmen began to advertise their crafts with weathervanes, a pen (for a lawyer or scrivener), a plow, a gloved hand, mortar and pestle, pig on a knife (see sketches), ship. As the country and the fashion grew, subjects were limited only by the ingenuity of the craftsman: heraldic designs, locomotives or trains, wild animals, wagons, jockeys on horseback, patriotic subjects, Indians, hunters, mythological figures, firemen. Some vanes even pictured a scene or told a story, picturing incidents involving several figures on a common base. Eventually, vanes were available cast in the round, cut from sheet metal, assembled from parts. Some still are, but we usually rely on the radio or TV to learn the weather nowadays.

The simplest weathervane is simply a flat silhouette standing against the sky. But more elaborate designs can incorporate chip carving, outlining, low relief or fully in-the-round elements. Some of the more familiar designs are sketched, but the sky is literally the limit.

The essentials are that the design present some surface to the wind, that it not be too fragile (if of wood, this is particularly true) and that it be possible to support it on a shaft in such a way that one portion—the rear end of most designs—presents more surface to the wind, thus pointing the nose portion into the wind. Wood must be reinforced, thick enough, and probably painted as well to reduce warpage. Carving technique can suit the ability of the carver. It is usually of little use to provide a great deal of fine detail; it will not be visible at a distance. Thus a technique that results in planes that catch the light is usually best—a modified form of chip carving, for example, as shown on several of the examples. Finishing had best be for endurance. Varnish will inevitably wear off. The ancients tended to use paint or stain, which weathered well. Also, their vanes were usually on lower buildings and more accessible. A good wood—pine, mahogany, teak—is the best base, either painted in the case of pine, or thoroughly oiled in the case of the others.

Fascination with the wind also led to a number of wind-activated pieces. A simple one was the Aeolian harp or wind harp (see page 13), simply a rectangular soundbox of thin wood made to fit a window width and bearing on its top a series of three or four fiddle strings that could be tuned. I have heard of, but never seen, other wind-activated sound devices like propeller-driven wheels rubbing on strings and wind-catching reed horns.

Propeller-operated toys were legion, most of them stemming from Pennsylvania Dutch designs. The commonest form is a man equipped with blade arms, on a common spindle, so they rotate like a windmill in the wind. Originally a frock-coated, square-hatted figure like that sketched, it was inevitable that this design would eventually become a traffic cop. Every farm boy at one time or another used to make an even simpler design—simply a rough-whittled propeller tacked to the end of a stick with a tail at the other end, the assembly in turn tacked to a vertical post. This became both a miniature windmill and a weathervane, because the propeller faced into the wind as long as the tail vane was made long enough. Wind-activated figures such as a woman churning, a man sawing, horses walking, a ship plowing through the waves or people performing other simple tasks, either singly or in groups, were devised by the ingenious, usually during long winter nights. Some of these vari-

Signs lend themselves to low relief carving. Here are a group from Old Somerville, N.J., a restored village. They can be merely painted and framed with carving, as is the ship chandler's sign at right; be a symbol, like the plow at right, the wheat sheaf design below, or the sun at center right. They can contribute an idea to the sign, like the angel at center, the butcher and pig below, the whale on the ship chandler's sign just below or the girl on the candle sign at lower right. Or they can be largely lettering, like the Quail Hill sign. The eagle at lower right was carved by Matilda Smith to go over an Indiana mantel. It is more than 30 inches long and 2 inches thick.

ations are also sketched to show the basic idea. All are based on the propeller connected to a crank, which runs either in a hole or a slot. If it is in a slot, a guided shaft can be made to reciprocate, as in the churn sketched. If it rotates in a hole, the toy operated must have at least two pivots, to allow for motion in two directions. Pieces that move should be light and loosely jointed, operated by a propeller large enough to turn the assembly easily and fastened securely to the crankshaft. The usual way is to thread the prop end of the crankshaft and hold the propeller with a nut on each side—but the propeller can be put through a tight drilled hole, bent at a right angle and secured to the face of the prop. Shafts can turn in holes, well oiled, drilled in maple or other hard wood, and there must be some form of thrust collar or stop to keep the shaft in position; else the thrust of the propeller will soon cause wear and locking of shaft against support post.

It is also advisable not to have *too* large a propeller, or to have some way of inactivating the wind toy in gales, or parts will be strewn in all directions. My father told of a mechanic friend who made a windmill of a man sawing wood. As a realist, he provided teeth in the

My favorite sign is this song without words in the park where the Oktoberfest is staged each year in Munich, Germany. People of many tongues gather there, so no language is adequate. Carved in pine 2 inches thick and about 18 inches high, it is painted in color and delivers its message as only an inspired sign can do.

saw. One night in a storm, the man sawed through the log. Obviously, a saw should be held so it does not bear on the log it is apparently cutting—and my father's friend should have provided an accessible stop for use in high winds.

It may be necessary to experiment with propeller size and blade width to suit the assembly being driven. If parts move freely, the device will operate in light winds with a relatively small propeller, but this leads to excessive speed when the breeze builds up.

Both vanes and mills must rotate on their vertical supporting shaft to face the wind, so they should have some form of tail element that steers them, and some form of pivot. For a vane, the simplest is simply a well-oiled hole and a smooth end on the shaft. To reduce the drilling effect and wear, a small plug made from the shaft material can be inserted and glued in the hole, so the bearing at the top becomes metal-on-metal. Another device is to solder on a washer so it will bear on the base of the vane. Still another is to run the shaft up the side and hold it with screw eyes or staples.

Similar bearings can be used in the base of a windmill, but it is usually better to form a more elaborate bearing, with a stop collar soldered in place below and a washer and nut on top, so the device will not lift off in case of a ground swell.

In either case, the support should not be at the center of gravity of the assembly unless a long tail vane is used; the device must present more rear surface to the breeze so the propeller of the mill or nose of the vane faces into the wind. Note that in the examples sketched, pivots are well forward to avoid such problems.

As I remarked initially, vane silhouettes can also be used as wall plaques, signs (name, number, etc.), or as surface decorations on a mailbox, plate rail, over a door or on a boat. I have therefore also provided (page 26) designs of silhouettes too complex and too fragile for vanes, but eminently suitable for a standing or appliqued decoration.

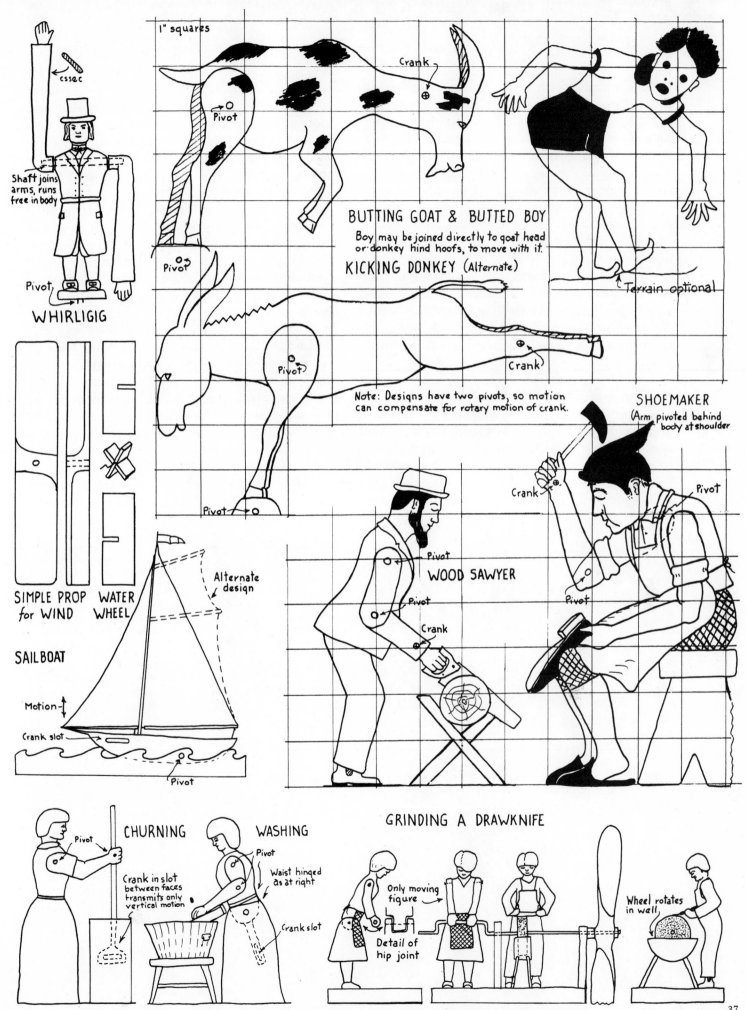

cssec

Shaft joins
arms, runs
free in body

Pivot

WHIRLIGIG

1" squares

Crank

Pivot

Pivot

BUTTING GOAT & BUTTED BOY
Boy may be joined directly to goat head
or donkey hind hoofs, to move with it.

KICKING DONKEY (Alternate)

Pivot

Crank

Pivot

Note: Designs have two pivots, so motion
can compensate for rotary motion of crank.

Terrain optional

SIMPLE PROP   WATER
for WIND   WHEEL

SAILBOAT

Alternate
design

Motion

Crank slot

Pivot

SHOEMAKER
(Arm pivoted behind
body at shoulder

Crank

Pivot

Pivot

WOOD SAWYER

Pivot

Pivot

Crank

CHURNING

Pivot

Crank in slot
between faces
transmits only
vertical motion

WASHING

Pivot

Waist hinged
as at right

Crank slot

GRINDING A DRAWKNIFE

Only moving
figure

Detail of
hip joint

Wheel rotates
in well

✳ Love Spoons from Wales and Elsewhere:

Scandinavians, Germans, Spanish, Latin American Indians All Make Them

The standard whittling "tricks"—ball-in-a-cage, fan, swivel, chain, pliers—have been familiar to me all my life as just themselves and nothing more. When Walter L. Faurot wrote his pioneering book, *The Art of Whittling*, in 1930, he devoted most of his pages to them; he'd always known of them, too, and probably assumed, as I did, that they originated in our own past. At the advanced age of fifteen or so, I applied the fan to birds' wings and tails, flying fish in a cage, flowers and even a Sioux headdress, and felt I'd advanced the art several steps. I described these advances in 1936 in my first book, and the WPA did me the dubious honor of copying some of them in a little booklet without credit several years later.

Then I began to see the fan variations from Sweden and Japan—far more elaborate than anything I'd done. The Viking spoons, supposedly made originally almost a thousand years ago, incorporated the wooden chain for a reason, as we shall see. The Chinese nested spheres in ivory, with as many as twenty-eight balls one inside the other, several surface-carved, far outclassed any ball-in-a-cage I'd

ever seen. And, just recently, a friend brought back from Wales some pictures of Welsh love spoons that have been made there for at least three hundred years, incorporating both the ball-in-a-cage and the swivel as integral parts and giving them a meaning instead of just celebrating them as tricks.

At this late date, I'm beginning to realize how little we really know of the origin of our standard designs, and how most have come down through the centuries, sometimes losing their basic meaning in the process. I described such a situation in a recent book, *The Modern Book of Whittling and Woodcarving*: the breadboard which some carver long ago circled with "Give us this day our daily bread," which later copiers shortened to just "Bread," although they retained the Old English lettering of the original and the circular form. In all of these designs, later makers copied the earlier ones; and, because wood is perishable, it is not possible to date such pieces as remain in many instances.

Now I've found excellent descriptions of Welsh and Swedish love spoons and pictures of several dozen types in various references,

Left—These three love spoons, made in a few hours each by the author, show some of the range of designs. The largest is a copy of the earliest known Welsh spoon, modified slightly for greater ease of carving by a class and hence is somewhat gross in appearance. It is in sugar pine about 1-1/4 in. square by 10 in. long. The smallest spoon is in blond limba (white mahogany) and substitutes an apple for the original comblike top (remember the Garden of Eden?). The center spoon, in mahogany, is a modification of a frequent design by lonesome sailors. Scales on the mermaid are produced with vertical cuts with a 1/8-in. half-round gouge, followed by paring away the edges beneath. Below—the availability of an apple suggested the old Chinese whimsy of a worm in the back, and cutting away the intertwined snakes to thin the spoon handle left a precut slab which yielded a pendant as a bonus.

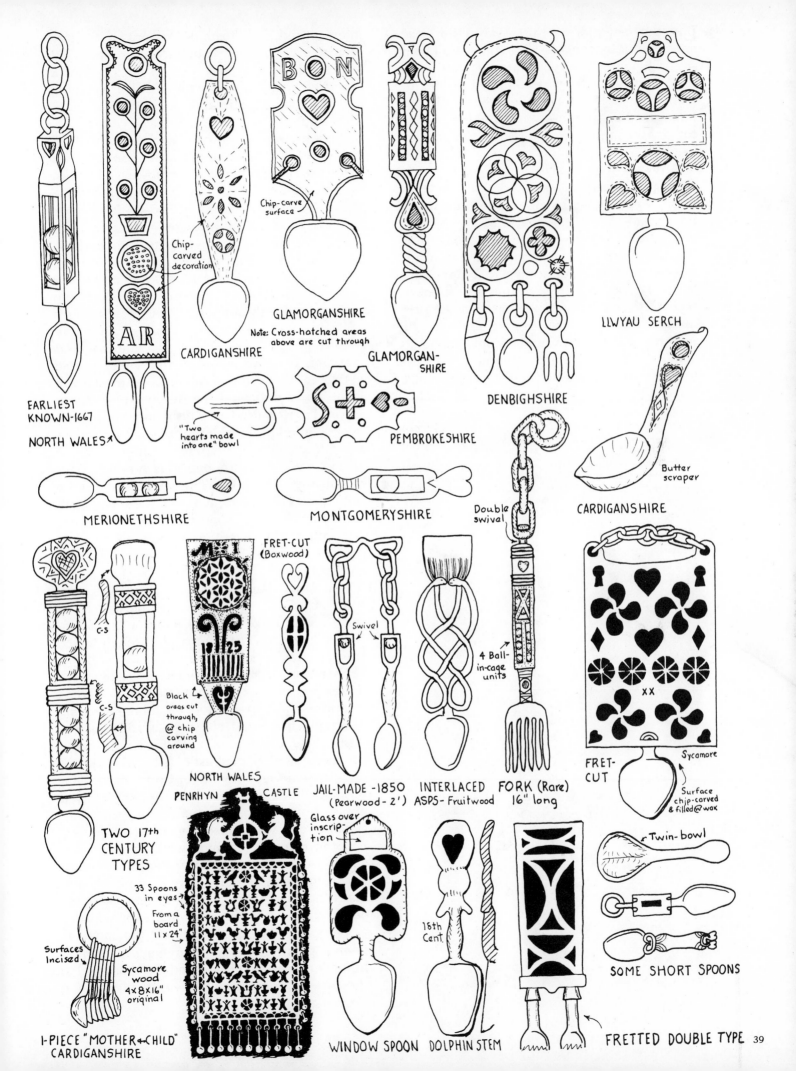

EARLIEST
KNOWN-1667

NORTH WALES

AR

Chip-
carved
decoration

CARDIGANSHIRE

Chip-carved
decoration

GLAMORGANSHIRE

Note: Cross-hatched areas
above are cut through

BON

GLAMORGAN-
SHIRE

DENBIGHSHIRE

LLWYAU SERCH

"Two
hearts made
into one" bowl

PEMBROKESHIRE

Double
swivel

Butter
scraper

CARDIGANSHIRE

MERIONETHSHIRE

MONTGOMERYSHIRE

C-S

C-S

TWO 17th
CENTURY
TYPES

FRET-CUT
(Boxwood)

Black
areas cut
through,
@ chip
carving
around

NORTH WALES

PENRHYN   CASTLE

Swivel

JAIL-MADE -1850
(Pearwood- 2')

INTERLACED
ASPS- Fruitwood

4 Ball-
in-cage
units

FORK (Rare)
16" long

FRET-
CUT

Sycamore

Surface
chip-carved
& filled @ wax

Surfaces
Incised

33 Spoons
in eyes

From a
board
11 x 24

Sycamore
wood
4 x 8 x 16"
original

1-PIECE "MOTHER & CHILD"
CARDIGANSHIRE

Glass over
inscrip-
tion

WINDOW SPOON

18th
Cent.

DOLPHIN STEM

Twin-bowl

SOME SHORT SPOONS

FRETTED DOUBLE TYPE   39

plus the fact that Swedish swains wore their spoons in a buttonhole when they went courting. The young lady countered with a yarn doll, and these were exchanged to plight a troth. Our ball-in-a-cage devotees could have had a traditional reason and a practical outlet for their output had they only known its origin!

Anyway, the Welsh love spoon, like its Viking counterpart (and possible ancestor), was a young man's proudest gift to his intended. It had all the symbolism of love gifts the world over, and showed the young man's devotion and skill, just as the modern girl's knitted neckties and socks were supposed to later. There were those coquettes, of course, who collected a row of spoons, just as girls I know collected fraternity pins and diamonds—and the swain who could make one could presumably make several if his affections varied. Inevitably, less gifted men hired

more gifted ones to make spoons, until they became just another commercial product, and the tradition and custom died out perhaps a hundred years ago. Now the Welsh are turning out the spoons again and "reviving" the tradition—but for the tourist trade.

Spoons are, of course, not the only love token. Many rustic and seaside communities have produced other types: chip-carved boxes, lockets, pins, scrimshawed ivory, macramé belts. They were in many cases an alternate for a declaration by a tongue-tied suitor, but were also made as love gifts for children, parents, wives and friends. Their basic idea, however, was as a prelude to courtship, to indicate a desire to "spoon" or to nest like spoons, hence the Victorian usage "spooning."

The ball-in-a-cage, incorporated in many Welsh designs, was called a "lantern" and signified the love captured that could not be set free. The number of links in a chain in some cases indicated the number of children desired or promised, as did the number of little spoons in addition to larger ones. Two spoons on one handle or two bowls in one spoon meant "We two are one," as did two balls within the same cage. The keyhole showed a willingness to provide a house, the spoon itself a willingness to provide food (sometimes this was emphasized with a knife and fork as well). The wheel meant a willingness to work for her, the spade a desire to "dig" for her and so on. The comma shape, usually in pairs, was common; it is a "soul" motif—possibly derived from the Chinese yin and yang or the Egyptian shapes depicting nostrils (through which the soul was believed to escape at death).

Extremely intricate designs eventually were developed, just as they are in any other art as it approaches its decadence. Some became relatively huge and elaborate scrollwork designs, the equivalent of an Eiffel Tower model in glued-together matchsticks; but the idea of one-piece design was largely preserved. Material could be local woods, fruits like pear and apple, nuts like pecan, maple and the occasional exotic woods used by lovelorn sailors. But the commonest wood was sycamore, because it cuts clean and carves easily. Inevitably, some later designs were assembled, and many actually were no longer spoons—they became forks or knives instead, even whistles or pairs of miniature shoes. But the shoe has been a persistent symbol anyway; it survives in modern wedding cakes and the shoes tied to the benedict's getaway car—probably even in

Other countries have their love spoons as well, best known among them the Scandinavian or Viking one at left. Made from a single piece of wood, this twin spoon has pierced carving, surface-carved bowls and is big enough to be usable. Legend has it that the newlyweds fed each other with the spoons, and the bride wore them about her neck while her mate went a-conquering. The spoon at right is simply an elaborate variation of the traditional Mexican ladle, made for the tourist trade, as are simpler versions of the Viking spoons. Designs are produced with gouges.

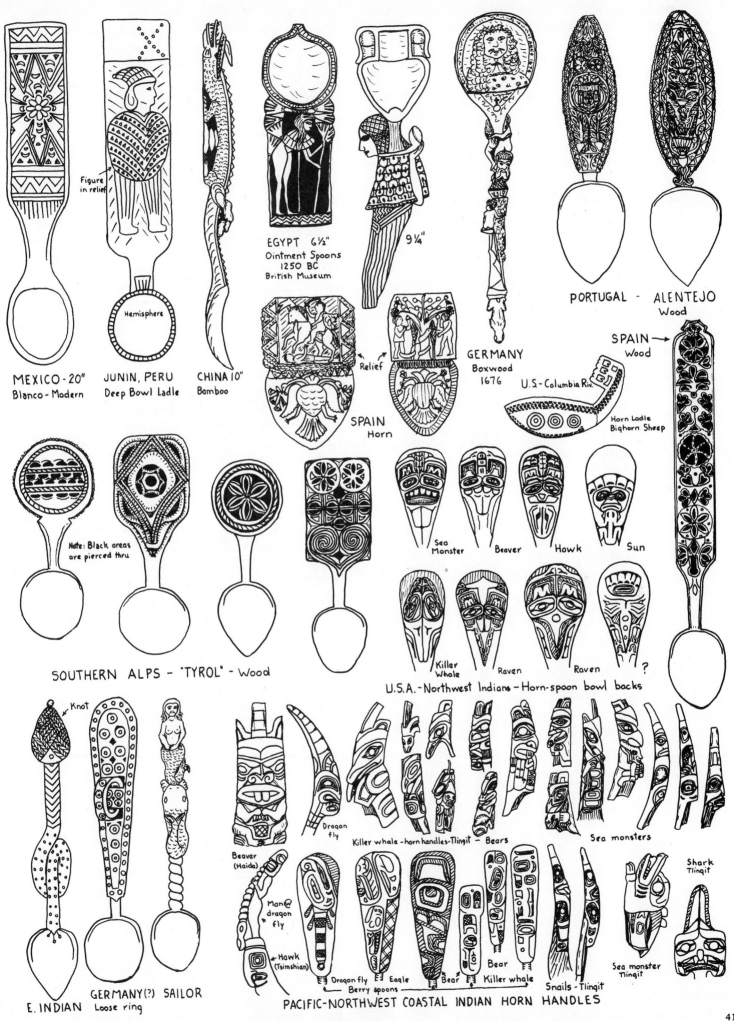

MEXICO - 20"
Blanco - Modern

Figure in relief

JUNIN, PERU
Deep Bowl Ladle

Hemisphere

CHINA 10"
Bamboo

EGYPT 6½"
Ointment Spoons
1250 BC
British Museum

9¼"

GERMANY
Boxwood
1676

Relief

SPAIN
Horn

U.S - Columbia Riv.

PORTUGAL - ALENTEJO
Wood

SPAIN
Wood

Horn Ladle
Bighorn Sheep

Note: Black areas
are pierced thru

SOUTHERN ALPS - "TYROL" - Wood

Sea Monster   Beaver   Hawk   Sun

Killer Whale   Raven   Raven   ?

U.S.A. - Northwest Indians - Horn-spoon bowl backs

Knot

E. INDIAN

GERMANY(?)
Loose ring

SAILOR

Beaver
(Haida)

Man &
dragon
fly

Hawk
(Tsimshian)

Dragon fly

Dragon fly   Eagle   Bear
Berry spoons

Bear
Killer whale

Killer whale - horn handles - Tlingit - Bears

Sea monsters

Snails - Tlingit

Shark
Tlingit

Sea monster
Tlingit

PACIFIC - NORTHWEST COASTAL INDIAN HORN HANDLES

the story of Cinderella. An early form of the shoe tradition can even be found in the Bible (Ruth 4 : 7). The Welsh converted this into a pair of carved shoes made into receptacles with sliding tops, one containing a lump of coal, the other a lump of sugar—so the newly married couple would not lack for food or warmth.

There is little to say about the technique of carving the spoons; the drawings are largely self-explanatory and will serve as a takeoff point for other designs. Some designs in "chip carving" (page 8) can be adapted, as well as others. Some designs are identifiable for area of origin. There are local design differences; in the British Isles, for example, a dolphin-shaped or crooked stem was from Caernarvonshire, large twin panels featuring the keyhole and heart were from Pembrokeshire, and so on. Some areas stressed fret-saw work and chip carving (page 8) of surfaces; others had intricate detail carving or incorporated several whittling stunts.

In any case, these designs offer a challenge,

Alaskan Indian horn spoons which I had upwards of thirty years before I found out what the designs were meant to represent. Many of these are quite elaborately carved, yet sturdy and usable.

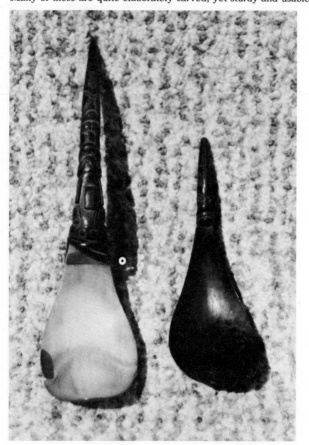

and a more practical application of some of our familiar tricks, although few of the spoons are practical. My only caution is the usual: Be sure your selected wood is straight-grained and that your smallest knifeblades are razor-sharp.

Spoons from Other Countries

The Welsh spoons led me to research other sources for spoon designs. Results are in the second page of drawings. Included are examples from the Southern Alps (the "Tyrol," once Austrian, now Italian), from Spain, Portugal (the Alentejo area on the southwest coast), Germany, India—all old, but none so old as two ointment spoons from Egypt that are more than 3,000 years old! There are also more modern designs from China, Mexico and Peru. These are probably not "love" spoons in the Welsh romantic tradition, but they were nonetheless for domestic use and some affection must have been involved or the necessary time to carve them would not have been spent.

The "sailor" spoon is my own composite of three motifs common in such spoons—the mermaid, fish and rope. Note the loose ring on one German design, and the formal carving of another. Most of the spoons, however, are examples of folk art, repeating what are commonly called chip-carving designs.

In sharp contrast are the horn spoons made a century or so ago by the Indian tribes along the northwest coast of North America—Tlingit, Haida, Tsimshian, etc.—the same tribes renowned for their totem poles. These, in fact, utilize the same design conventions. The outer ends of the horns of bighorn sheep were split, then heated and formed into bowls. The bowls were cut to shape, and the horn tip and bowl bottom carved in low relief with formalized depictions of birds, fish, sea monsters, animals and occasionally man. Many of the handle designs were carved through to the open core, making pierced designs. Flat bones from whales and walruses were also carved into berry spoons, with symbolic designs on the spatulate handles. I have owned two of the horn spoons for thirty years and only now have found that they depict sea monsters, and one has a hawk on the bowl! In the bowl designs, by the way, the elaborate designs above the eyes are the ears, positioned there because of the limitations of material.

✳ The Carved Spanish Colonial Door:

Traditional Revival Makes These Modern

Note: Details of designs are obscured on some doors, because photos are converted from color.

Western and southwestern Americans are becoming more and more conscious of the impressive doors of Latin American churches and haciendas, carved by the Indians under Spanish tutelage and repaired or duplicated as they disintegrated in the centuries since. These are typical examples, except for that at right, which is a modern copy on a mansion in Santa Cruz, California. Beyond it is a section of one of the massive doors at the Carmen church in San Luis Potosí, Mexico. Below, from left to right, are the upper halves of the doors to San Diego church, Guanajuato, Mexico, the doors to the chapel in the state museum at San Luis Potosí, Mexico, and the restored doors of a church in León, Nicaragua. All have classical floral motifs except for the portrait heads on the American door, which is also the only one without an arched top.

A Whale of a Carving Project:

Seagoing Mammals Provide Many Possible Designs

The whale is a particularly popular subject for carvers along the Northeastern coast of the United States, particularly poses of the sperm whale. They range from small examples in ivory appliqued for decorations on women's purses and tiny ones for pendants and charms to relief carvings several feet long for wall plaques and signs. The blunt-headed shape of the sperm whale also works out well for a weathervane (page 34), and the carving is relatively simple. In fact, many "carvers" produce them with a bandsaw and power sander, using chisels or knife only for the eye.

There are exceptions to the standard pattern, however, as pictured here—a great blue whale carved by Don Riemer, Kendall Park, N.J. After a heart attack, he decided to undertake "a fairly large woodcarving, but one which would not be too demanding physically nor so detailed that it would be exasperating mentally." He decided on a whale, and his wife drew him the necessary pattern. It is carved from $1\text{-}\frac{7}{8} \times 15 \times 45$-inch sugar pine, with an inset eye carved from holly. It turned out to be exactly what the doctor ordered for Don—something satisfying to do during recuperation, without being too strenuous.

Don's comments led me to the sketches reproduced here of most of the major whale types, as well as some associated designs. I modified the mermaid to make a Welsh love spoon (page 38), and made several of the dolphins, another popular East Coast subject. The latter, because of his playfulness and willingness to perform in oceanariums, is frequently illustrated and thus offers many sources for designs.

Usual practice is to make the whale as relatively higher relief, even half-round, and to finish it simply with wax or varnish and wax, depending upon the wood. Except for the killer and the humpback, whale color is relatively unimportant anyway, so a slight darkening along the back is usually all the coloring that is desirable.

Whale motifs may also be used for scratch or scrimshaw carving and for surface decorations on a variety of objects. A whale-handled letter opener is another example of the whale incorporated in a design and is unusual in that it comes from the West Coast rather than the East—which is only proper, because they see far more whales than we do these days, particularly during the semiannual migrations. But nostalgia is a powerful force—as the fishing shack habitat suggests. Many of these picturesque scenes have been produced, often based on pictures or sketches of scenes long gone, just as present-day scrimshaw makers frequently use sailing vessels and whale hunts for motifs—although they have not existed in reality for more than a hundred years.

Left—Fishing shack and appurtenances; about 2 × 2 in., painted. Below—Whale motif letter opener, by John Virgil, in oak (sketch on page 69). Bottom, 45-in. great blue whale, in sugar pine, by Don Riemer. It has an inserted eye of holly, at far right of the closeup.

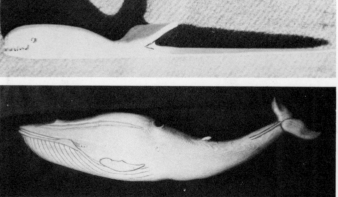

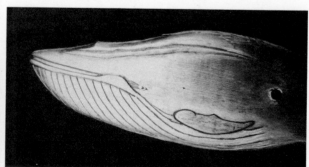

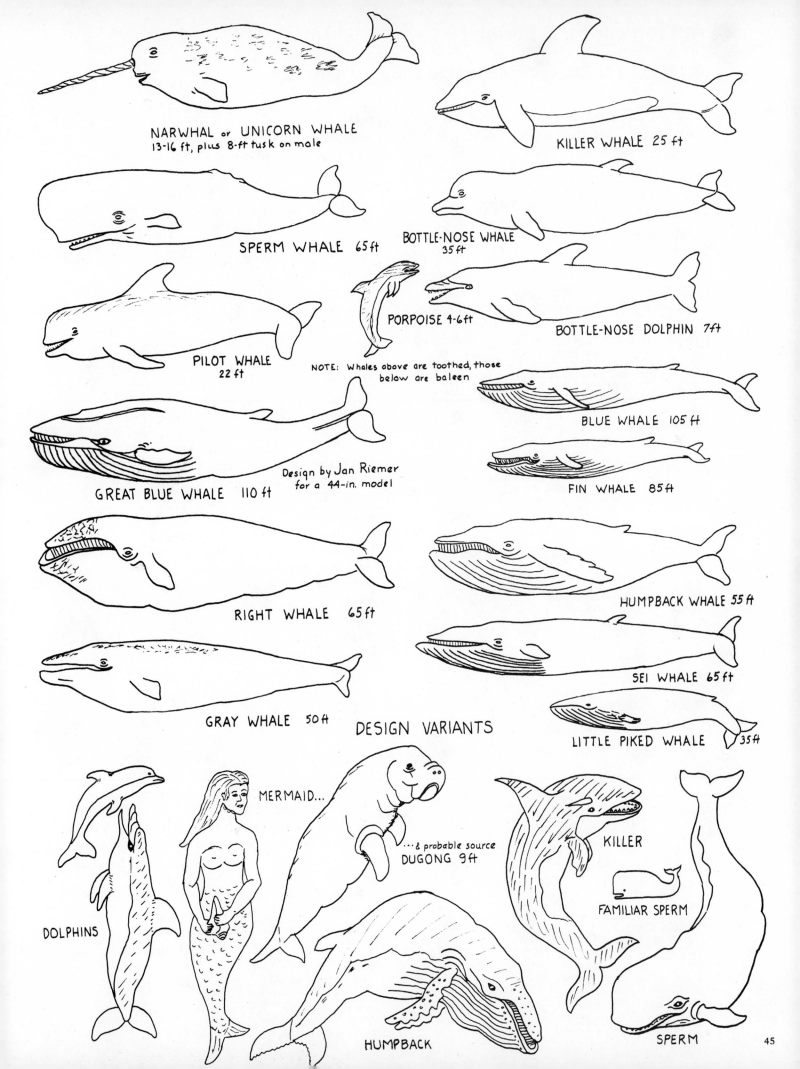

NARWHAL or UNICORN WHALE
13-16 ft, plus 8-ft tusk on male

KILLER WHALE 25 ft

SPERM WHALE 65 ft

BOTTLE-NOSE WHALE 35 ft

PORPOISE 4-6 ft

BOTTLE-NOSE DOLPHIN 7 ft

PILOT WHALE 22 ft

NOTE: Whales above are toothed, those below are baleen

GREAT BLUE WHALE 110 ft

Design by Jan Riemer for a 44-in. model

BLUE WHALE 105 ft

FIN WHALE 85 ft

RIGHT WHALE 65 ft

HUMPBACK WHALE 55 ft

SEI WHALE 65 ft

GRAY WHALE 50 ft

DESIGN VARIANTS

LITTLE PIKED WHALE 35 ft

DOLPHINS

MERMAID...

...& probable source DUGONG 9 ft

KILLER

FAMILIAR SPERM

HUMPBACK

SPERM

45

✳ A Tropical-Fish Mobile:

Whittling and Balancing Seventeen Different Woods

When an English naturalist saw my Bali-bird mobile, he mentioned that natives in Antigua wove straw fishes for mobiles. This set me to thinking of the clouds of tropical fish over Buccoo reef in Tobago, thence to this mobile. The conventional mobile is usually an odd number of elements—three, five, seven—but I had the idea of using a different wood for each fish and my initial list totaled twelve. One way to approximate the swirling mass of color of fish over a reef would be to tint them—and this would more nearly depict greens and blues that are so common; but I prefer natural wood colors, which meant that my mobile would be predominantly brown, with some whites, reds and even black as possibilities. By now, my list had grown to seventeen, enough for two or even three normal mobiles.

These seventeen tropical fish, when windswept, produce action similar to that on a reef. (This makes a group photograph almost as difficult to sort out, so detailed photographs follow.)

I wanted the mobile to be compact, which meant small fish, and I decided (as usual) to abandon scale and make each fish from whatever scrap of whatever wood seemed most suitable. This did make it possible to get some color and stripe effects from the wood itself. Zebra wood makes a good sergeant-major if the stripes are run vertically; cherry is a good color for a squirrelfish; ebony has a good color for a frogfish, who will also add a note of ugliness to the composition. Lignum vitae growth wood provides the light-colored tail of the jewelfish, while the heartwood gives an interesting pattern for the body, which in real life is iridescent purple with white spots along the back. Cocobola has a long, lateral figure, which made a good sailfish. I could have approximated the striping of the huge sail by running the grain vertically on this fin (which is one of the few separate elements glued in, the other two being antennae on the frogfish), but I chose to run grain the long way of the body.

Of course, it is advisable to remember grain to provide maximum strength in the thin cross-section of the fins and tail, but this problem can be minimized by leaving those parts abnormally thick, and thinning the edges to give apparent lightness to the composition. In some cases, however—abnormally long or wide fins—it is preferable to adapt grain to them. In the angelfish, for example, I used walnut, and, because of its tendency to split, the grain had to run the long way. Also, this particular scrap was quite thin, so the angelfish is really a two-sided low relief, while the puffer and the dolphin are fully three-dimensional. (This difference is, incidentally, of relatively little importance, as far as appearance is concerned; it is preferable, in fact, to have the large flat fish thin and light so they will be activated by drafts more easily. When the mobile is hung, there are so many elements that the observer is unlikely to make detailed comparisons.)

Shapes were adapted from pictures in fish identification books and sawed out on a bandsaw. Some modifications may be necessary to eliminate or merely suggest threadlike appendages, for example. Details can be cut more closely with a scrollsaw, which will also

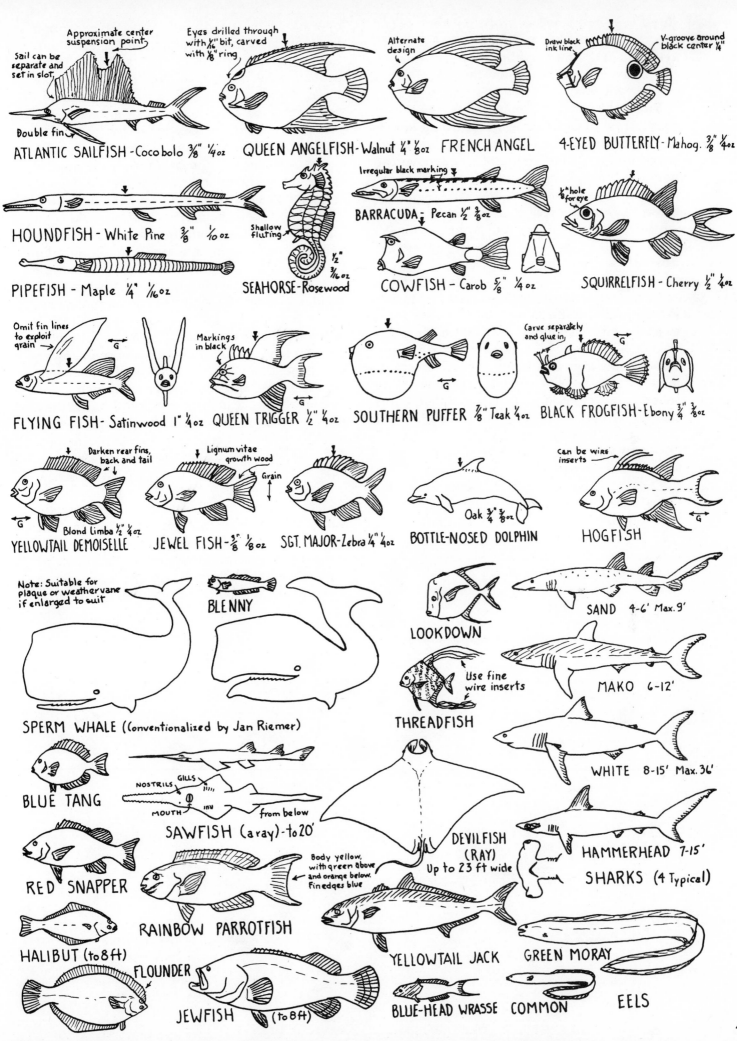

ATLANTIC SAILFISH - Cocobolo 3/8" 1/4 oz

Sail can be separate and set in slot

Approximate center suspension point

Double fin

QUEEN ANGELFISH - Walnut 1/4" 1/8 oz

Eyes drilled through with 1/16" bit, carved with 1/8" ring

Alternate design

FRENCH ANGEL

4-EYED BUTTERFLY - Mahog. 3/8" 1/4 oz

Draw black ink line

V-groove around black center 1/4"

HOUNDFISH - White Pine 3/8" 1/10 oz

PIPEFISH - Maple 1/4" 1/16 oz

SEAHORSE - Rosewood

Shallow fluting

1/2" 3/16 oz

BARRACUDA - Pecan 1/2" 3/8 oz

Irregular black marking

COWFISH - Carob 5/8" 1/4 oz

SQUIRRELFISH - Cherry 1/2" 1/4 oz

1/4" hole for eye

FLYING FISH - Satinwood 1" 1/4 oz

Omit fin lines to exploit grain

G

QUEEN TRIGGER 1/2" 1/4 oz

Markings in black

G

SOUTHERN PUFFER 7/8" Teak 1/4 oz

G

BLACK FROGFISH - Ebony 3/4" 3/8 oz

Carve separately and glue in

G

YELLOWTAIL DEMOISELLE

Blond Limba 1/2" 1/4 oz

Darken rear fins, back and tail

G

JEWEL FISH - 3/8" 1/8 oz

Lignum vitae growth wood

Grain

SGT. MAJOR - Zebra 1/4" 1/4 oz

BOTTLE-NOSED DOLPHIN

Oak 3/4" 3/8 oz

HOGFISH

can be wire inserts

G

Note: Suitable for plaque or weathervane if enlarged to suit

BLENNY

SPERM WHALE (conventionalized by Jan Riemer)

LOOKDOWN

THREADFISH

Use fine wire inserts

SAND 4-6' Max. 9'

MAKO 6-12'

WHITE 8-15' Max. 36'

BLUE TANG

SAWFISH (a ray) - to 20'

NOSTRILS GILLS

MOUTH

from below

DEVILFISH (RAY) Up to 23 ft wide

HAMMERHEAD 7-15'

SHARKS (4 Typical)

RED SNAPPER

RAINBOW PARROTFISH

Body yellow, with green above and orange below. Fin edges blue

YELLOWTAIL JACK

GREEN MORAY

HALIBUT (to 8 ft)

FLOUNDER

JEWFISH   (to 8 ft)

BLUE-HEAD WRASSE   COMMON

EELS

47

serve to remove excess wood between dorsal fins or the wings of the flying fish. A saw will also help in thinning the fin and tail portions of the blanks, particularly in the hard woods where whittling is a chore at best.

From the whittling standpoint, the job is mostly rounding surfaces and showing details with V-grooves. Remember that the width, depth and apparent shape of a V-groove can be varied to suit the design. Thus around the pectoral fins—those at the sides of the head—in most cases it is easiest simply to indicate their position and shape with V-grooves. Use narrow grooves to suggest the ribs of the fins, and a broad V-groove to outline the fin itself, this V-groove having a vertical side against the fin and a broad flat side fairing into the side of the fish, so it looks as if the fin is standing away from the body below. A similar V-groove will make the gill stand away from the body. In some cases, it may be worth while to carve the fins in the round (as on the dolphin), or to whittle the fins separately and glue them into drilled holes. I made the dolphin, incidentally, in an "action" pose and fully in the round because he is, in a sense, the centerpiece of the design.

The variation in wood characteristics provides a challenge. You may be surprised to find that all the woods can be whittled, albeit the very hard ones require a great many more cuts and somewhat frequent knife resharpening. Also, the very hard woods generally have less tendency to split than the more familiar

ones like walnut and mahogany. An exception is cocobola, which tends to split like walnut. Satinwood also tends to split and give grain problems because of its "figure." On lignum vitae, the growth wood is much softer than the heartwood, so cutting across from one to the other must be done very carefully.

To make the eye, it is easiest to drill the pupil right through the fish, unless the head is quite thick. In every case, however, I used drilled holes for the pupil, and simulated the iris by cutting a channel around the hole. The squirrelfish has an abnormally large eye, so in this instance the pupil hole was larger and the iris edge was simulated by a V-groove well outside it. Also, the frogfish has a fat head and a ridge around the eye; this can be represented by leaving a ridge of wood around the eye when the head is shaped. The mouth, in most tropical fish, is almost abnormally small, but a few have long mouths, which are best as sawn slots, because this lets the light through.

Fin ribs are a painstaking job. I found they had to be carved with the knife; a V-tool or veiner made too many tears on the across-grain edges. Also, to simulate the points of the ribs at the outer edge of the fin, a scrollsaw was very helpful.

The fish weigh so little that they can be suspended from monofilament nylon thread, which partially disappears if the mobile is hung in a light area. Drilling a hole at the balance point and inserting the end of the thread with a good plastic cement in the hole

Downward from top: Four-eyed butterfly (mahogany), yellowtail demoiselle (blond limba), Atlantic sail (cocobola) and barracuda (pecan).

Jewel (lignum vitae), flying fish (satinwood), queen trigger (unknown red hardwood), and Southern puffer (teak).

gives the least visible support for the fish, but may be difficult to glue in. An eye can be formed on the end of a pin and this glued in the hole. It will look less natural, but will be more secure. To find the proper point, I use two straight pins held against the body or fin from opposite sides. Actually, if the fish is not quite balanced, so it hangs slightly nosed up or nosed down, the mobile may look more life-like. In the sketches, I have indicated the support point I found; it may vary slightly in yours because of differences in blank thick-ness or carving. The nylon thread, by the way, can be purchased at any notions store—it is used in sewing synthetics and is very durable and much stronger than cotton thread.

When the glue has set firmly and the fish hangs to your satisfaction, it can be varnished (matte or satin finish) or waxed. (I prefer waxing in this case because of the beauty of some of the hard woods.) Do *not* sand the fish unless you have splintery or rough spots. The small planes left from whittling will catch the light and create some illusion of scales. To carve individual scales takes an inordinate amount of time and in my opinion is not worth the effort; it is excessive detail. In the case of the flying fish, I felt that even veining the "wings" was excessive. This particular fish, because its wings extend so far over its head, presents a problem in balance, particularly since the balance point is between the wings and therefore hard to fit with the nylon fila-ment. It may be better in this case to support

the fish by a long-shanked eye that can be bent to balance (as I finally did), or by a double thread through the tips of the wings.

Assembling the mobile is a matter of balanc-ing weights and colors of wood. Even with a delicate postal scale, I could not get the weights with total accuracy—they obviously vary more than is indicated by the weights in the drawing. (The drawing, by the way, shows wood, thickness and weight for the fish I selected; you may prefer some of the others sketched or some of your own design.)

Generally speaking, mobiles are assembled by suspending the elements from whiffletrees, which are in turn balanced and suspended from larger whiffletrees. Slight differences in the weight of the elements on the two arms of the whiffletree are readily compensated for by moving the "center" support point of the whif-fletree slightly. Also, a pair of elements sus-pended from a whiffletree arm can be bal-anced by a single element on the other arm, and elements may also be suspended from the support point—as I did with the seahorse and the dolphin. (These two, by the way, are not fish; the seahorse is a crustacean and the dolphin is a mammal.)

The conventional mobile is basically in a plane created by the two arms of the major whiffletree. To increase the concentration of fish, I made mine three-dimensional by using two major whiffletrees crossed at right angles. One of these, by coincidence, has pairs, so four fish are on each side of the major whiffletree;

Black frogfish (ebony), squirrelfish (cherry), and cowfish (carob).

Seahorse (rosewood), sergeant-major (zebra), pipefish (maple), houndfish (pine) and queen angel (walnut).

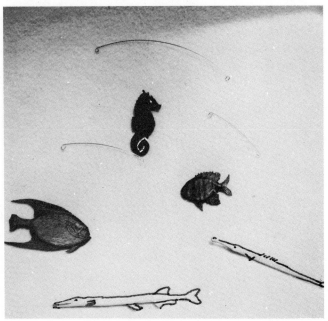

the other has two fish balanced by one, so six fish make up the total. It is also possible to make endless variations on this basic pattern—one heavy fish can balance three or four light ones, for example, or single fish can be hung from other parts of the whiffletree—or even from other fish.

To start assembling the mobile, begin with the bottom elements. Select a suitable pair—probably a round fish and a long one—it is best to have the long ones at the bottom of the mobile so they have clearance. Make whiffletree long enough so the two will clear each other's suspense cords—you'll want the long fish to hang below the other anyway, so the whiffletree need only be long enough so the cords are a bit over half the length of the shorter fish apart. Whiffletrees can be made of music wire, which is tempered and polished steel and obtainable from a hardware store in wrapped 1/4-pound coils. I used No. 10 wire (0.024 inch diameter) for all but the two major whiffletrees, which were No. 18 (0.041). The minor whiffletrees need only have eyes formed at the end; it is easier and more graceful to let the wire retain its coil curve than to attempt to straighten it. But close the eyes, or they'll snag other filaments and each other.

The nylon filaments from the fish are knotted temporarily into the eyes. Then another nylon filament is knotted at the center of the whiffletree and slid until the fish are balanced, then glued to prevent further slippage. This is an important step; unless it is done initially, the units will slip and slide during later steps of assembly and cause endless nuisance.

The second row of whiffletrees will be longer than the first, to allow clearance for the total width of the widest elements of the first, unless one of the balancing elements is something like the ebony fish, which alone can equal two other fish and their whiffletree. (It is usually helpful in planning the assembly to retain the heavier fish for second-stage balancing.)

The top whiffletrees must be both heavier and much longer than the second row, of course. I made mine a bit too short, so I found it necessary to straighten them out somewhat to separate the elements—and still had some occasional contact of adjacent fish. When I sold it, I therefore replaced them with longer and stiffer coat-hanger wire.

Once the entire mobile is assembled, hang it and begin to adjust the heights of individual fish so they are not all at the same level and so that the positions of the larger fish balance those of the smaller ones. This is a matter of what looks well. When you're satisfied with the relative heights, double-knot the nylon, glue the knot to the eye and cut off the excess filament. It may also be necessary to make some adjustments in whiffletree height; this is a nuisance but becomes possible by cutting out the knots and restringing. Finally, add elements like the seahorse and dolphin from whiffletree centers if you have noticeable blank spots—and hang your mobile where drafts, but not people's heads—can move it lazily.

Even a single fish can be made into a mobile, of course, so you can produce yours with fresh-water fish, a favorite breed or some of the other patterns I have sketched. It is also possible to carve each fish much more elaborately and in an "action" pose, although this is likely not to repay the effort because the mobile needs flat surfaces to catch vagrant airs, and in-the-round fish as well as action poses work against you in that respect.

Some in-the-round carvings make better mobiles than they do standing figures, incidentally. In one show, I entered an ebony baton which was basically four female figures, one above the other, and representing the four seasons of the year. The judge, a sculptress, asked the show manager for a piece of black thread and a tack, so the baton could be suspended from the ceiling rather than lying on a table—and awarded it a prize. I have also used a Lazy Susan topped with a circular mirror to display standing carvings so the observer can see all sides without picking up the carving and risking damage. (Some people are unreliable—fragile parts "come off" everything they touch!)

Dolphin in action (oak) is the "centerpiece" of the mobile, and properly hard to photograph.

✳ With Animals, the Silhouette Is the Key:

Low-relief, Appliqué, Intarsia Examples

Animals and birds usually have distinctive silhouettes, as they are naturals for low-relief carving, for plaques, appliqués, wall panels, even for free-standing sculptures. These are a miscellaneous group in various woods and techniques as examples. All six were made about the same time, although one did not suggest the other to any degree.

Simplest of the group is the black skimmer, carved in white pine and oil-painted as a wall decoration for a boat in Florida. It has more detailed feathering than it really needs but will be mounted in the close quarters of a cruiser cabin and hence will be viewed at 3 to 6 feet at most. The anatomical detail may serve to interest people more concerned with an accurate depiction of a favorite local bird than with esthetics. The blank was sawed from ³/₄-inch wood, with grain running from beak to tail, of course.

The pair of cardinals and the lion (sketch on page 52) were much more difficult to carve. Rosewood provided a desirable color and figure, as well as a lovely natural finish, but rosewood is by no means easy or soft to whittle. Setting-in of the outline is best done with a ¹/₈-inch firmer and grounding with ¹/₄-inch flat gouge and firmer; that reduces wear and tear on the fingertips when details are whittled.

The magic bird in the big plaque is so highly conventionalized that it is barely recognizable as a bird at all. However, it provides a wide range of surfaces and shapes, as well as an excursion into typical Maori motifs. This shape, as a matter of fact, was the one that von Däniken used to "prove" that beings from outer space came to the Earth as astronauts—although to me, and I suspect to the Maori, it is simply an explanation of how their island was populated, with Pourangahua, a Maori god, arriving on his magic bird—a story like that of Sinbad and the roc.

I selected mahogany for the piece, and felt that carving tools were preferable to the knife because of the areas involved. The whorls and spirals that are characteristic of Maori carving are difficult in any wood, but particularly so in mahogany because of its tendency to split. Incidentally, the Maori seem to use the spiral to indicate a movable joint of the body—witness the placement of these elements on the body of the god. The bird's claws and head have cross-sections quite similar to that of a conventional molding, the concave shape making a gouge essential.

The cockerel differs from the other design in that it is intarsia—a series of carved wood sections joined on a walnut background. As intarsia often is, this design is in various woods, but unlike most intarsia, it is quite high relief—almost half-round, with shaping of

Black skimmer as a detailed but unpainted silhouette (below), and painted with oils (right). Feather detail was provided because the carving was hung against a cruiser cabin wall and will always be seen at close range. I prefer it uncolored.

parts carefully carried out, but detail only on pinion feathers and the elaborate tail. Most difficult are the legs, because of their delicacy. The tail is close behind (no pun intended). I found the legs and tail to be basically whittling of a scrollsawed form, although tools can be used on the tail to remove unwanted wood in back.

The tiger and zebra plaques were primarily an effort to test the distinctive grain of a piece of zebrawood I discovered. They are interesting, but the grain figure doesn't do for them all it might be expected to. Further, the wood is difficult to work, because darker portions of the figure are much harder than the lighter ones, so carving is alternately hard and easy, with constant sudden changes along a single cut.

Top—Pourangahua on his magic bird coming to New Zealand. Note Maori-style whorls at joints and shell-insert eyes. Mahogany, 1 × 12 × 12 in. Above—Two experiments with zebra wood in low relief. About 3 × 3 in. before mounting. Below—Cardinals and recumbent lion in rosewood, about 3 × 5 in. Right—Intarsia cockerel (see sketch).

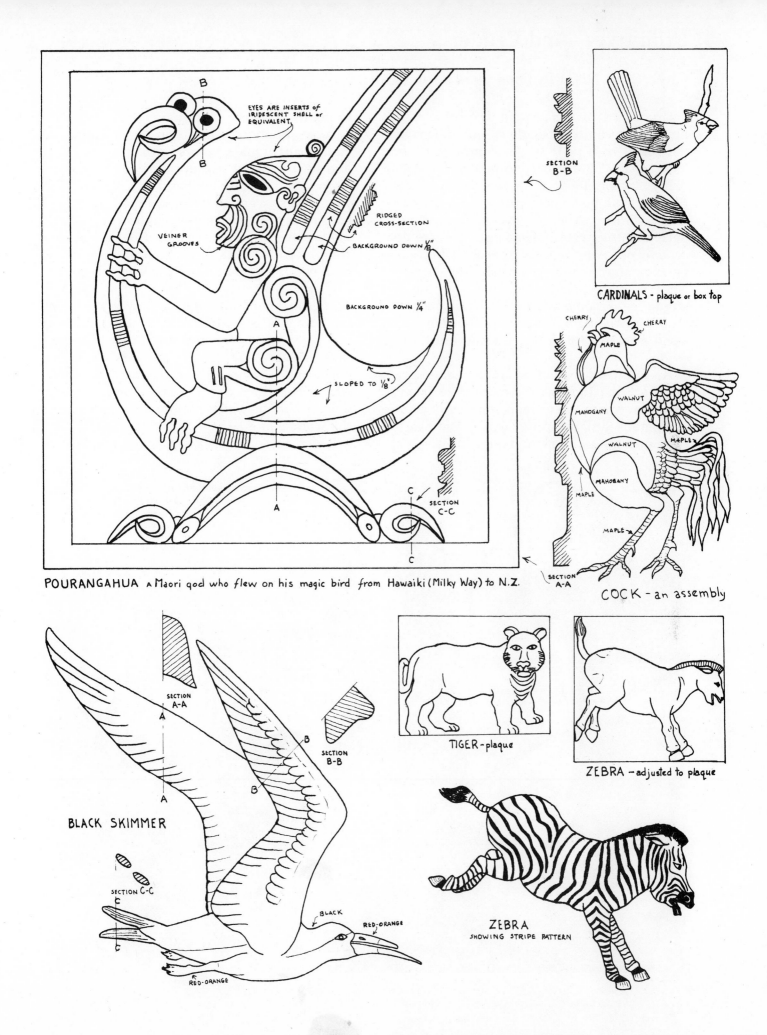

EYES ARE INSERTS of IRIDESCENT SHELL or EQUIVALENT

RIDGED CROSS-SECTION

BACKGROUND DOWN ⅛"

VEINER GROOVES

BACKGROUND DOWN ¼"

SLOPED TO ⅛"

A

A

B

B

SECTION C-C

C

C

POURANGAHUA a Maori god who flew on his magic bird from Hawaiki (Milky Way) to N.Z.

SECTION B-B

CARDINALS - plaque or box top

CHERRY

CHERRY

MAPLE

MAHOGANY

WALNUT

MAPLE

WALNUT

MAHOGANY

MAPLE

MAPLE

SECTION A-A

COCK - an assembly

TIGER - plaque

ZEBRA - adjusted to plaque

SECTION A-A

A

A

SECTION B-B

B

B

BLACK SKIMMER

SECTION C-C

C

C

BLACK

RED-ORANGE

RED-ORANGE

ZEBRA SHOWING STRIPE PATTERN

✳ Primitive—And Crude:

Cuna (San Blas) Indians Carve for Utility

Crudeness in design and execution is not limited to primitive people by any means; it is the result of a poor sense of proportion and lack of skill. But primitive peoples are more likely to produce crude carvings because they've had no opportunity to see art other than their own. A sense of design leads them to decorate utilitarian objects and to make decorative ones to wear or venerate, but some peoples simply never develop the "knack." They produce pieces of obvious purpose and strength, as some of our Colonial ancestors did, using available wood and knowing which wood was best for each purpose—but they're crude.

An interesting exception to the general rule are the Cuna Indians of the San Blas Islands, Panama, where the women appear to be quite competent designers; they design and execute their own *molas*, some quite fanciful and elab-

orate. (A *mola* is a cloth panel decorated with reverse appliqué—insertion or stacking of cloth strips of many colors, with upper ones cut and sewn back to reveal the lower ones—and worn as a front or back band on a blouse.) The women also wear gold rings in their noses and gold necklaces, as well as beadwork wristlets, anklets and upper-arm bands. But the men are content with "white-man" clothing and wear no jewelry. They make quite good dugout canoes (most of the San Blas live on offshore islands and commute almost daily to the mainland to garden patches and for water) and one-piece seats for their houses, but they rarely decorate either and do almost no pure "pleasure" carving beyond occasional dolls. And what they do is quite crude, without evidence of the well-developed design sense of the women.

The men do, on occasion, show glimmerings

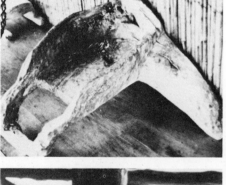

Far left—Three typical San Blas stools, hacked out of stumps with no decoration and little effort to square up bases—-the dirt floor takes care of that. Left—A surprisingly lifelike eagle or hawk, possibly copied from a picture. Below—The idol and walking stick are in sharp contrast: The idol is traditional, while the stick is modern and painted in true colors. Each is a single piece. The chief seated on a one-legged stool shows the usual flat face and square-topped head, depicting the ceremonial head scarf.

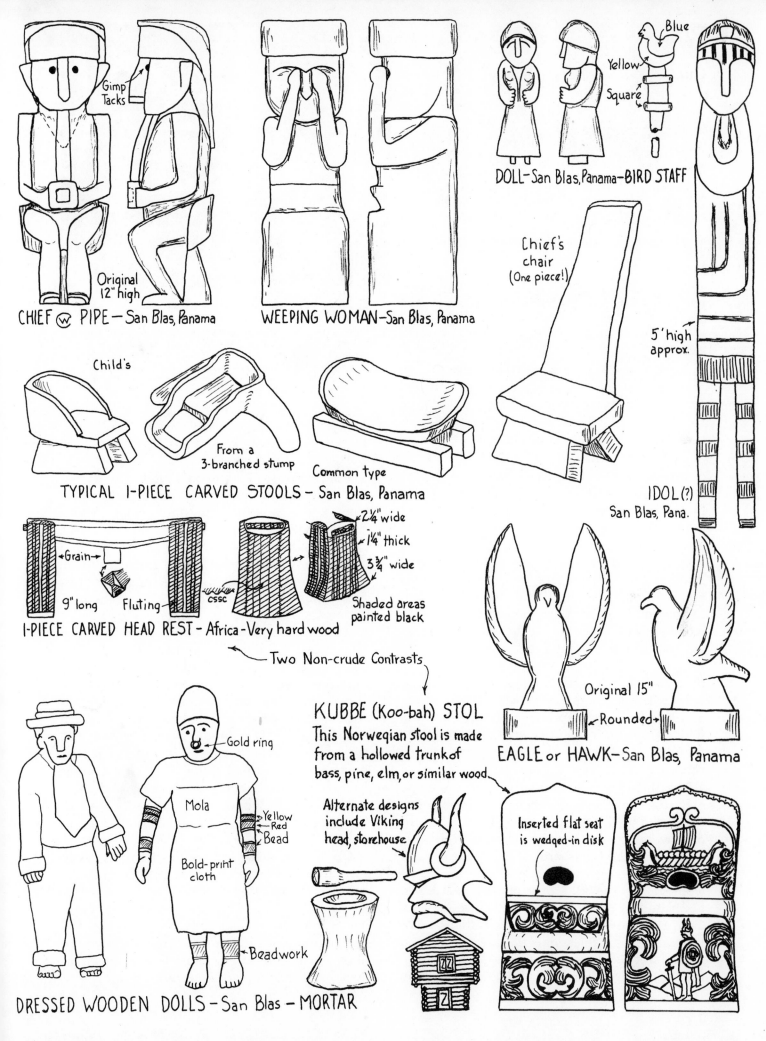

CHIEF w PIPE — San Blas, Panama

Gimp Tacks

Original 12" high

WEEPING WOMAN — San Blas, Panama

DOLL — San Blas, Panama — BIRD STAFF

Blue
Yellow
Square

Chief's chair (One piece!)

5' high approx.

Child's

From a 3-branched stump

Common type

TYPICAL I-PIECE CARVED STOOLS — San Blas, Panama

IDOL (?) San Blas, Pana.

←Grain→

9" long   Fluting   cssc

2¼" wide
1¼" thick
3¾" wide

Shaded areas painted black

I-PIECE CARVED HEAD REST — Africa — Very hard wood

Two Non-crude Contrasts

KUBBE (Koo-bah) STOL
This Norwegian stool is made from a hollowed trunk of bass, pine, elm, or similar wood

Original 15"

←Rounded→

EAGLE or HAWK — San Blas, Panama

Gold ring

Mola

Yellow
Red
Bead

Bold-print cloth

Beadwork

DRESSED WOODEN DOLLS — San Blas — MORTAR

Alternate designs include Viking head, storehouse

Inserted flat seat is wedged-in disk

Above—Typical dolls and a figure of a weeping woman, pictured in one-piece carved seats for children, which are like low-backed rockers. Left top—An African headrest, heavily decorated and painted, a sharp contrast to San Blas seats. It is made of three pieces; San Blas pieces are units. Left—This very crude model of a glass-bottomed raft has a woven-reed roof and is assembled piece by piece, which is unusual; it was probably made with the idea that the owner of the raft would buy it (which he did).

of artistic imagination, as in the carving of the chief with the pipe or the group in the glass-bottom barge. Both resulted from their contact with a Pittsburgher named Tom Moody, who achieved the impossible a few years back and rented a three-acre "coconut" island for a small hotel consisting of seven guest cabins and a couple of other buildings, all of bamboo. In the course of his ticklish negotiations, Tom gave each of the three tribal chiefs a long-stemmed Bavarian pipe, so I found one carving depicting the chief sitting on his taller stool and puffing his pipe. Tom also has a barge with which to take his guests fish-watching, and this has been reproduced after a fashion, with very crude figures and a woven-reed roof. (Two of the figures have horse or dog shapes!)

Yet the chief, the crying woman, the eagle and the seats show strength and vitality enough to justify their inclusion here. The bird on a walking stick is quite accurate in proportions, and the seats are all very sturdy and usable, although they'd never do on a hardwood floor—the idea of a plane surface that accurate has not yet influenced these carvers. Tom had the idea of having the Indians carve bases for his tables like their wasp-waisted mortars of hardwood stumps—and had to refinish the bases himself so they didn't rock on

his wood floors. (The Indians thin the central portion for knee comfort.)

For contrast, I have included two widely differing designs, one from a supposedly primitive people, and the other dating back so far it probably was primitive as well. Both of these, however, have graceful curved shapes and decoration; they come from peoples with an inherent sense of design. The African headrest has a rounded bottom, for comfort of the user rather than because the maker couldn't carve a straight line. It would never occur to a San Blas man to put this much effort into a seat—or even a favorite dugout—which lasts about ten years. The Scandinavian *kubbe stol* is even more elaborate than the African headrest, and shows great ingenuity in utilizing a natural shape. It is deeply carved, tinted with stain to make the design stand out and is now being made in the United States by Halvar Landsverk and others in Minnesota. Weight is a bit over 25 pounds with outer walls about 2-inches thick. The flat seat is usually upholstered.

Obviously, there are few instructions if you want to copy the San Blas pieces. Just grab the nearest chunk of wood and let 'er go! But you'll find that you have a great many "civilized" inhibitions; you'll try to improve the design and make it more accurate—and you're likely to end up with something which is at least as primitive and even more crude.

✳ Primitive but Not Crude:

American Indian Carvings Are Strong, Original Designs

Traditional designs of peoples all over the world are suffering from the leveling process that accompanies our mechanized civilization. One country or people preempts another's ideas if there is a possibility of cash reward, and quality and individuality suffer in the process. Indians, like everyone else, have been influenced by the buyer: the tourist who wants a cheap memento of his trip, the trader who wants multiple copies of a popular piece or who takes designs from one area to another to cut costs—and by the white man in general, who flaunts his higher standard of living by "collecting" anything and everything, his gadgets and his culture. The Indian abandons his own crafts to emulate the white man in using machinery and better tools, and cheaper materials like plastics and print cloth.

No one is to blame for this; the world has never stood still. But, as a result, the distinctive and handmade articles that once differentiated cultures are rapidly disappearing. A number of the pieces shown here were carved by older men who have since died, and younger men have been unwilling to take the time necessary to learn the technique involved, and to follow it.

The pipes, for example, were made from scraps of hormigo wood left over from marimba keys. The wood grows on the Guatemalan coast and was toted on men's backs to the highlands. These five pipes and the lion are the last of the pieces made by an Indian near Chichicastenango, and were lying forgotten in the corner of a trader's store there. The pipes are meticulously made, with a tinplate lining

Right—A variety of Indian designs are shown on these wooden plates from Panama. The plate is hollowed in the conventional way, then carved in low relief. Design is smooth and gilded, while background is textured with vertical gouge lines, then blackened. Below—Zuni fetishes and a fetish necklace. Materials are shell, coral and various semiprecious stones. Below right—Pipes and a lion carved from hormigo wood in Guatemala. Stems are bamboo and bowls are lined with tinplate.

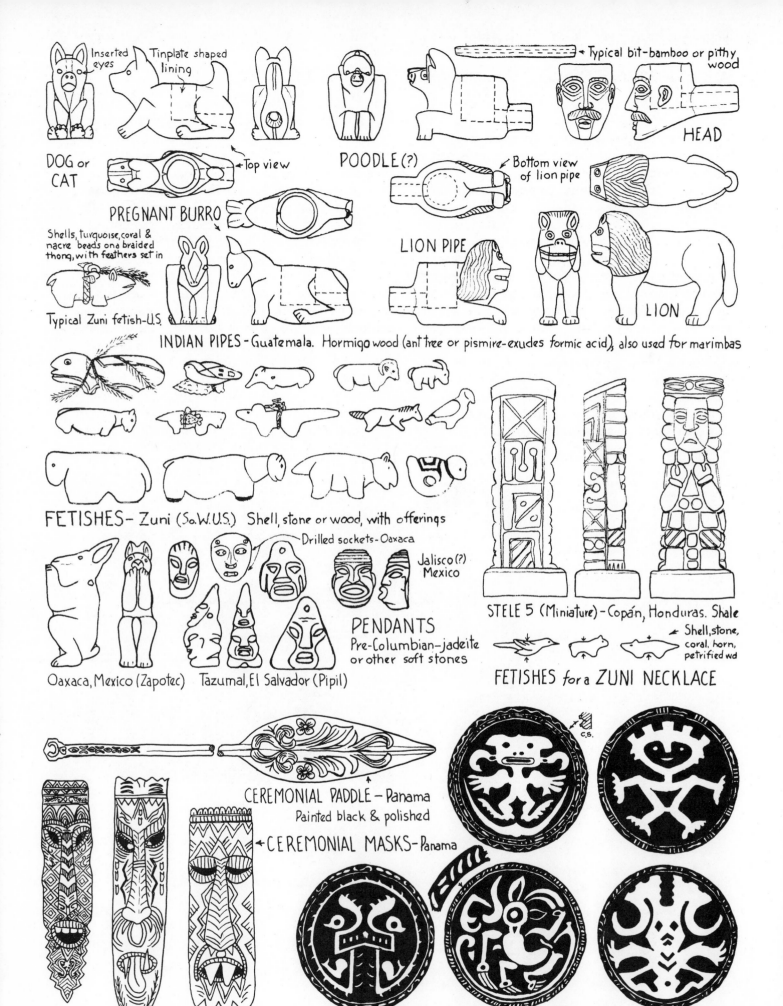

Inserted eyes — Tinplate shaped lining

DOG or CAT

Typical bit–bamboo or pithy wood

HEAD

POODLE (?)

Bottom view of lion pipe

Top view

PREGNANT BURRO

Shells, turquoise, coral & nacre beads on a braided thong, with feathers set in

Typical Zuni fetish–U.S.

LION PIPE

LION

INDIAN PIPES – Guatemala. Hormigo wood (ant tree or pismire–exudes formic acid), also used for marimbas

FETISHES – Zuni (So.W.U.S.) Shell, stone or wood, with offerings

Drilled sockets–Oaxaca

Jalisco (?) Mexico

PENDANTS
Pre-Columbian–jadeite or other soft stones

Oaxaca, Mexico (Zapotec)   Tazumal, El Salvador (Pipil)

STELE 5 (Miniature) – Copán, Honduras. Shale

Shell, stone, coral, horn, petrified wd

FETISHES for a ZUNI NECKLACE

CEREMONIAL PADDLE – Panama
Painted black & polished

CEREMONIAL MASKS – Panama

DECORATIVE TRAYS – Panama. Background recessed, scalloped, blackened in the tobacco chamber, and inserted eyes of semiprecious stones. The designs are simple and relatively easy to carve, but powerful and distinctive, and the resulting pipes are light and compact. The Indians smoked sections of penny hand-rolled cigars in them.

Similarly, fetishes were once the proud possessions of Indian families in our own Southwest, particularly in the pueblo areas. Zuni craftsmen made the best ones, good enough that other tribes traded for them. They were usually soft stone, turquoise, coral, abalone shell, and similar materials, although some were made of wood. They carried decorations of offerings of shell, coral or turquoise beads, feathers and miniature arrowheads, particularly the "prey" fetishes, images of animals frequently hunted by the Indians. Fetishes were "fed" regularly by being dusted with a mixture of cornmeal and ground turquoise and other ingredients—and rewarded with added decoration when a hunt was successful. An Indian once told me: "If you don't believe in it, it's just a carving of an animal; if you believe in it, it becomes a fetish, with power."

Almost all early fetish designs were very simple, with foreshortened legs and ears, blunt noses and little or no detail. They were not in exact proportion but did depict the general outline of the animal, real or imaginary, and emphasized its physical characteristics: a mountain lion had a heavy, powerful neck; a horse had a blocky head and strong back; a bear was bulky and globular. In some respects, the fetishes and the Guatemalan pipes have similar designs.

Carving primitive figures of this sort is not difficult for the modern craftsman, but maintaining the simplicity and power with lack of detail *is*. The tendency is to be too accurate and too detailed. Pieces were made with crude and simple tools, so every bit of material removed was an effort, but the maker's belief in the piece made him keep at it until the shape was what he had in mind. His work thus was "primitive"—but decidedly not crude.

Left and below—Masks and a paddle carved by Panamanian Cocle Indians. Right—Small masks and a hare carved in soft stone in Mexico and Honduras; they are "instant antiques" for tourists. Below right—Miniature copy of Stele 5 at Copán, again carved from soft stone for tourists.

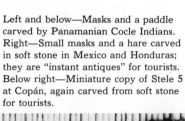

❋ Those African Animals—Typical and Atypical:

Great Diversity Characterizes Tribal Designs

Like most Americans, I have always tended to think of Africa as more of a large country than as a continent, forgetting that it includes such diverse peoples and cultures as the Egyptians, Moroccans, Arabs, Libyans, as well as the myriad of individual black peoples, each with its own way of life. Too, I have been conscious of "African" woodcarvings as something decorators favored for primitive contrast with our otherwise opulent and sophisticated living spaces. Gradually, however, I have come to realize that the crude and blocky pieces which tourists bring back from Kenya and Tànganyika may represent the quantity, but not necessarily the quality, of the work in the primarily black-populated countries, and that there is as much diversity of design in black Africa as in any other continent. The crude ebony figures of animals and people are representative only of a limited area of East Africa—and not always that, because pieces that sell to tourists are produced in increasing quantities and with less and less attention to quality; thus they became familiar. Money is a powerful incentive there as anywhere else.

Consider, if you will, the typical Kenyan animals like the springbok, giraffe and rhinoceros—all standard, readily available "tourist" items, like India's elephants. They are blocky, simple and undecorated except for spots like those on the giraffe, burned on hastily with a hot wire, or the inlaid eyes of the crocodile at right—a very regrettable and spiritless piece. They are also often out of proportion and crude in form when compared with other "typical" national designs. Compare the springboks, for example, with the two contrasting deer styles from Norway, which have continuous flowing lines and suggest the lightness and speed of the animal. There are no rough or clumsy sections, and the thinness of the legs is exaggerated. Beside them, the Kenyan animals look primitive and hasty. The Norwegian animals look graceful, fragile, painstakingly done—and probably sell for ten times as much.

This is by no means typical of all Africa, however, or even of East Africa. Look at the water buffalo, the cobra, or the stone crocodile and fish. Or the unusual action pose of the leopard and its atypical support point. Or the stylized panels from Benin and Dahomey (West Coast). Or the bas-relief animals from Dahomey, which are practically caricatures and very enjoyable to look at.

A number of American carvers have copied East African animals, because they seem relatively simple and strong, at first glance. Like most animals, they start with a sawed silhouette, which need only be chamfered along the edges and smoothed up, then notched here and there, and presto: a finished carving. But it isn't that simple. Note that many figures

Contrast between East African and Scandinavian approaches to carving animals are illustrated by these examples. The Kenyan springbok is heavy in the hooves and muzzle and has less flow in its other contours than either of the Norwegian designs.

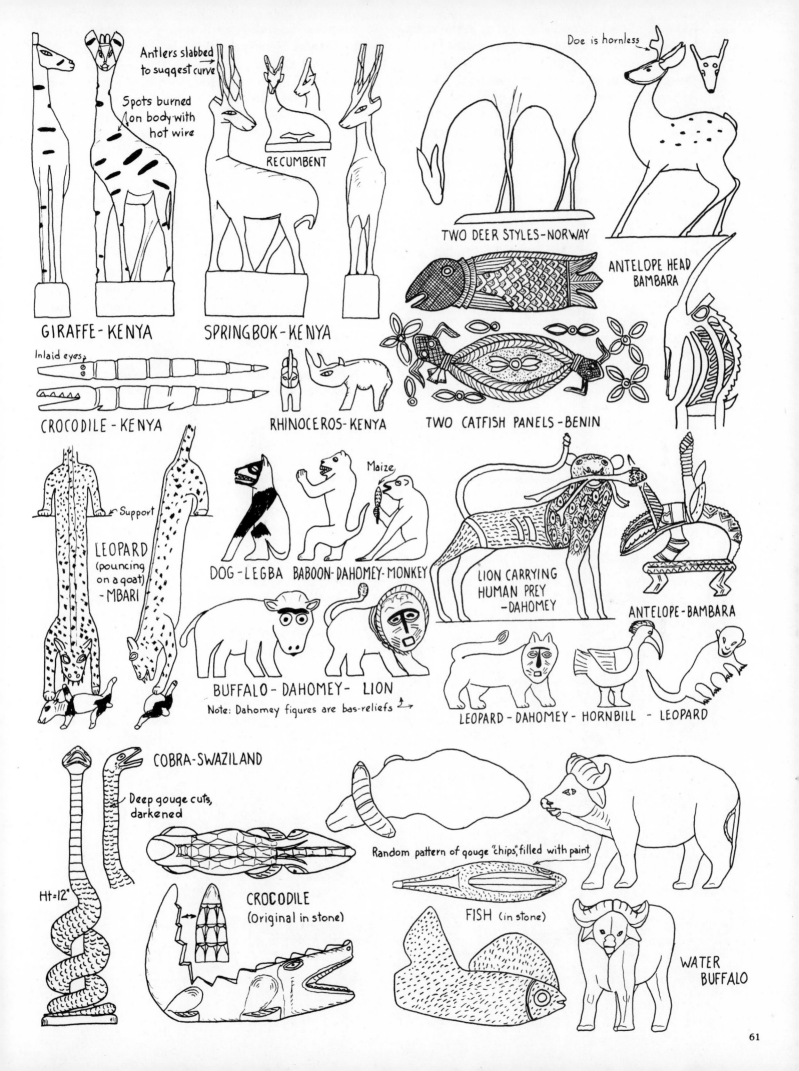

Antlers slabbed to suggest curve

Spots burned on body with hot wire

RECUMBENT

Doe is hornless

TWO DEER STYLES-NORWAY

ANTELOPE HEAD BAMBARA

GIRAFFE-KENYA

SPRINGBOK-KENYA

Inlaid eyes

CROCODILE-KENYA

RHINOCEROS-KENYA

TWO CATFISH PANELS-BENIN

Support

LEOPARD (pouncing on a goat) -MBARI

DOG-LEGBA

Maize

BABOON-DAHOMEY-MONKEY

LION CARRYING HUMAN PREY -DAHOMEY

ANTELOPE-BAMBARA

BUFFALO-DAHOMEY-LION

Note: Dahomey figures are bas-reliefs

LEOPARD-DAHOMEY-HORNBILL-LEOPARD

COBRA-SWAZILAND

Deep gouge cuts, darkened

Ht=12"

Random pattern of gouge "chips", filled with paint

CROCODILE (Original in stone)

FISH (in stone)

WATER BUFFALO

have the head turned slightly, as in the springbok, or a full quarter-turn, as in the giraffe; and the legs are usually carved integral with the base. These factors, necessary if the East African style is to be achieved, tend to make the carving just as difficult to make as one of a local pig. Carving the legs integral with the base adds time and complexity even if you drill and scrollsaw out the waste wood, but this design gives the composition much greater strength and stability, and looks much better than a base applied later.

Wood can be selected to suit yourself, of course, but if you plan a polished finish, as on the water buffalo, or a surface design that is crisp and clear, as on the cobra, fish, or leopard, a harder wood is preferable to a softer one, and one with a decided figure may compete with the surface pattern. A stronger wood means less likelihood of breaking spindly elements—like the horns or legs of the Norwegian deer, which should be done with the grain.

We often think of African carvings as black,

because so many are made of ebony. But blackness is no particular advantage; in fact, may be a disadvantage if the piece is in a dimly lighted room. However, black does offer a very good contrast if yellow or white pigment is to be rubbed into the surface design, as was done on the fish. After all, the Kenyan uses ebony because there is a great deal of it available, and it adds value to the finished piece. But, as you can see from the photographs, the African carver is not restricted to ebony; in the cobra the carver reversed the color scheme and used a light hardwood, then filled the pattern with a dark pigment. In some of the books I've read about the "old Africa," the authors spoke again and again of the skilled native carver and how he selected both color and grain of the wood to suit the piece and the personality of the ultimate user or recipient. This was even true if the carved object was a bowl, let alone a *mwiko* (household idol). But then, the old Africans, like primitives everywhere, understood that wood has a soul and used wood in rough blocks rather than as dressed lumber from a yard.

Most of these figures can be done with the knife alone; decoration, however, is produced with a veiner and flat gouges. The leopard's spots can be painstakingly produced with gouge scalloping in free forms and various sizes—or can be done simply with paint. On the other hand, a small gouge will simulate the scales of the cobra or the fish and provide three-dimensional shadows and texture that paint cannot. This is also true of the stylized Benin fish and Dahomey lion, but the Legba dog is better done with a surface finish or selection of a two-tone wood like walnut, utilizing the lighter growth wood for color patches. The crocodiles may also be scaled with a series of gouge cuts darkened with stain or pigment.

Left—Cobra from Swaziland. Below—A crude springbok from Kenya and a water buffalo from West Africa. Bottom—Animals from Kenya seem crude when compared with stylized designs from the West Coast.

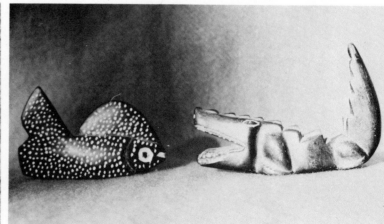

✳ Misinterpretation Can Be Fun:

Or, How to Make Several Carvings from One Blank

These figures are primarily for fun—a series of exercises in misinterpretation, as it were. It began when I made the minotaur—and found that some observers somehow missed the fact that it was a bull's head and a human body! They saw the bull's head and assumed an unusual pose, and that's all. The minotaur is mahogany, with holly horns inserted, and provides a real test in anatomy, both because of the pose and the mixture of species. As whittling projects go, he's tough, in my book.

The wolf in sheep's clothing is a very simple design, developed originally by the Pennsylvania Dutch. He is largely a chamfered silhouette, with the legs merely inserted dowel sections set at appropriate angles. But his tail is not carved—it is black fur, appliqued after the entire figure is stained black. Also, in a further mixture of media, a coat of white sheepskin is made to slip over the whole animal, the head going through a hole so the animal looks at first glance like a white sheep with black legs and head. He's really quite convincing, and is reminiscent of Red Ridinghood. Sketched with him are two side views of our currently endangered species, the gray wolf and the timber wolf, which differ little from some breeds of dogs.

The other figures on the page were the result of a present in Cooperstown, N.Y., when I taught there in 1974. A whittler dropped in for a morning with my class and eventually identified himself as from Ohio and handed out a batch of hand-sawed walnut blanks in return for the materials he'd been furnished in class. I brought several blanks home and, never having seen the original finished animals, decided I'd let my fancy roam. (The dachshund is an exception; his shape is so distinctive that it doesn't suggest much else.) But from the hound blank I was easily able to get a donkey, from a dog blank both a dog and a cat, and from a bird blank three different kinds of birds, one of which actually is a shy woodpecker who hangs from a drape. I wouldn't suggest walnut as a regular whittling wood, however; it's a bit hard on fingertips, although it provides very good natural color and finish without sanding or tinting. All that was necessary was a bit of wax.

Bill Higginbotham, who carves caricatures of people rather than animals, has shown me a similar idea. He makes a number of poses from the same basic blank, which I'd have real trouble doing; most of my figures of people are caricatures, whether or not I intend them to be.

These exercises in misinterpretation have

Right—Minotaur, legendary guardian of the Cretan labyrinth, was half man, half bull. This suggests a muscular human body in a human, rather than animal, pose. Even so, casual observers see only the bull head, suggesting that perhaps the proper composition would be a bull's body, with human upper torso, crowned by a human head with bull's horns. Far right—This walnut blank was for a tired hound dog, but made an enjoyable donkey, with slight misinterpretation (see sketches). What was wood for a lop ear makes a luxurious mane.

led me to a further study—to determine the anatomical differences that make a dog different from a donkey, or from a cat, and even the slight difference in various species of birds. It's relatively easy to make a basic simple bird, and rather difficult to produce one that looks like anything else, but I have, through the years, made dogs that persisted in looking like horses and cats. The answer is, of course, that it is easy to make a basic animal silhouette, but nearly as hard to get a likeness as it is with people; the individual placement of ears and eyes varies, as does the exact shape of the body. The best answer is to precede each development of a new design with a little careful research. Some—perhaps most—of that can be done with pencil and paper rather than with the knife, and for most of us, a little drawing ability is long overdue. I spent years carving a piece, then drawing an outline around it to get the sketch, which somehow now seems to be backward.

Below—Three identical blanks in walnut make three different birds, with a little adjustment to get the swallow's wingtips. Legs are added, made by twisting together four small-diameter copper wires, and inserting one end of the assembly in holes in the body and spreading the other ends to make claws to suit.

Bottom left—Further experiments with blanks. The dachshund retained his identity, but the dog blank also produced a cat (see sketches). Below—The wolf in sheep's clothing is a composite, with a rather crude wolf body carved from 3/4-in. wood with dowel legs and a glued-on black tail. When the sheepskin cover is applied, however, he becomes a momentarily convincing sheep.

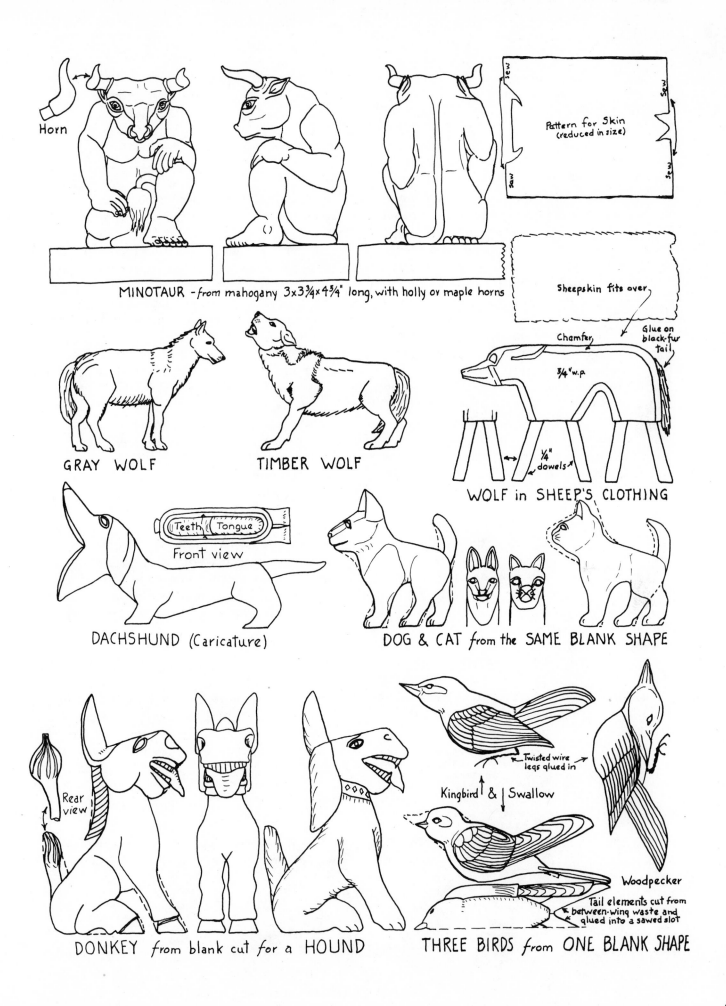

Horn

MINOTAUR – *from mahogany 3x3¾x4¾" long, with holly or maple horns*

Pattern for Skin
(reduced in size)

Sheepskin fits over

Chamfer

Glue on
black-fur
tail

¾" w.p.

¼"
dowels

GRAY WOLF

TIMBER WOLF

WOLF in SHEEP'S CLOTHING

Teeth Tongue

Front view

DACHSHUND (Caricature)

DOG & CAT *from the* SAME BLANK SHAPE

Rear
view

DONKEY *from blank cut for a* HOUND

Twisted wire
legs glued in

Kingbird & Swallow

Woodpecker

Tail elements cut from
between-wing waste and
glued into a sawed slot

THREE BIRDS *from* ONE BLANK SHAPE

❋ Some Selected Small Animals:

Details Suit Size and Shape

This group of animals is based primarily on the selection I made to supplement my collection during the 1974 Whittler's Wanderjahr. Most are therefore from Germany, but I've added several other challenging shapes—six from the Far East and three from our own Southern Highlands.

The three Indonesian birds caught my eye in a shop in Vollendam, Holland—probably left over from Holland's one-time empire. They are in a hard, dark-red wood, each a single piece, with no decoration except artificial eyes and natural finish. I was intrigued by the poses and the tying in of the bird with the base.

All of the group of animals below the drawing come from one shop in Oberammergau and are obviously products of the same designer. They are in linden, very small, very fragile and beautifully executed in angular lines, with light tints on backs and separately carved and inserted horns. Kids and fawns have tint spots.

These pieces contrast sharply with the rounded forms of the mule, kangaroo, and bear cub from the Southern Highlands (North Carolina and Tennessee), all done in harder fruit woods and wax-finished. The German colt is so blocky that he almost looks like a kid.

In recent years, it has become quite the fashion for Americans familiar with Japan to collect netsuke, the carefully carved little knobs that Japanese gentlemen once wore on pursestring thongs so the thong could be tucked under the obi, or sash. The two I have sketched are at least 150 years old. The toad is a hard brown wood with artificial eyes and the badger is ivory, now a dark yellow-brown.

They're fun to carve and offer an interesting variation to the usual flat designs on bolos and neckerchief slides.

The Chinese dog is bigger, also an antique in a hard, red wood, and has a T-shaped slot in the belly so it can be hooked over a sash or other projecting knob as a decoration. It is a very complex and distorted pose, with the head turned 180 degrees over the back and a ball held playfully in the front paws.

Ivory has always fascinated me as a carving material because it lends itself to detail and miniature carving, with little danger of splitting or breakage except from sudden changes of temperature in large pieces. I found three pieces in Germany, a swan and Pied Piper at Neuschwannstein Castle (see my Piper, page 157) and a split walnut ball from Ehrbach in Oldenwald which can be opened to show two forest scenes. The latter is particularly interesting because each side, rather than being one deep and complex pierced carving, is really three thin panels, each carrying part of the scene and mated so the panels behind can be seen through the one in front. Each has deer and trees and grass, intricately carved so that the assembled panel looks like a scene in perspective. It led me to try something of the same sort in wood—the result being the Pied Piper of Mittenwald (see page 157). (Incidentally, the ball has hinge and dowel of ivory.)

Ivory carving is, of course, a specialty, and the material is so hard that saws and files work better than knives for much of the cutting. German carvers now do most of the work with a dental burr. Even so, the cost of ivory carvings has more than tripled there in the past ten years, and the number of carvers is steadily declining. (The Piper cost about 80 marks, the forest scene 90 and the swan about 25—not much by American standards, with the mark then at 2.50 to the dollar.) All of these pieces are challenges if done in wood in larger size.

Left—Note conventionalized face, tail and markings on this Chinese antique dog. Belly is slotted to hook on a sash.

Far left—Three Indonesian birds integrate with bases, to protect legs and tails. Each is one piece, except for eyes.
Left—Walnut ball with ivory forest scenes actually shows five deer on each side, carved in thin pierced and stacked panels.

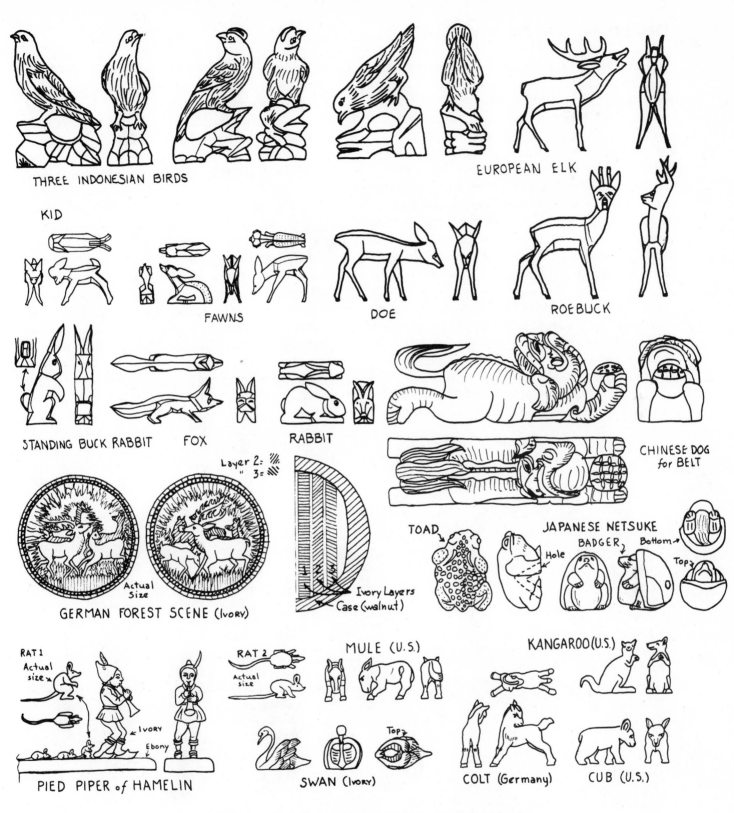

THREE INDONESIAN BIRDS

EUROPEAN ELK

KID

FAWNS

DOE

ROEBUCK

STANDING BUCK RABBIT   FOX   RABBIT

CHINESE DOG for BELT

Layer 2:
" 3 =

GERMAN FOREST SCENE (Ivory)

Actual Size

Ivory Layers
Case (walnut)

TOAD

JAPANESE NETSUKE

BADGER   Bottom

Hole

Top

RAT 1
Actual size

RAT 2
Actual size

MULE (U.S.)

KANGAROO (U.S.)

Ivory

Ebony

PIED PIPER of HAMELIN

SWAN (Ivory)

Top

COLT (Germany)

CUB (U.S.)

Miniature animals (shown near actual size) are in basswood and tinted.

67

✳ Common Animals Uncommonly Carved:

A Gallimaufry of Fauna and Ideas

Every tribe that carves inevitably produces animal, bird and fish forms, usually copied after local fauna, but sometimes highly imaginative, sometimes very simple and sometimes highly stylized, sometimes for fun, sometimes for play, and sometimes for worship. (These days, an increasing number are for tourists.) There is a great deal of imagination in the design of the parrot from New Guinea, much decorative sense in the Balinese birds and the Trobriand fish, evident stylizing in the birds from Guatemala. The piece can be innately humorous, like the Costa Rican monkey musician or the Guatemalan burro; it can be on a high artistic level like the flamingos (or cranes) and the bull; it can even be useful like the fish dish or the whale (photo on page 44). The only thing this group of fauna has in common is their uncommon design quality.

As in most animal carvings, the silhouette itself usually provides identification, leaving the carver free to let himself go on design or decoration if he dares. Thus we have surface patterns ranging from the detailed feathering of the quetzals and the hair of the monkey to a plain surface like those of the flamingos, swan, bull, burro, and Balinese birds. The surface may be suggested, as in the iguana and penguin, the hen and ferret from Russia, and the Mexican bird; it can be intricately patterned as in the alligator from Ponape, or converted into a pattern for an object, as in the fish from Trobriand. Some carvers make use of prominent figures in the wood, as in the American flamingo and Guatemalan swan; this, however, is relatively uncommon. Successful use of the lighter-colored growth wood, as in the Costa Rican bull, is rare. So, surprisingly, is actually distorting the figure to achieve a special design, as in the ferret and hen from the Soviet Union, the Mexican bird, Balinese fish, and Guatemalan burro. The blocky fig-

Left to right—Quetzael, Guatemala; flamingo or crane, Bali; flamingo, U.S.A., and fish, Bali; fish, Trobriand Island; bird group, Bali.

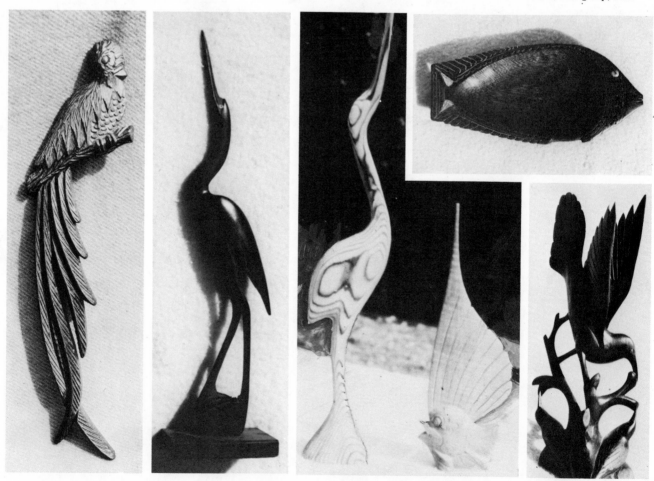

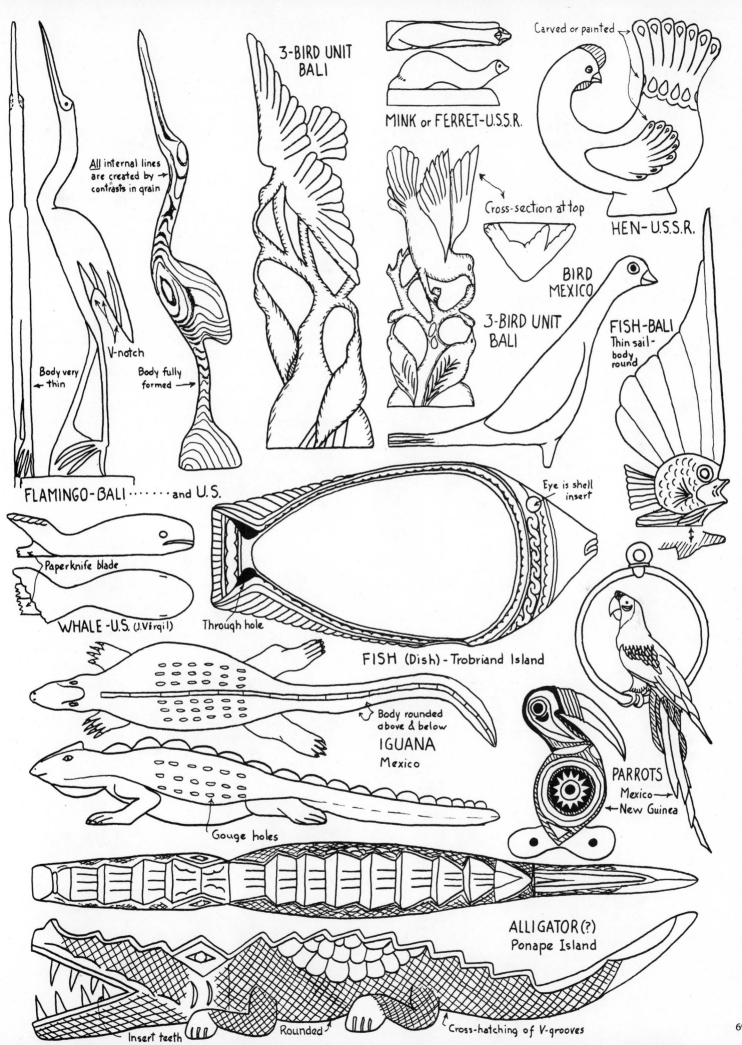

3-BIRD UNIT BALI

All internal lines are created by contrasts in grain →

V-notch

Body very thin

Body fully formed →

FLAMINGO-BALI ······· and U.S.

MINK or FERRET-U.S.S.R.

Carved or painted →

HEN-U.S.S.R.

Cross-section at top

BIRD MEXICO

3-BIRD UNIT BALI

FISH-BALI
Thin sail-body round

Paperknife blade

WHALE-U.S. (J. Virgil)

Eye is shell insert

Through hole

FISH (Dish)-Trobriand Island

Body rounded above & below
IGUANA
Mexico

Gouge holes

PARROTS
Mexico →
← New Guinea

ALLIGATOR (?)
Ponape Island

Insert teeth   Rounded →   Cross-hatching of V-grooves

69

ure, like that of the bull, was once common but now is relatively rare. Most native carvers seem content to carve as accurate a portrait as their skill and inclination will allow.

This is not intended to be a complete representation. There are other very well designed fauna in the chapters on American Indian and African animal carving (pages 57 and 60), as well as elsewhere in this book and my earlier ones. My intent here is to provide an idea of the possible variety of poses, techniques and finishes possible. The two flamingos or cranes illustrate how the same silhouette may be handled differently. The two fish on the first panel, or the two saurians, provide similar comparisons, as do the two parrots—although in these instances the subject is the same, but the silhouette, while readily recognizable, is different.

The ability of Balinese carvers to combine graceful bird forms with foliage in any available piece of wood is fascinating, but is born

partly from necessity. Their ebony must be imported nowadays—they've carved all their own—so every scrap is precious and hence is used if possible. Wide use, regardless of area, of the veiner and gouge in surface decoration is also worthy of note; most of these figures are basically projects for chisels rather than the knife. The only ones finished with color are the Soviet hen and the New Guinea parrot; the other carvers relied on their skill and the wood to get their effects. Of course, the carver of the penguin did use a darker stain to represent the bird's dark coat. The Trobriand carver, like the Maori, used a shell insert for the eye, the bull carver made the horns of a very white wood and inserted them, and the Ponape carver made separate teeth and inserted them—all for effect, but none attempted to produce a three-dimensional oil painting as so many American carvers do.

Most of the problems in producing these pieces are self-evident. In each case, the blank can be sawed to shape, thus saving an enormous amount of work. And it can be formed with three or four tools—all some of these carvers have. Most of these designs will repay selection of a good wood, so the piece can be given a final low gloss. Most have delicate parts, so will not take kindly to hammer-and-tongs production; most foreign carvers seem to be willing to make many small cuts over a longer period of time than we do to achieve their effects.

Below—Swan and burro, Guatemala; dog fattened as a living "hot-water bottle," Pre-Columbian Jalisco, Mexico. Right—Penguin, Guatemala; monkey, Costa Rica; bull, Costa Rica; iguana, Mexico; and alligator, Ponape Island. The Mexican dog is pottery but can easily be made in wood—and is too good a subject to miss.

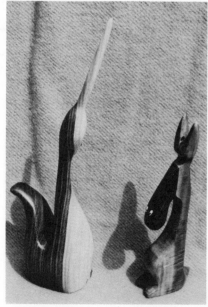

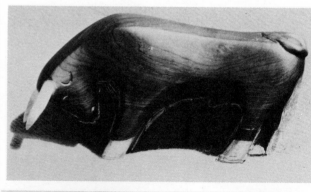

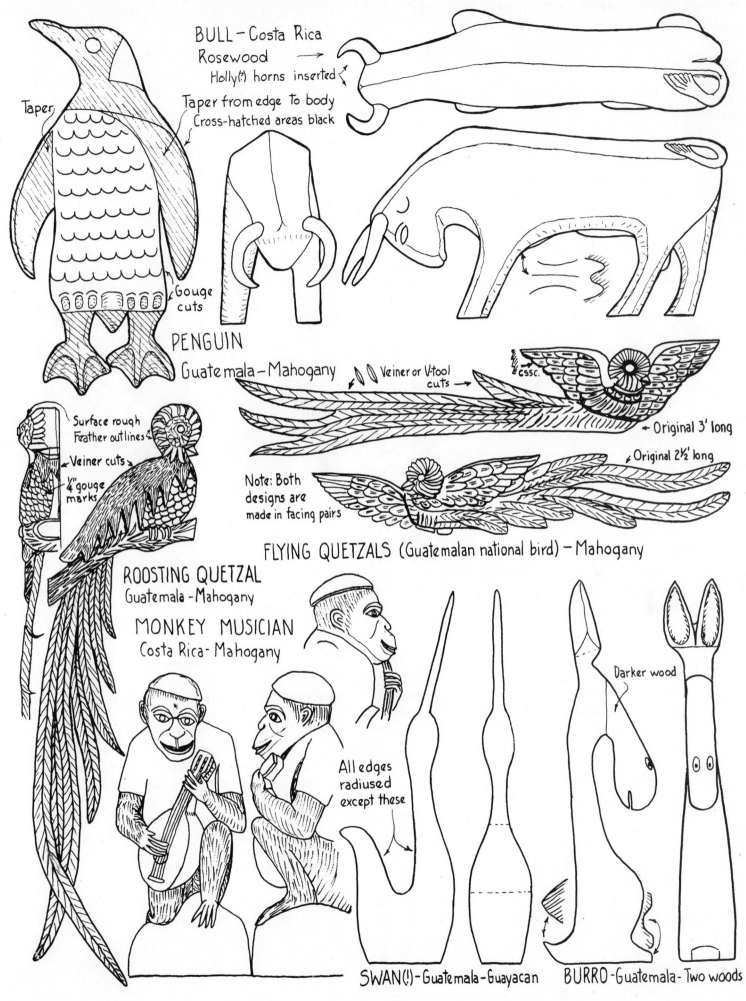

Taper

BULL – Costa Rica
Rosewood →
Holly(?) horns inserted

Taper from edge to body
Cross-hatched areas black

Gouge
cuts

PENGUIN
Guatemala – Mahogany

Veiner or V-tool
cuts

cssc.

← Original 3' long

Original 2½' long

Surface rough
Feather outlines

Veiner cuts

¼" gouge
marks

Note: Both
designs are
made in facing pairs

FLYING QUETZALS (Guatemalan national bird) – Mahogany

ROOSTING QUETZAL
Guatemala – Mahogany

MONKEY MUSICIAN
Costa Rica – Mahogany

Darker wood

All edges
radiused
except these

SWAN(!) – Guatemala – Guayacan   BURRO – Guatemala – Two woods

✳ The Descent from Ararat:

Animals in Low Relief—How They Grew

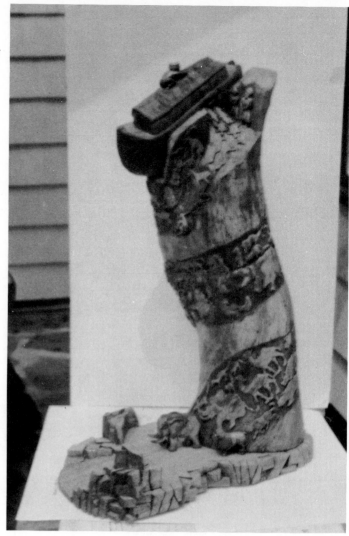

Ideas for future carvings are often the greatest result of a visit to another carver. The "Pied Piper of Mittenwald" is one example (page 157), and this column is another. In one Oberammergau shop, I saw a 5-foot carving in the form of a cross, with the Ark across the top and two or three diagonal bands of paired animals on the lower limb. The animals were moving *up*—and this struck me immediately as backwards, because the animals should be moving *down* from an Ark in the elevated position. In other words, the pose should not be the conventional ones of the animals entering the Ark on the low ground where it was built, but of the animals leaving the Ark after the Flood, when it came to rest atop Mount Ararat.

This carving was the result. It is about 3 feet high, made in a section of apple trunk about 12 inches in diameter at the base and with the base of a branching bough at the top. The extra wood there made it possible to carve the Ark as if it were jammed into rocks at an angle, and to show the animals descending from it in low relief in a continuous helical band. It also offered several interesting problems, including showing the figures of Noah and his wife frontally in relief and some animals from above in relief nearby, because I wanted Noah to be standing near the ramp watching the unloading. By cutting a channel for the ramp and leaving high "peaks" on either side, it was possible to achieve the desired result. I carved alligators, turtles and snakes on the ramp and nearby (their *top* silhouette is most important), doves against one wall, Noah and Mrs. Noah against the other, then had a natural transition from top to side views for the rest of the helix.

Another challenge was to utilize the various bulges of the trunk, as well as the excrescences of natural growth resulting from trimmed twigs and the like. This necessitated designing the pathway as I went to take advantage of the surface, so the helix is not a perfect spring shape nor a constant width. Details can be distinguished in the photographs.

Because of the Ark angle, it was possible to add Og, King of Bashan, who in some legends was a freeloader for the trip, clinging atop the

Ark and fed by Noah through the window. (He has a wedding ring for a crown.) Also, to simulate the animal group arriving on more level ground, I added a base of 2-inch blond limba (white mahogany) in free form, utilizing the pieces cut from the corners to build up simulated rock formations on both sides of a central path. This also suggested an animal or two on the path, so in the bottom of the helix I carved only one elephant and one lion (who seemed the logical leaders for the descent), and carved the other lion and elephant in the round, with half of the lion's hindquarters removed so he fitted tightly against the column, and the elephant standing free. There are fifty-two pairs of animals on the ramp and path, selected at random to suit the blemishes, and in a variety of poses, both for interest and again to suit the surface shape. With Noah, Mrs. Noah, and Og, there are thus a total of 107 figures on the piece.

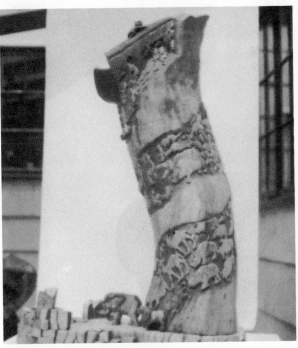

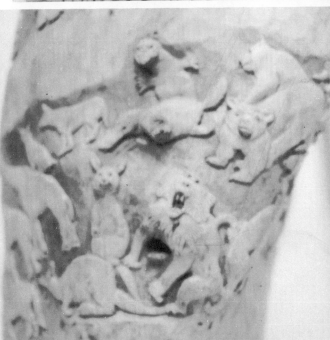

Natural surface excrescences are incorporated in the design; note mandrills at left and above left. Two animals in-the-round exit the ramp (below), and Og (atop the Ark) is also in the round, with an old gold wedding ring for a crown.

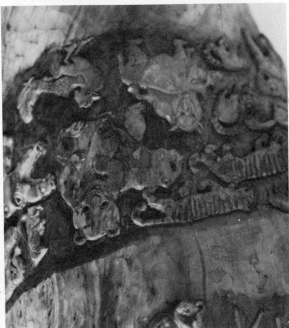

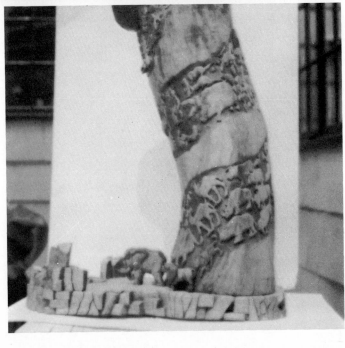

73

✳ Contrast in Bird Carving:

One Sculptor Shows No Feathering; Another Shows It All

Birds are a woodcarving tradition. They range from polished fruitwood turkeys and rough-shaped gulls on bits of driftwood through "Audubon" birds with precise feathering and coloration, to conventionalized eagles and major sculptures. In recent years, waterfowl decoys have become particularly popular, so there are literally hundreds of carvers—and, luckily, ten times as many collectors. There are specific books on techniques and several big annual shows. Certain carvers capture the lion's share of the blue ribbons; their names have become synonymous with excellence. Many birds are so well done that one expects them to fly, and they are "decoys"

only for collectors' pocketbooks. Their quality is often more in the painting than in the carving.

These are basically "folk art," a classifica-

Below—Snowy owl carved integral with its base to make a 22-in. sculpture of elm. Here again "Chippy" Chase uses the natural figure of the wood to create a stump projecting from a pool, with the bird just alighting or preening. No feathering is delineated, although the grain lines suggest some, and even wing edges are smooth outlines. Note the eyes, which are simply rounded hollows with a central pillar. There is no coloring and no artificial claws. The result is a work of art that almost comes alive.

Right—A snowy owl copied from the photo below. The carver has lost the wing bulges and flare—thus has lost power and life. He has also lost boldness in the eye representation, failed to show claws as well, made the stump too prominent.

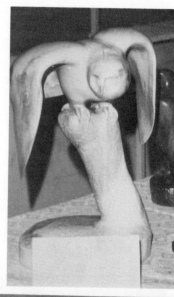

Below left—Green heron 19 in. high, carved in one piece of olivewood log by "Chippy" Chase, emphasizes natural color and figure of the wood, which has a greenish tone. There is no feather delineation nor artificial eyes or legs, although the mouth line and some "pebbling" or texturing of the feet is suggested. The free-standing water-plant leaf is characteristic of the carver's style—delicate, airy, natural, yet unmistakably wood.

tion which has been recognized by connoisseurs for many years but has only recently begun to attract the general public. However, among bird carvers, there are some who also have attracted attention and gained recognition in artistic circles. Two have recently had important shows, and their work differs so markedly that it is interesting to draw contrasts.

One whom I have long admired is Charles G. "Chippy" Chase, of Brunswick, Maine, who makes birds to scale, often in tableau, and usually in a single piece of wood. His work is distinguished by meticulous care and precision; it often includes some natural habitat element like a cattail, rock, or pond, but has no artificial color, glass eyes, or even more than a suggestion of feathering. He occasionally suggests a surface texture with a rasp, planes, or gouge cuts, but in general his surfaces are smooth and show the natural wood color and figure. He works from stuffed models, uses templates for greater accuracy, selects his wood to suit the bird on occasion, and corrects major surface checks and knotholes, but

otherwise relies on form, pose and the natural beauty of the wood.

A Harvard graduate of 1930, Chippy went on the McMillan Arctic Expedition in 1931, tried law school, investment banking, math teaching and engineering. He began by whittling small figures of famous baseball players but soon shifted to birds, and has been carving them exclusively since 1951. His work has been shown in a great many galleries and one-man shows; a recent big show was at the Farnsworth Museum, Rockland, Maine, and he was commissioned to make a large eagle in walnut for their permanent collection. He works only on commission and normally has at least a six-month backlog, although his work sells for well into four figures. He is recognized as "one of the world's outstanding bird sculptors." His studio is a tiny old farmhouse on the coast at Wiscasset, with a lean-to shed full of logs of walnut, ash, and some exotic woods, from which he selects to suit his fancy.

In sharp contrast, both in technique and intent, are the lifelike habitats produced by Gilbert Maggioni and Grainger McCoy. Nine of their creations, involving perhaps thirty-five birds or other animals, were exhibited at the American Museum of Natural History in New York in 1974. Each is an assembly depicting life-sized birds at an instant of peak tension in flight, hovering, attacking or

Red-shouldered hawk attacking a copperhead snake, as Mr. McCoy assembles it for exhibition. The life-sized bird will be supported only by its left claw, above which it will be delicately balanced with outspread wings. Wings have glued-on individual feathers and groups, textured and tinted by pyrographic needle and oil paints so exactly that the bird looks like a real one mounted by a master taxidermist.

feeding. A red-shouldered hawk grips a copperhead snake. Mallards forage for food. A peregrine falcon swoops down on a family of green-winged teal. A green heron poses midstream to spear a fish. Also, in similar action poses are wood ducks, the gadwall, the red-tailed hawk, the turkey, ring-necked pheasants, mourning doves, the black skimmer and the willet, as well as feather groups, partially assembled birds, and some tools.

All these birds are characteristic of South Carolina's coastal inlets and marshes, where their creators live. Gilbert Maggioni, born in 1921, is a Georgian, but settled in Beaufort, South Carolina, in 1946 after four years in the

Companion red-shouldered hawk attacks the snake from the side (its upper wing tip can just be seen at lower right in other photo) and is cantilevered out from one claw so it actually trembles when visitors pass. Feather technique is more evident in this closeup. Ducks in the exhibit have iridescent feathered areas and the like; faithfulness to the live bird and its habits and habitat are outstanding. The objective seems to be to instruct rather than to impress or entertain.

Navy. He now operates an oyster-canning business and has painted as an avocation since 1939. But many years of duck hunting finally pushed him into decoy carving in 1967, and he almost immediately went on into much more elaborate depiction of action, working out techniques and solving problems as they arose. He has had one-man shows at the Gibbes Art Gallery in Charleston, South Carolina, and at Telfair Academy, Savannah, Georgia, and has shown his work during 1969–1973 at the Waterfowl Festival in Easton, Maryland, and the Atlantic Flyway Exhibit in Salisbury, Maryland. Grainger McCoy carved his own decoys, but his interest in "serious" bird carving began when he met Gilbert Maggioni in 1968. In 1970, with his B.S. in biology from Clemson University, he moved to Beaufort and studied with Maggioni. Now he has converted a country store on Wadmalaw Island (south of Charleston) into a studio and home.

Their birds are so accurately detailed that they look like the work of master taxidermists. They are primarily of basswood (linden). Some are hollow to cut weight, and they may have as many as 500 to 600 feathers or feather groups individually carved and attached. Some rock, sand and plantlife are used to complete each tableau, although certain grass stems or the like may be replaced by brass tubing or carved wood to provide support for a bird. Even oysters and quahogs are carved rather than real, and some tall grass and the like is cut from brass shim stock and painted. Painting is, of course, very meticulous, utilizing techniques developed by Mr. Maggioni to duplicate the effect of light on feathering. Some feather and color effects are obtained by burning the wood surface, so no natural-base paint can be used. A present problem is the old familiar one—to prevent the oil colors from spreading onto the bare wood or burned areas.

The accompanying pictures may begin to draw the sharp contrasts between the work of the two "schools"—one emphasizing extreme detail and the other almost none, but both recognized as outstanding. It was amusing to hear New York TV commentators try to categorize the Maggioni and McCoy tableaus and failing totally. They have still to recognize that art may not be solely the product of a "school"—that it can be precise rather than impressionistic and abstract, realistic rather than a montage of soup cans and auto tires or junk.

✳ Cuckoo Clocks Are a Tradition:

Design Elements Standardized for Fast Carving

Clock mechanisms have been enclosed in decorative cases for several hundred years, and some kinds have been familiar articles of furniture or decoration as well—mantel and grandfather clocks, for example. Some mantel clocks had carved wooden cases, but many had additions of other materials or were totally of metal, porcelain or pottery and were quite formal—except, perhaps, for some of the old French clocks which replaced the navels of dancing nymphs. Grandfather clocks, likewise, were quite formal, the most elegant probably being the William and Mary style.

There are, however, folk art clocks emanating from the Black Forest area of Germany. Some are faced with scrollsawed and painted frames. Better known, however, are the familiar cuckoo clocks, in many sizes and with greater or less elaborate carving, but usually with mechanism that opens a door and allows a cuckoo to emerge and bow while a pair of whistles powered by miniature bellows whistle a two-note call to accompany the hour strike.

This mechanism was invented by Anton Ketterer in the Black Forest in 1730, and has been varied to include an added pipe and a quail to whistle the quarter hours, or some other variation. (The cuckoo call, by the way, is a musical third.)

Traditional motifs for the relatively high relief carving on cuckoo clocks have to do with the Black Forest—oak, maple or grape leaves, game birds, rabbits, deer, hunting dogs, bears,

Below left—Made in 1907, this cuckoo clock is typical of the medium elaborate types. Much more elaborate and larger ones are made, as well as the small tourist types. It has both cuckoo and quail behind small upper doors, and a detailed eagle motif at the gable peak, carved in high relief. Other designs are oak leaves and acorns. The pendant for this clock is at left. Below Right—A simpler frame for a clock of the modern type. Two possible interpretations of the silhouette are shown. The bird at gable end is separately carved and applied, and the bird at the base is looking straight forward—at least in my interpretation of the silhouette.

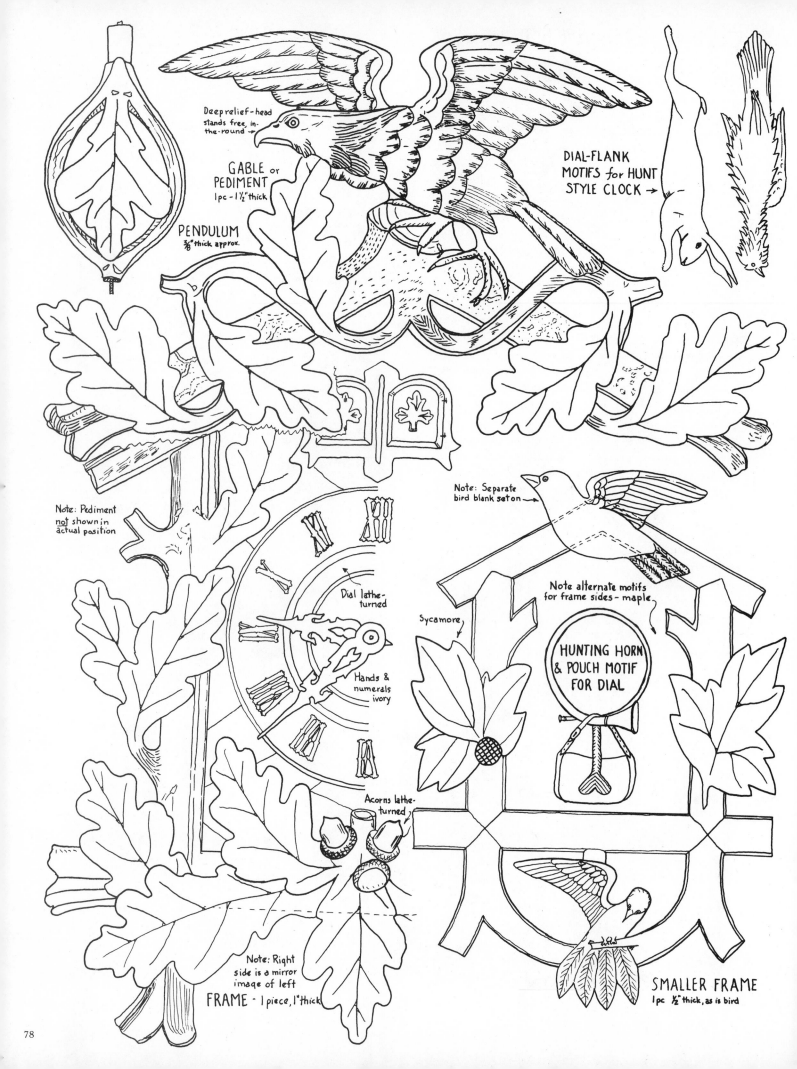

Deep relief—head
stands free, in-
the-round

GABLE or
PEDIMENT
1 pc - 1½" thick

PENDULUM
⅜" thick approx.

DIAL-FLANK
MOTIFS for HUNT
STYLE CLOCK →

Note: Pediment
not shown in
actual position

Note: Separate
bird blank set on →

Note alternate motifs
for frame sides - maple

Sycamore

HUNTING HORN
& POUCH MOTIF
FOR DIAL

Dial lathe-
turned

Hands &
numerals
ivory

Acorns lathe-
turned

Note: Right
side is a mirror
image of left

FRAME - 1 piece, 1" thick

SMALLER FRAME
1 pc ½" thick, as is bird

hunting dogs, shotguns, game pouches, *Jaeger* (huntsmen in traditional costume), and eagles for the gable end over the face. Designs are usually very complex and busy.

Interestingly enough, few American carvers make their own cuckoo clocks, probably because the mechanisms are not readily available. Even carved clocks are rare. But the new digital clocks, with their many shapes and sizes, should be a cinch to enclose—and certainly many electric clocks have such poor cases that they cry for enclosure. Hence these designs.

When I visited a cuckoo clock factory in Triburg, West Germany, in 1973, I was surprised to find that most of the carving is still done by hand, even that for the cheap clocks made in quantity. One shortcut is to saw the blank for the entire clock face as one piece; another is to mount five blanks on pins side by side on an inclined plank about 2 inches thick and carve the same areas on all five simultaneously, working tool by tool. Still another is to design the foliage so it can be produced in the fewest-possible cuts with fairly large tools, and to use linden wood because of its ease of cutting and relative lack of resistance to cross-grain cuts. Bold gouge slashes do most of the shaping.

I "liberated" a small frame and bird shape and brought them back home, but only about a year after my return did I get around to carving them. By then I had forgotten the precise design and my photos of the carvers at work didn't supply anything but pictures of roughing cuts, so I had to make up my own designs to fit the blanks. This turned out to be fun, as well as instructive. I've shown two variations of the design to fit the German blank, as well as details of the design of a much older clock, purchased by my father the year of my birth—1907—for $12.50 from Sears, Roebuck, as I recall. (Here is another opportunity to bewail inflation.)

Actually, while intricate in design, the cuckoo clock decoration is rather easy to carve. Frame members are simply chamfered into an approximate half-round, to simulate a portion of a vine or limb, and leaf veins (rough veiner cuts) are put in to finish off the basic gouge curls of the leaves. My old clock has two and a half acorns at the base; these are turned separately and applied. The pediment or gable end is very carefully done; though it has a simplified form, it is a quite exact depiction of the eagle's head and legs, as well as feathering.

Questions I Wish My Friends Hadn't Asked

I'd like that carving and I'd buy it, but I don't like pine. Can you copy it in mahogany or ebony? For the same price?

This carving has an empty hand. Shouldn't the hand have something in it?

Why do you carve rosewood? Isn't it hard?

Why is that bird just plain wood? Wouldn't it look better if you painted it?

Couldn't you finish that faster with a sander?

Corollary: Why don't you use glossy varnish instead of wax?

Why did you leave tool marks? Were you in a hurry to finish it?

When are you going to have a cut-price sale?

Why don't you put things in a gallery? They only charge a third of the sales price. Can't you use money?

Why didn't you exhibit in our church show?

What artist gave you that idea?

Couldn't you make it stronger in plastic—or iron?

How long did this carving take?

Why don't you make something at popular prices—under a dollar?

You cut all that out with a dental drill, didn't you?

Why don't you carve stone, so your work will last longer and be worth something?

If I bring my kids over some afternoon, will you teach them to carve like you do?

Why don't you make carvings that will sell—in a store?

Our ax is dull. Will you sharpen it? And a couple of paring knives, too?

Why doesn't our local library have your books? I can't buy them all.

When I tried to carve once, the wood broke. Is there some trick to it?

Some time when you aren't busy, will you make my kids some toys? The ones in the store cost too much.

How come you can make things like this and I can't? I'm as smart as you are.

Can't you find a better way to waste your time than whittling?

Doesn't your wife object to all the mess you make around the house?

Is that head supposed to be the Mona Lisa? The two sides of the face don't match.

I suppose that's a good way to pass the time, now that you're retired. But why don't you get a part-time job somewhere?

Who helped you write your books?

Below—Redhead duck (painted with oils) on a scrap of driftwood, by Edward Clist; and owl with pyrographed feathering, by Joseph Averso. Both carvers are from New Jersey.

✳ A Potpourri of Panels about People:

Carvers Preserve National Traditions

Since Stone Age man, carvings, particularly low-relief panels, have recorded and preserved our history. These, from various countries, are typical. Some are old, some new, but all are people-oriented; they tell a story or show a situation. Two are religious, that at right from the church in Brienz, Switzerland, center of woodcarving, and that below from Bali, showing a goddess and a demon in pierced work.

Below—Copy by E.J.T. of a fifteenth-century woodcut showing a woodcarver. Veiner lines on walnut, with white-pigment fill. Bottom—One of two large panels in the Manila Hilton hotel, showing Filipinos at work. It is mahogany, about 4 × 6 ft. Bottom right—Detail from the Oseberg wagon in Norway, showing a man being prevented by a woman from striking a rider. Right—Three panels and a cup from Chotjkowow, near Moscow, U.S.S.R.

80

✳ Pierced Carving in Japan:

Intricate Panels Typify a Traditional Craft

The Japanese have long been masters of intricate decorative carving, particularly of panels, a skill shared by the Chinese (who probably taught the Japanese and learned from the Koreans) and the East Indians. This specialty has been applied in temples, shrines and fine houses both for walls and for screens. Many are pierced to pass light and air or provide ventilation with some privacy.

One of the least known but, paradoxically, most important of these pierce-carved panels is over the door of a stable in Nikko (below)! It is the source of the familiar three-monkey carvings.

Many other shrines and temples also have magnificent panels and decorations, and motifs are usually floral or animal rather than religious. Good examples are the three long panels of Japanese cypress from Shitaya Shrine in Tokyo, photographed by Donald P. Berger. These were carved in the thirties (although the shrine is much older; it has a history of 1,200 years) by Mokoyurido Keiun. They are double-sided, because they are under the eaves of a roof which covers a well of sacred water with which visitors purify themselves before entering the shrine.

Pierced areas in these panels are much larger than they would be in Indian work, where open areas are usually filled with ornamental tracery or a pattern of screen. Relief is quite deep. The open spaces make for easier carving but do increase fragility and the danger of warpage. Also, the screen filling of India serves another purpose: It keeps birds out, which in Japan is of no importance because the "building" is simply a roof on four pillars.

The carver has achieved considerable realism; his water seems really to flow and his leaves to blow in the breeze. The panels also have a light look and feel, and achieve deep relief without undue thickness.

It is essential in planning such a carving to select a wood that cuts clean, is relatively knot-free, as well as able to withstand the effects of exposure. Small knots are of course of relatively little importance; the design can usually be modified slightly to miss them. Woods like basswood, cedar, teak, cypress, primavera (white mahogany) and mahogany will work well, although the mahoganies may tend to warp unless restrained and the basswood will deteriorate rapidly unless painted and protected from the weather. Fruit woods in general are not too good because of their proneness to insect attack. Also, the design should be such that pierced areas do not extend into the ends of the panel and it is advisable to frame the finished work with a sturdy panel to inhibit movement.

It may be advisable not to cut out all the pierced areas initially, but to do heavy and rough cutting first. This is, of course, difficult if the panel is to be double-sided, but support for projecting elements can usually be provided by leaving filaments of wood until the carving nears completion. Oriental carvers rarely find this necessary, because they use light tools and make many cuts; time is not as important to them as it is to us.

The familiar three monkeys originated from this panel at the Stable of the Sacred Horses, Toshogu Shrine, Nikko. An in-the-round carving of a cock with tail appliqued down the supporting post, in the lobby of the Hotel Jujiya, Miyanoshita, Japan.

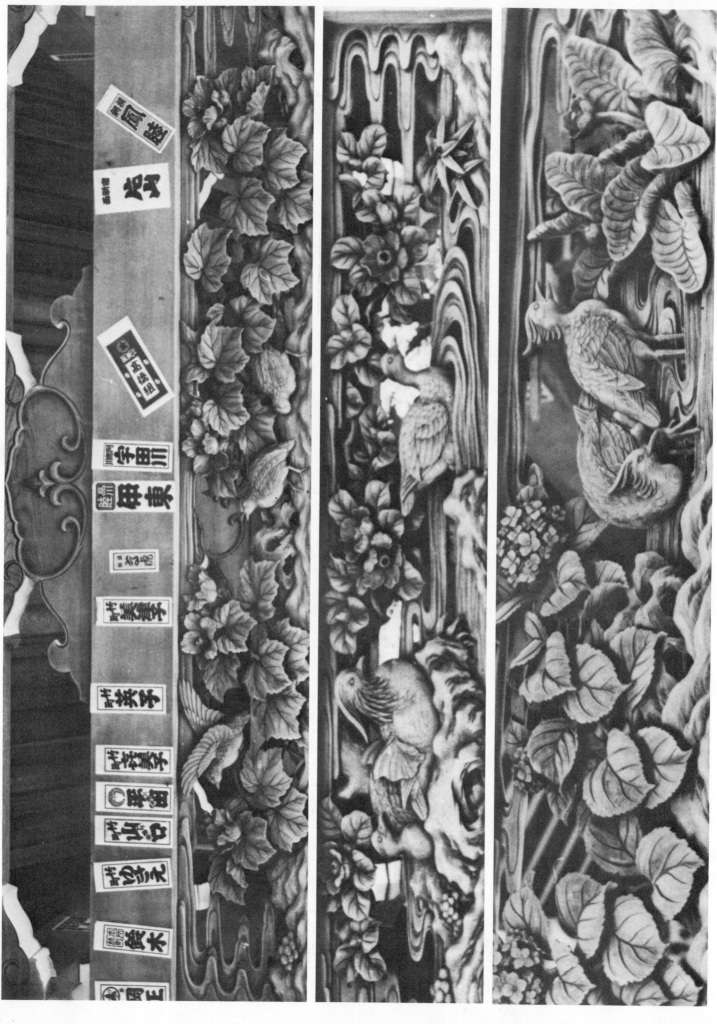

Three of the four panels on the **Shitaya Shrine**, with full-length patterns below. Photos by Donald P. Berger.

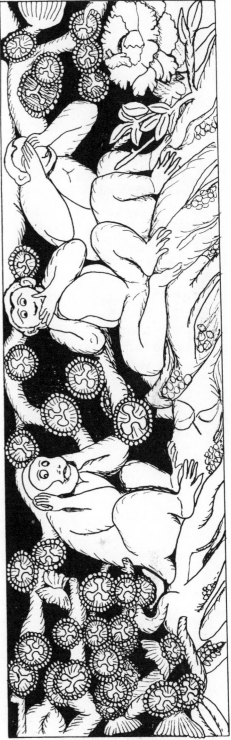

THREE-MONKEY PIERCED PANEL
Origin of the familiar "See no evil, speak no evil, hear no evil." Stable for Sacred Horses, Toshogu Shrine, Nikko, Japan

Note: Black areas are cut through

Left-BIRD PIERCED PANELS
Shitaya Shinto Shrine, Tokyo, Japan

✳ Don't Forget Multipart Assemblies:

Sometimes the Background Holds the Carving Together

Appliqué is usually just the placing of a relief carving against a suitable background, either of other wood or of a contrasting material such as sacking, glass, or metal. The background, in that case, is primarily to set off the carving against the wall where it is hung. But there is another form of appliqué in which the background is vital to the composition, where the carving has several parts and the background holds them together. Contrast, for example, the model sloop and the trout. The trout, which is in-the-round, can be set against a suitable background, or even hung as a mobile with no ill effects; it is self-sufficient. The sloop, on the other hand, is really four parts—three sails and a half-hull—which must be assembled on a background to hold them together and complete the work.

This is true also of the pair of assemblies which I titled "Just Passing Through" and "Emergin'" in my third book. (All four of these pieces were pictured in that book, by the way, but after I'd seen several copies of the two latter ones, I realized that I should have provided drawings with them in the interest of anatomical accuracy.) These assemblies *must* have a contrasting rough background to emphasize the smoothness of their contours, as well as to supply the missing "space" in which the entire figure is assumed to be. They could be mounted against glass, to the greater confu-sion of the viewer, against a wall or window—but less effectively, in my opinion.

From a practical standpoint, mounting a relief carving on a separate background makes the whole job a great deal easier; it is not necessary to do a lot of preliminary grounding, then work to get suitable level or flatness or color or tone or texture to the background. This can all be done separately before mounting. Also, the piece will in most cases be easier to handle and carve, with no background to get in the way of the tools.

The half-thickness ship model is very familiar among the boat fraternity. It was once used primarily to show prospective owners the hull shape, or for tank-testing of a new silhouette, but eventually became more often an ornament for the yachtsman's den or study, or a wall decoration at his yacht club. A pleasing element in such models is the assembly of contrasting woods. (In the model shown, the hull is maple above the waterline, mahogany below, while the sails are white pine.) An entire nautical scene can be built up, of course, but the danger there, as well as in many other assemblages of carvings, is that a multicolored painted background tends to submerge the carved elements.

Another common assemblage of recent years is one incorporating flying birds, or a combination of flying and standing birds,

The usual in-the-round carving requires no background, but may have one for accent; the tinted-pine trout at left, for example, is on a walnut disk that leaves his head and tail projecting. But some carvings, particularly low-relief ones, may require a background to hold the parts together, as in the sloop at far left. Its white-pine sails are in-the-round, while its hull is a half-thickness assembly of maple above the waterline and mahogany below, mounted on $1/2 \times 4 \times 6$-in. mahogany.

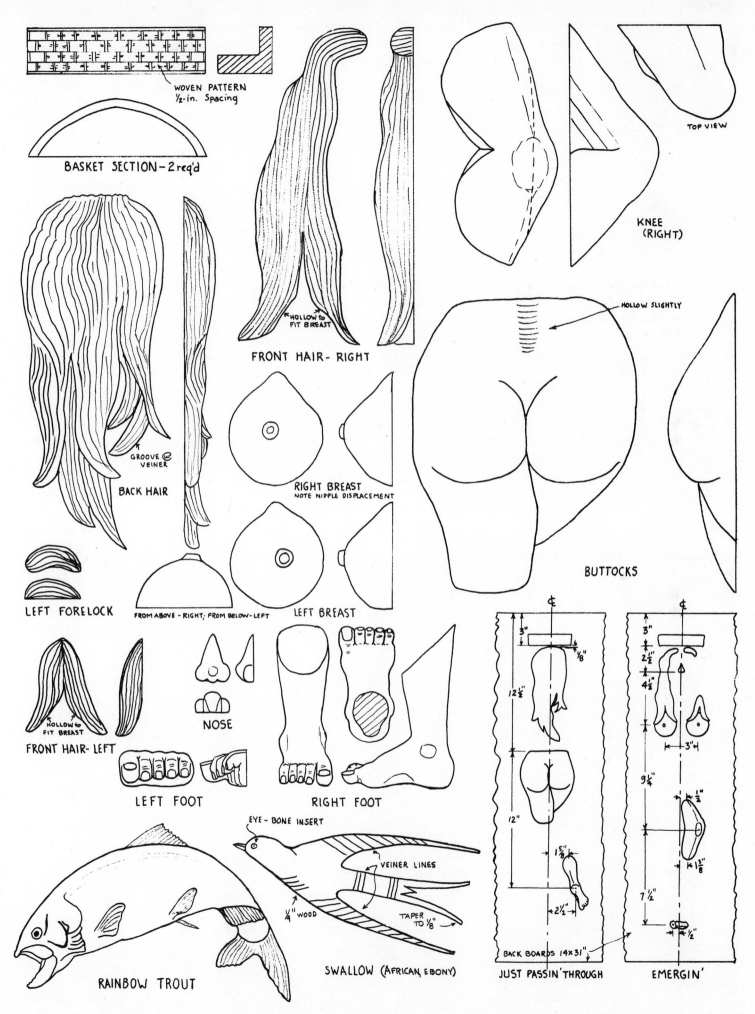

WOVEN PATTERN
½-in. Spacing

BASKET SECTION—2 req'd

BACK HAIR

GROOVE @ VEINER

LEFT FORELOCK

FRONT HAIR-LEFT

HOLLOW to FIT BREAST

LEFT FOOT

RAINBOW TROUT

FRONT HAIR- RIGHT

HOLLOW to FIT BREAST

RIGHT BREAST
NOTE NIPPLE DISPLACEMENT

FROM ABOVE - RIGHT; FROM BELOW - LEFT

LEFT BREAST

NOSE

RIGHT FOOT

EYE - BONE INSERT

VEINER LINES

¼" WOOD

TAPER TO ⅛"

SWALLOW (AFRICAN, EBONY)

KNEE (RIGHT)

TOP VIEW

HOLLOW SLIGHTLY

BUTTOCKS

JUST PASSIN' THROUGH

3"
12½"
12"
1⅝"
2½"
BACK BOARDS 14x31"

EMERGIN'

3"
2½"
4½"
3"
9¾"
1½"
1⅛"
7½"
½"
⅛"

against a painted or collage background. Any birds will do; I have shown a simple African silhouette as a sketch because it can easily be graduated in size to make a dramatic and simple group. This particular one is in ebony, but a browner wood might be more normal. It is also a simple silhouette design, which is often more effective than an elaborately detailed half-thickness bird for mounting against a background.

It should be mentioned here also that it is becoming increasingly common to make dioramas, a three-dimensional assemblage with forced perspective, in which may be included three-dimensional and relief carvings, the in-the-round pieces in the foreground standing on some kind of base—either the ground, a floor, or some other suitable support, while the relief figures are mounted on the background, which can represent a sky, the wall or a row of buildings. This is a familiar museum display and requires especial care in placing the objects so scale is maintained. A figure suited to such a display is the trout, which could be portrayed "dancing" on the surface of a lake or stream, with a background of the bank including flying birds or the like. It is very important in such assemblages that the background be subdued in color.

The twin panels represent a much more difficult kind of assembly, because they deal with the human body as well as having a touch of whimsy which can be easily destroyed—for example, by drawing in the outline of the body on the panel. They are an excellent exercise in anatomy and a lot of fun, but must be quite precise in proportion and positioning, or some of the effect is destroyed. In contrast to my usual preference not to duplicate a piece (which is why chess sets hold no attraction for me), I did make three of each of these panels, the extra sets going to a señora in Mexico in return for a favor she did me and to the young man who delivers my Scotch because of his insistence that he had to have them to go on opposite sides of the restroom door in his game room. The pair in Mexico were mounted there on the halves of an ancient mesquite shutter which still carries the original Spanish hand-wrought hardware as well as the usual wormholes and rotted areas. Mesquite is very heavy, so each assembly probably weighs 40 pounds, but is supported quite easily by hand-wrought nails driven into the adobe wall of a very Spanish *sala*. They have occasioned their share of comment there, plus the usual conjectures that she is a ghost passing through a door, or the personification of an Indian legend about the girl who disappeared into the waterfall after her lover rejected her. My own set, by the way, is mounted on 150-year-old pieces from the interior of a barn, while those for the Scotch-man (!) are on rough modern, but rather knotty, pine, antiqued in the rough. The body elements are mahogany, sanded smooth, flat-varnished and waxed to a dull glow for contrast. In the Mexican assemblies, I used small vegetables and fruits, native-made and hand-tinted from bread dough, for the objects in the basket and liked the effect so well that I came back and whittled and painted duplicates to replace the colored glass marbles in my own. Now I have a similar set to do for the third pair.

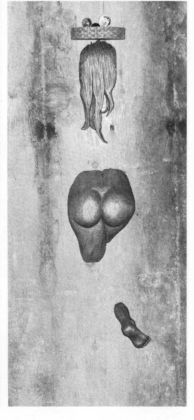

"Emergin'" (far left) and "Just Passing Through" (center) are two fanciful assemblies of polished mahogany against rough background (about 14 × 31 in.) for contrast. The background is essential, both for contrast and to hold the composition together. The background for another pair was made by cutting in half an ancient Mexican shutter, still bearing the original hand-wrought hardware as well as the marks of a couple of hundred years of usage and water. The fruit and vegetables in the baskets (here colored glass marbles) are brightly colored miniatures made by pressing dough into shape and letting it dry. They can be whittled and painted instead.

Possible—A Carved Jigsaw Puzzle:

Animal Panel and Furniture Blocks

The conventional jigsaw puzzle formerly included recognizable silhouette shapes. By adapting this idea to a plain surface, or by sawing a low-relief carving along natural parting lines, an interesting puzzle can be developed. I even had one that was nothing but a plain countoured surface sawed into uniform squares—and it was a devil to assemble!

Below is a traditional Chinese puzzle, made by jigsawing a block into pieces of furniture. It offers some opportunities for carving, as long as the outer contours of the elements are not removed. It can also be made more complicated by lengthening the block from 3⅝ to 4¾ in., as shown—an increase from thirteen to twenty-two pieces, largely by splitting one area (No. 2) in half vertically.

The puzzle at left offers more possibilities, however, in that each element is an animal which can be surface-carved or low-relief shaped. I added two animals to the original Italian design, and made it in ½-in. teak (pattern on page 89). Any low-relief scene or pattern (without repetition) could be cut similarly into miscellaneous shapes or along natural lines of the carving, as mentioned earlier. Also, two different scenes can be carved on opposed faces, as long as the sides of the blocks are not disturbed. A further application of this "puzzle" idea is intarsia, as described in the next article, which adapts some designs of M. C. Escher.

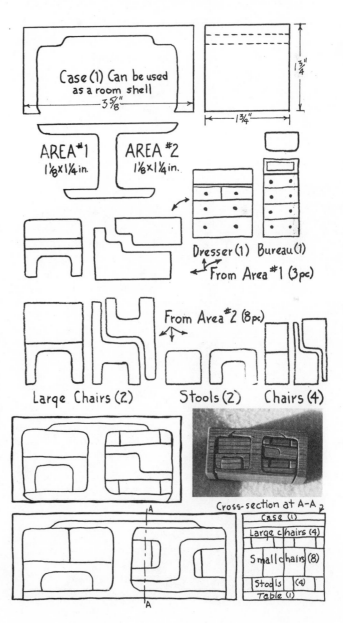

Case (1) Can be used as a room shell — 3⅝"

1¾"

1¾"

AREA #1
1⅛ x 1¼ in.

AREA #2
1⅛ x 1¼ in.

Dresser (1) Bureau (1)
From Area #1 (3 pc)

From Area #2 (8 pc)

Large Chairs (2)   Stools (2)   Chairs (4)

Cross-section at A-A

Case (1)		
Large chairs (4)		
Small chairs (8)		
Stools	(4)	
Table (1)		

❋ Escher Adapted to Wood and 3-D:

Intaglio and Intarsia Reinforce Low Relief

M. C. Escher, who died in 1972, became a favorite of the American younger set in his later years, probably because his works are so intriguing. A Dutch artist who was also a draftsman and mathematician, he seemingly enjoyed the production of intricate patterns, many of which involved repetition of units, distortion, or technical impossibility—like making water apparently run uphill. His interlocking designs, in which the "background" is the same element as the foreground, or the spaces between a repeated design motif evolve into another, are particularly intriguing to me.

Not being of the younger set, my interest in him grew from a reproduction of his "Sky and Water—I" which I saw in a newspaper (see sketch). It seemed to be exactly the idea I needed to execute a fireboard (mask for an unused fireplace). It combined birds and fish, which made sense, both because they were hobbies of the friends who commissioned the piece and because it was to be installed in a dining room. I also realized that the woodcut would lend itself to translation into three dimensions and would be ideal for viewing

from above; it is rarely that a carver is asked to produce a piece that is normally placed well below eye level—and this one had to stand on a hearth. Further, the design could readily be widened to suit the size of the opening.

Because of the relationship of birds to spaces to fish, I felt that intaglio should be used. This is the opposite of relief—like the carving of a mold—and was once quite familiar in jewels and metals. It is still fairly common in Italy for cameos, in Scandinavia for the making of butter and cookie molds (see photo) and elsewhere in the making of molds for plastics, rubber and metals (tin soldiers, for example). Much of the carving in metals and semiprecious stones is now done with dental burrs or hand grinders. Burrs can be used in wood also, but tend to tear the fibers and make extra work in finishing, so I elected to do the entire project by hand. The background at the top could be routed, but it is of varying depth and therefore offers some complications in addition to the usual ones of avoiding the design.

This offers some challenges, including the necessity of thinking "inside out." Intaglio is

Left—"Sky and Water—I", a woodcut by M. C. Escher, inspired this 30 × 34-in. teak fireboard (screen for the opening of an unused fireplace). It is placed on the floor at a slight angle (leaning back about 15°) so the observer does not have to stoop to look at it, set on walnut blocks and supported by rear aluminum legs which fit into the fireplace opening.

Below—Test panel 1 × 6 × 20 in., of white pine, formerly a stove-side shelf (hence the burns) which is now a mantel panel over a kitchen fireplace, surrounded by cookie cutters and butter molds.

ANIMAL JIGSAW (ITALY) Animals can be low-relief carved

PERSIAN HORSEMEN (Escher) Dark sections intaglio or other wood

FISH & NEWT MOTIFS (Escher)

SKY & WATER I
Birds in low relief;
fish in intaglio (Escher)

Edge of original

FLYING HORSES (Escher) Cross-hatched horses in intaglio

FISH & LADY-BUG MOTIFS (Escher)

much more difficult technically than relief, because the surfaces are harder to get at and are largely concave, so tools tend to dig in. It requires small bent gouges if you have them, or special tools ground from sawblades if you don't.

I first tried the fish in intaglio in a piece of white pine that had been a shelf beside our kitchen stove—and had several burn marks to prove it. I liked the fish so well that I added a cow and bird also in intaglio, and thus I had an interesting panel which my daughter hung *over* her farm kitchen fireplace. Each figure was about 6 inches long and $3/8$ inch deep at the deepest.

Escher's original, made in 1938, had a fish like this, but merely cross-hatched instead of detailed. His panel was 44 cm, or about $17\frac{1}{2}$ inches, square, mine almost twice that. I was proposing to magnify and lengthen the design to 30×34 inches, so had to add some detail and take more care with anatomy. Also, I wanted to use the figure of the wood to represent water. My plan was to have the fish in intaglio, as if they were within the water, while the birds would be in relief, as they would be if flying in air. I debated the problem of blending the two for some days, and finally settled on the idea of reducing the depth of the intaglio as the carving neared the horizontal center line, then increasing the depth of the background toward the top, so the increasingly detailed birds stood out correspondingly. Maximum depth in both instances was $3/8$ inch at top and bottom, shading to about $1/8$ inch at the center line. A 2-inch border would hold the whole thing together at the surface level, like the "water" and like Escher's original design.

I was fortunate enough to find a length of 1-inch teak 15 inches wide, dressed, so I could glue two sections together, then brace the joint with a couple of lengths of $3/4$-inch aluminum T-bars at each end of the back. The T-bar also provides a device for either hanging the panel or for putting on back legs so it can be stood up. I set the panel on twin $2 \times 3 \times 5$-inch walnut blocks, with a groove in each at the proper support angle (leaning back about 15 degrees), and provided a $3/8$-inch-diameter back support bar on each end. The bar runs from a hole in the T-bar near the top of the panel and down to the floor level at about 30 degrees with the vertical, then back and up slightly into the walnut block, thus forming a rough triangle. Teak this wide is hard to come by these days, and the piece I had was the end of a plank, so it had a check. To my relief, it was possible to glue and clamp the check, and hold it with an aluminum back strap screwed in place.

The newspaper reproduction I had was about 5×5 inches, so it was necessary to enlarge it by the method of squares. I usually do this directly on the wood, but in this case I did it first on drawing paper, then transferred it to the wood with carbon paper. This was helpful later in an unexpected way: Interlocking designs like this are surprisingly difficult to keep clear in your mind's eye, and a same-sized reference is helpful during carving when each cut destroys a guide line. The transferred design (ratio: $1/8$-inch squares on original; $3/4$-inch squares on copy) was emphasized with a fiber-tip pen, then bottom intaglio designs were carved, so my arms and sleeves rubbing on the panel would not erase the designs—and might help to build patina on the flat surface.

The bottom fish was carved in great detail, 6 inches long, with scales delineated and the like, and each successive row of fishes was less detailed. The bottom fish is about $3/8$ inch deep at the center, shading to about $3/16$ inch at the edges, with the flat edges of fins about $1/8$ inch below the surface. The rough fish shapes at the center line, on the other hand, are barely $1/8$ inch deep, to carry out Escher's original idea. Tools were $1/16$-, $1/8$-, and $1/4$-inch flat firmers, veiner, and a series of gouges of several different sweeps (curvatures), from $1/8$ to $1/2$ inch.

At the top, the background within the border was roughed down in a slope from about $1/8$ inch at the center to $3/8$ inch near the top border. Then the bird figures were cut free, principally by outlining with a $1/8$-inch firmer and $1/4$-inch flat gouge, then cutting waste away with a $1/2$-inch flat gouge and firmer. Background was cleaned up and smoothed, then scalloped with a $1/2$-inch long-bent flat gouge.

Low-relief carving of the bird shapes was the final operation. After the other carving, this seemed easy, and I did parts with a knife for the fun of it. As before, the top bird is executed in detail, showing pinions and feathering, with less detail on birds nearer the center line, so there is progressive loss of detail, as well as form. The entire surface—and the back—were finished with flat varnish. This acts as a seal (remember there's a fireplace flue behind the piece) against moisture variations and temperature variations as well, and brings out the color of the teak, but adds no objectionable shine. It also makes it possible to apply an oil stain like Minwax without getting overloading of color on end-grain and edges. I used dark-walnut Minwax on the surface of the lower half and border, flowing it on and wiping away any excess after a few minutes. Despite the manufacturer's recommendations on the can, the Minwax *will* penetrate a varnish, given a minute or two, yet not fast enough to make end-grain problems.

The border, by the way, was left surface height all around, and cut across horizontally by veiner lines $1/4$ inch apart. Along the top and bottom, I made the lines of diminishing width toward the edges, and I carried the design into the border slightly on each end of the center line. I kept stain *out* of the veiner lines, wiping it out immediately if my brush slipped, and wiping excess *parallel* to the lines. (These lines, incidentally, are better if a bit ragged and not exactly of constant width.)

Then, with a small brush, I "antiqued" both birds and fish, which simply means applying a little stain to the cut lines, just as dirt will settle into them, given time. Bird wings and backs were also darkened, to help mold them and make them stand out against the light background. (I have applied this technique on panels for a number of years, using walnut stain on teak, mahogany, and other dark woods, and suitable lighter colors on lighter woods, such as apple. (The Germans make a whole series of stains, based on sal ammoniac, particularly for this purpose.) For inside use, the finish is simply wax, but for outside, it must be marine-varnished or the equivalent, unless it's teak, which can simply be oiled.

When I'd delivered the panel, I found I was itching to try another Escher design, so I made the flying horses in a mahogany panel $1 \times 9 \times 12$ inches. Alternate horses—in this case facing in the same direction—are in relief and intaglio, and the intaglio ones are darkened to

Right—Flying-horse design, converted from an Escher repetitive pattern. Lighter horses are in low relief, darker ones in intaglio, with some modifications—it is possible to "cheat" slightly by making wing-pinion definitions as grooves rather than ridges, and mouths and nostrils as depressions rather than mounds, as they would be in a true reversal or mold. The wood is $1 \times 9 \times 12$-in. mahogany.

Below—A table of blond limba (white mahogany), stained mahogany, incorporating an Escher-derived design below the inset glass top. The panel (below right) is of Persian horsemen facing in opposed directions and could readily have been made as a relief-inlay combination, except for the bridles, which cross parts of the opposed figure. It is executed in intarsia—really a jigsaw puzzle of $1/4$-in. wood—with the light horsemen maple and the dark ones mahogany. Copper reins are appliqued for the maple horsemen, silver ones for the mahogany, in each case glued in veiner grooves. Horsemen are individually carved in low relief, then fitted together and glued on $3/4$-in. plywood. The assembly is inset in a socket in the table and surrounded by a $1/2$-in. border covered with brown felt to support the cover glass and seal the edges. (Photo is slightly foreshortened at bottom because of camera angle.)

make them recede still more than their approximate 1/8-inch depth. (At the same time, I discovered there were several books picturing Escher's work and having English text, while the one I had was in Dutch, which tends to add complications. These books are mostly paperbacks and relatively inexpensive. Since that time, *The World of M. C. Escher*, by J. L. Lecher, et al., has been published by Harry N. Abrams, Inc., 110 East 59th St., New York, N.Y., 10022, containing 270 pages and over 300 illustrations. (It is very comprehensive, but costs $15.)

My third "Escher" was to be a simple try at intarsia in a small panel, but my wife suggested that I expand it into the top for a table next to my recliner and thus led me into a great deal of work. This is the "Persian Horsemen," with riders facing in opposite directions. I had originally intended to follow the intaglio-relief approach on it, but changed over to intarsia, which resembles nothing so much as a jigsaw puzzle in various materials. My plan had been to use 1/4-inch maple and mahogany for the two, and I'd found a scrap of a good brown mahogany at the local cabinetmaker's. But with expansion to table-top size—about 13 1/2 × 19 inches, I had to supplement the mahogany with another piece of lighter color and finish it to match the color of the original.

Anyway, each horse and rider was sawed by hand individually, carved in low relief, then fitted to the preceding ones by whittling to precise shape. It is theoretically possible to cut stacks of blanks on a jigsaw and match them without such fitting, I suppose, but my pattern at that time was not quite that accurate. I used a cardboard template, but this permitted slight inaccuracies in drawing and sawing that necessitated the knife work. Further, the maple was quite hard and the mahogany quite soft, so the differences in cutting pressure required were

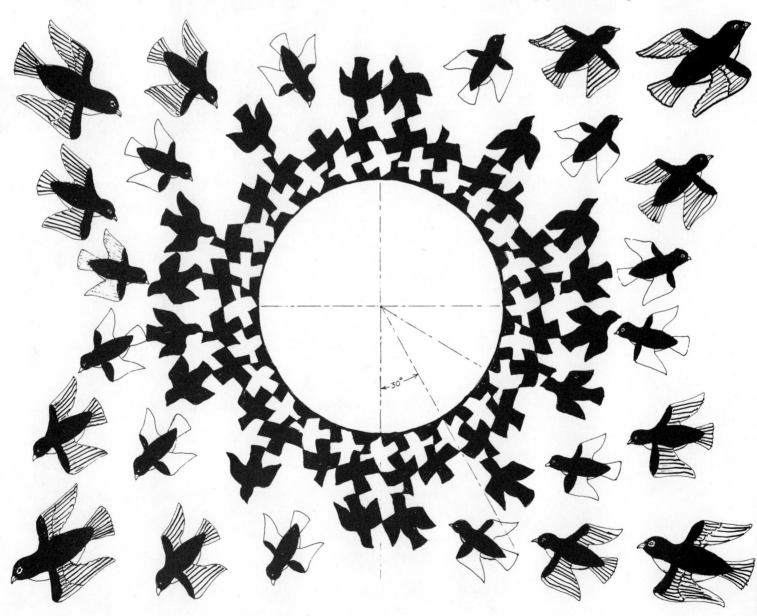

Flying-bird panel, 14 × 17 in., of 2-in. blond limba (thick enough to match the inserted barometer body). It was derived from an Escher panel that is slightly wider in proportion and has an added row or two of crosses at the center, because the clock mounted in the original was slightly smaller in proportion and was merely a pair of hands and knobs for the hours. (The inner rings of crosses were, however, spaced more widely and may have been an adjustment to suit the insert, since they reverse the otherwise converging pattern.) Background is rounded down at edges and the surface roughened with flat-gouge scoops. Blond limba was selected because the wall on which it is mounted is dark paneling. Barometer incorporates a thermometer and a hydrometer.

a constant problem. I glued finished pieces to ³/₄-inch plywood as they were completed to avoid mishaps with broken legs and arms—sometimes before the next ones were fitted, thus adding complications. And the bits and pieces of heads and legs required to fill out the edges were an extra nuisance, so much so that I suffered with each cut of the table saw when we finally cut the panel to size to fit the table made for it. (It was inset, with a brown-felt border to support a cover glass and seal against entry of dust, spilled drinks, etc.)

When the carving was complete, I added reins of copper wire on the maple horses and of silver wire on the mahogany ones, in each case gluing them into veiner grooves and inserting the ends in drilled holes. It is also possible to make bridle and stirrup elements this way, but I stopped while I still had my sanity. Also, as a penance, I made my own variation of a traditional Italian animal puzzle (see sketch) and of a Chinese puzzle on a jigsaw (see page 87).

Some months later, another friend, an emigre Dutchman who had known Escher, commissioned a background for an indoor barometer. Again I went to my references and found that Escher had indeed made such a design and had actually executed it as the background for a clock. It involves birds flying in and out of a central circular path, and chang-

ing from a bird with outstretched wings to a cross as the design becomes smaller and more compact (see sketch). I had to modify the shape slightly to fit the board I found, in this case blond limba (white mahogany) about 2 × 16 × 22 inches. Again the full-sized drawing was a great help in sorting out details when I began carving, in this case all in relief, with the background down about ¹/₈ inch at the center and slightly over ¹/₄ inch at the edges, plus a rounding off along the extreme edge so the outer birds were emphasized even more. In this design there is also a progressive reduction in detail as bird size diminishes toward the center. I also emphasized the modeling by antiquing the bird bodies against the light-wood background, making the central less-defined shapes quite dark. The technique was the same as that described for the initial panel, but, because of the lighter wood, I used a German stain of appropriate contrasting color.

I have by no means exhausted Escher as a source. I recently made two bird panels (page 173). A younger carver who visited me is working on still another Escher design, involving lizards translated from two dimensions to three. It's in poplar (gum), and he'd been at it for several months. It includes hands in three dimensions, so is good practice from several angles. Look up Escher at your local library and you'll see what I mean.

✱ Just for the Fun of It:

Fifty Pieces to Carve for Pure Pleasure

Most carvings tend to be very serious projects, but occasionally I see one that looks like pure fun and has an idea I intend to adapt at first opportunity. This group is largely such ideas—and many of them I haven't gotten around to as yet. None of the pieces is particularly difficult; design and method of carving are evident.

There are such detailed and stylized shapes as those of the armadillo and frog, as contrasted with the flowing, almost abstract, lines of the bear and the pig, the strict utility of the bull-head napkin ring and the mouse magnet, the straightforwardness of the hen and the komodo dragon, the challenge of the little Bavarian people, the lacy tracery of the Thai dancers as compared with the formality of the Spanish lady, the demure shyness of the U.S. S.R. girl (who has no definite features), or the pure abandon of Laurie Nichols's imaginative animals. Twice, I have selected a cypress knee to provide an Alpine background for the little people, and both times it has become something else; "Flight," pictured here, was almost such a background. I've added similar pieces carved by others, as well as two versions of a sea otter. The first, and larger, is based on the shape of a fragment of ironwood, the second a more formal design made possible by the tiny abalone shell I found in Carmel, California.

For good measure, I have included a number of photographs on the next two pages that suggest projects; many are similar to those dealt with in more detail in *The Modern Book of Whittling and Woodcarving* (1973).

Below and bottom right—These little animals are from Costa Rica. The hen is lifelike; the rosewood armadillo is very well designed; the frog is stylized, with a deep mouth that could take a match packet, a placecard or the like. Bottom left—These little people, from Bavaria, are of pine with paper-wound wire arms and are painted. I have made tables for an Alpine village scene against an appropriate cypress-knee background. Right—The sea otter, in rosewood, I designed to fit a tiny real abalone shell from Carmel, Calif. (Compare this with the "improvisation.") The girl is in two contrasting Russian stones, but suggests similar figures in contrasting woods. Center—These silhouettes of shadow dancers are in thin tortoise shell, but could be in horn or thin wood and make a good window decoration. Below them is an antique mother-of-pearl panel from an old Spanish album; note the raised central figure.

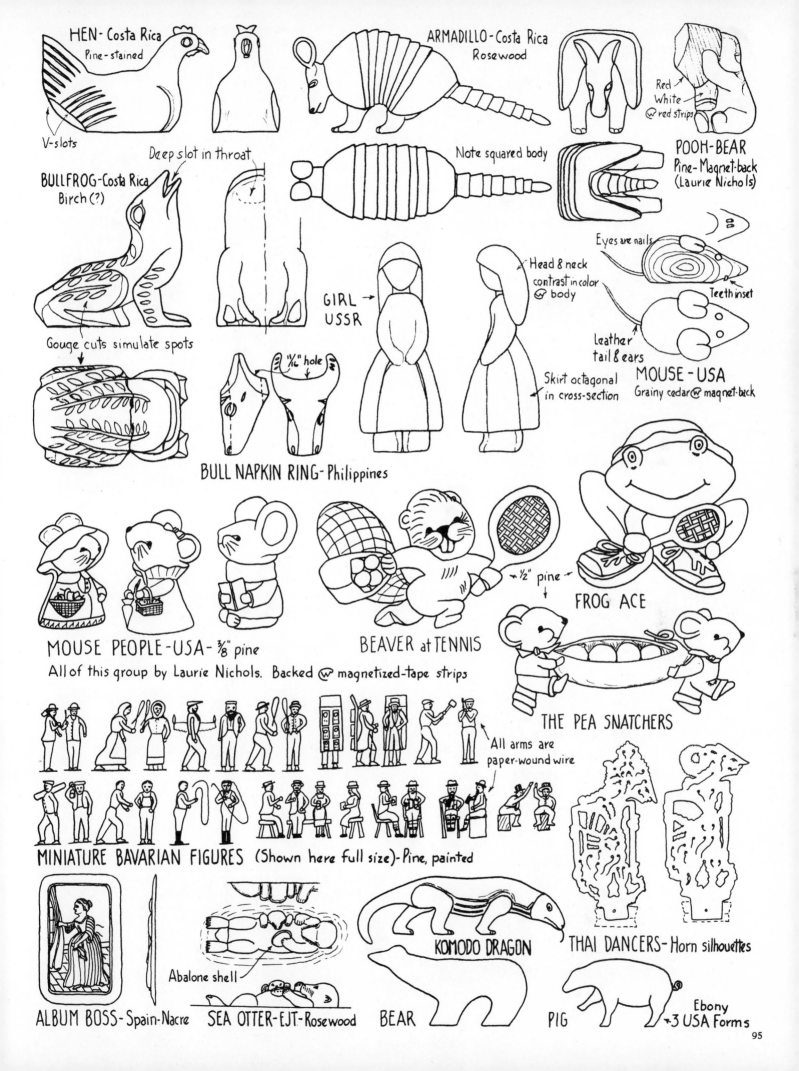

HEN- Costa Rica
Pine-stained

V-slots

ARMADILLO-Costa Rica
Rosewood

Note squared body

Red
White
@ red strips

POOH-BEAR
Pine-Magnet-back
(Laurie Nichols)

BULLFROG-Costa Rica
Birch(?)

Deep slot in throat

Gouge cuts simulate spots

GIRL
USSR

Head & neck
contrast in color
@ body

Skirt octagonal
in cross-section

Eyes are nails

Teeth inset

leather
tail & ears

MOUSE-USA
Grainy cedar @ magnet-back

¹¹/₁₆" hole

BULL NAPKIN RING- Philippines

MOUSE PEOPLE-USA- ³/₈" pine

All of this group by Laurie Nichols. Backed @ magnetized-tape strips

BEAVER at TENNIS

½" pine

FROG ACE

THE PEA SNATCHERS

All arms are
paper-wound wire

MINIATURE BAVARIAN FIGURES (Shown here full size)-Pine, painted

ALBUM BOSS-Spain-Nacre

Abalone shell

SEA OTTER-EJT-Rosewood

KOMODO DRAGON

BEAR

PIG

THAI DANCERS- Horn silhouettes

Ebony
-3 USA Forms

95

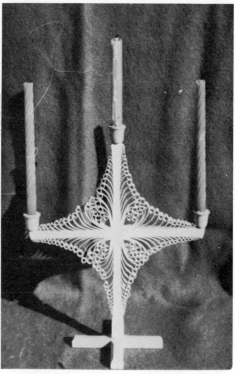

A study in contrasts—The Balinese girl, in ebony, my mounted copy of an old Welsh love spoon in mahogany, a German salad set in lime, and a Swedish candelabrum in pine, with whittled curls. Compare the grace of the girl and the candlestick with the solidity of the other two designs.

Below—Surface scratching has returned to favor. The two gourds are from El Salvador, the string of gourds from Peru. Color contrast is obtained by cutting through a dark-coated surface, as in the Philippine napkin ring at far right. The older Peruvian design does not have this contrast. The scrimshaw pieces are excellent examples, done by Eskimos and brought round the Horn in 1910.

Below—Hanko's circus, as well as the dragon and animals at bottom, were exhibits at the Claremont, Calif., NWCA show in 1974. The circus includes railway cars and wagons and represents several years of work. The dragon, bear and pig are typical of modern "streamlined" pieces in which details are not defined and the surface (in these cases black) brought to a high polish.

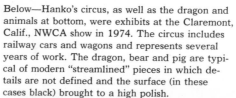

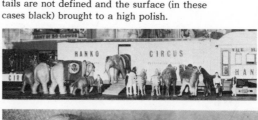

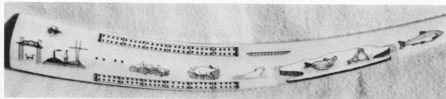

Laurie Nichols of Pittsfield, N.H., makes designs like these freehand, carves them in pine or basswood, and tints them with thinned acrylics. Much of her work is done with an Exacto knife; in this particular case, the flexibility of the blade makes it possible for her to carve a curved surface rapidly. Many of her figures are backed with magnetized self-adhering tape, so they can be used to hold notes on a steel surface—as, for example, a refrigerator—so they are in demand by women visitors to shows. All of her work has a whimsical touch; her subjects usually are humanized animals, particularly frogs and rodents like the mouse and the beaver.

Five Improvisations: That at left I made from a cypress knee and titled "Flight"; it suggests a mother, two children and a dog (a natural bulge on the far side) fleeing from danger. At bottom right is a sea otter, the combination of a piece of California ironwood and a real abalone shell. The dog head (?) at bottom left is in eucalyptus and was shown at Claremont, Calif. The male head at right is in driftwood and the sea serpent in manzanita; both were made by Rick Cain.

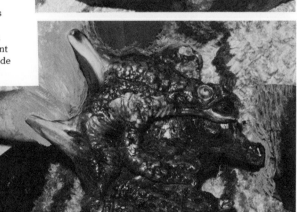

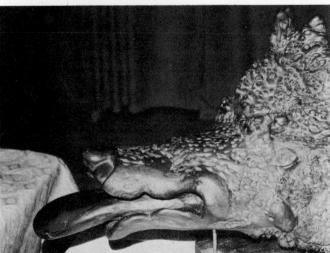

❋ Simplicity Builds Strength, Cuts Time:

Salvadorenos Show How to Cut Corners

These carvings, except the Don Quixote panel, were selected at a state handicraft store in San Salvador primarily to show the variety of native work, and the Don Quixote panel was added because of its great contrast with the others. Inadvertently, however, these examples all illustrate how simplicity in design can give strength to a carving—and how the same simplification can cut carving time radically. These pieces look dramatic and distinctive, but they are produced with relatively few tools, perhaps even on a production line. The makers have dozens of shortcuts to make carving faster.

Decoration on the plate rim and details of the Mayan panels are done largely with a couple of gouges and a veiner; glyph patterns on the plate rim are repeated with only slight modification, but *look* quite different. None of the pieces has any laborious elements like surface texturing. None even has a rigid design; the two Mayan panels are halves of other pairs, but are near enough alike in "feeling" that they can be hung together. While the central element of the plate is a well-executed design, it is not exactly balanced and varies from plate to plate in the three "look-alikes" I saw. The border was never exactly laid out; the carver simply worked his way around by eye.

This could all be coincidence, of course; presumably the pieces were carved by different people and their patterns thus should differ. This is, however, an even more important factor: These pieces were made to be sold, so shortcuts had to be taken to keep cost low. To reinforce this point, let me give you the retail prices in American dollars: Don Quixote $10, plate $4, ashtrays and panels $2 each! Granted that the Salvadorean standard of living is not as high as ours, those prices are almost ridiculous by American standards. But the most important lesson to be learned from them is that their makers have a basic under-

Left—Slight variations in designs incorporating Mayan heads and glyphs provide endless variety, yet permit use of unlike panels in pairs. Design looks complex but is basically simple, and much of the decoration is straight cuts with two sizes of gouge. Note thinning of nose. Each panel is $5/8 \times 4 \times 18$ in.

Below—Don Quixote panel, in mahogany, $3/4 \times 13^{1/4} \times 20^{1/4}$ in., is very simple in execution, yet has a dramatic impact that a more complex design might well lose. The windmill seems like an afterthought or footnote rather than a part of the composition. Note that background has no details beyond gouge shaping.

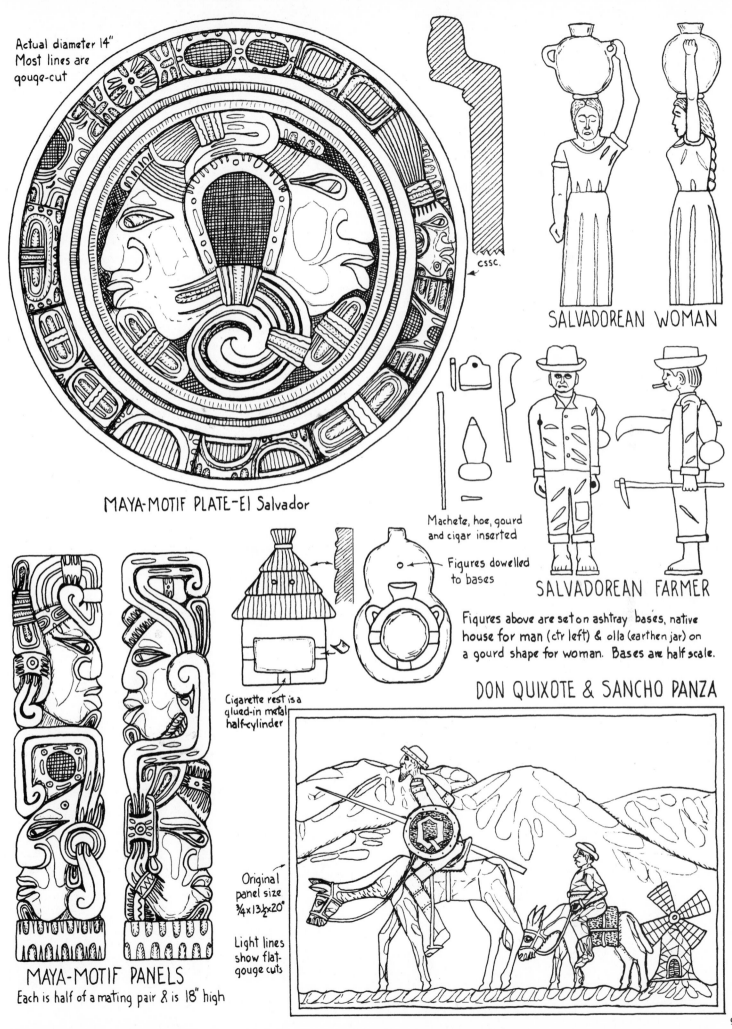

Actual diameter 14"
Most lines are
gouge-cut

MAYA-MOTIF PLATE—El Salvador

cssc.

SALVADOREAN WOMAN

Machete, hoe, gourd
and cigar inserted

Figures dowelled
to bases

SALVADOREAN FARMER

Cigarette rest is a
glued-in metal
half-cylinder

Figures above are set on ashtray bases, native
house for man (ctr left) & olla (earthen jar) on
a gourd shape for woman. Bases are half scale.

DON QUIXOTE & SANCHO PANZA

MAYA-MOTIF PANELS
Each is half of a mating pair & is 18" high

Original
panel size
¾ x 13½ x 20"

Light lines
show flat-
gouge cuts

standing of economies so that they have learned to get dramatic effects with a limited expenditure of time and effort; if there is one thing that can be criticized in the typical American carvings I've seen, it's that the carver has vastly overdone the detail.

The Quixote plaque provides an ideal example of what I'm talking about. Don Quixote and Sancho Panza are quite well detailed and carefully designed to illustrate the story. The windmill, on the other hand, seems to be an afterthought added for those viewers who need it to recognize the two characters; it is not set into the background but stuck on a slight rise behind Pancho's burro, belying the knowledge of drawing that the carver obviously had.

The plaque is a cartoon, a stark statement of the basic situation of the story, the clumsy armor, flea-bitten Rosinante, oblivious Sancho, ascetic Don. But note that the sky is perfectly plain—no clouds, no texture, no anything. And the mountains are merely outlines, textured slightly with a gouge that has very little sweep. There are no houses, no trees, no shrubbery, no birds, no other windmills, not even a real road beneath their feet, nothing but the mountain outlines and that absurd windmill. Yet the plaque is dramatic, powerful, decorative, a testimonial to the fact that simplicity gives strength—as every cartoonist knows. He eliminates detail to make his point, and this carver has done the same, in contrast to most of us. How many panels have you seen in which the needles are shown on pine trees, the shingles and panes on distant houses, and a lot more detail that the eye simply does not pick up in the background when there is something worth seeing in the foreground? A well-carved bird or animal, person or object, the principal element of many American panels I've seen, is lost in a maze of detail in the background—more background than is necessary—and a waste of time, if time is important.

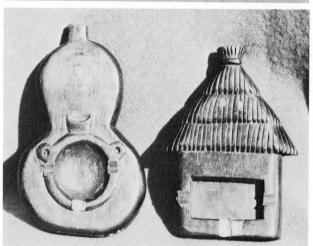

Left—Male and female *campesino* figures are about 5 in. high, go on appropriate ashtray bases, the man on a house, the woman on the *olla* or pot. The figures would actually be better on plain bases. Below—Again the Mayan head motif, arranged in the base of a serving plate. Glyphs form the rim pattern. Designs can be executed with very few tools.

✱ A King-Sized Chess Set:

Large Pieces Help the Audience

There is a persistent legend about a chess game played with live men—when captured, they are killed as the game progresses; the idea was converted to a popular novel a few years back. And a town in Italy annually stages a pageant game with elaborately dressed human figures. In more practical and everyday terms, however, several European cities have outdoor chessboards with heroic figures—kings perhaps 2 feet high—some made from tree stumps, others assembled from trimmed lumber and carved to a greater or lesser degree. Stuttgart, Germany, has two such sets in one park, which I saw in 1963, as well as giant checkers. Stockholm and Paris have them, too.

In 1973, the president of McGraw-Hill, Inc., New York, saw and photographed a giant set in use in Stockholm and decided a similar one might be a good addition to the sunken plaza of his company's new building in Rockefeller Center. I was commissioned to design and build a suitable set, which was first used July 1–3, 1974, in noontime games played by national champions.

A "board" with 2-foot squares suggests a king about 3 feet tall—which, if turned in the standard Staunton pattern, would weigh upwards of 100 pounds! Any elaborately carved pieces would take an eternity to produce, as well as costing a fortune and being far too fragile. So I designed pieces which are essentially shells, suggesting the traditional shapes of the Staunton pieces, but weighing far less, even though the base material is 2-inch lumber and the king is 16 inches square. My designs turned out to be primarily cabinetmaking, because actual woodcarving was limited to the faces of the king and queen, the knight's head, crenellation on the rooks, and shoulder patches on the kings of the company symbol in low relief. All joints were butted rather than mitered, for greater strength and to make full use of available widths of material. I was surprised to find that the set could be made of maple for the "white" pieces and mahogany for the "black" at only about 15 percent more cost than for all pieces in white pine, painted, because of recent increases in the cost of pine.

There are a number of abnormalities which must be considered in designing a set which is so large. Pieces should be nestable for storage and able to withstand battering. Pieces must have natural and evident hand grips. They must be readily distinguishable so players are not confused; there's a vast difference between playing on a conventional board and

First day of play in Rockefeller Center, with twin clocks, the same announcer as for the Fischer–Spassky matches, and international champions playing. The "board," 16 × 16 feet, is in an open-air plaza, one floor below the street, and surrounded by galleries, which makes it possible for several hundred spectators to see the game. The board is 2-foot squares of contrasting indoor-outdoor rug, the men maple and mahogany in natural finish. (Wagner International Photos.)

surveying a 16 × 16-foot playing surface. Also, players tend not to leave the board between moves, so some pieces should double as seats, and it doesn't hurt if some double as footstools as well.

My ultimate design was for 2-inch lumber (1⅞ inches when planed) in three basic patterns. The knights and bishops are merely a back and two sides, the queens and knights are tapered crosses, and the pawns and rooks are truncated pyramids—the latter can be stacked like ice-cream cones, and the others nest together nicely so the complete set can be transported on a 4 × 6-foot hand truck. Any one of these three forms could have been used as the basic shape for all pieces, but I felt that having this variety would reduce the chance of mistake in play. I also adhered to the general and traditional Staunton outlines, while making the pieces somewhat more modern in feeling. The king has the identifying cross on his crown, the queen a ball, and these figures have definite faces. As a matter of fact, although the king has a handgrip under the back rim of his crown, he balances better if the carrying hand is tucked under his chamfered chin.

While the sets I've seen in use are played on a concrete "board," this set required a board which was also portable; the plaza has other uses. So the "board" is indoor-outdoor rug

Because the set must be stored nightly, pieces are designed to nest, the pawns and rooks being stacked, and the others interlocked, to make one compact hand-truck load. Pieces are varnished and waxed to resist abrasion.

material in 2-foot squares, dull gold and dark brown.

In the interest of reducing weight and material cost, the pyramidal rooks and pawns have shells of ⁵⁄₄-inch wood (1⅛ inches planed). All pieces are assembled with both glue and long No. 12 woodscrews, countersunk and topped by cross-dowel plugs of the same wood. (Queens and knights, because of their cross design, are glued and doweled rather than assembled with screws.) As completed, the set weighed about 600 pounds, the white king weighing 39 pounds and the mahogany one 31; the queens each weigh 26 pounds, (some mahogany was especially heavy!), the bishops 20 and 15, the knights 12 and 10, the rooks 31 and 26, and the pawns 15 to 17— the black pawns were also heavy mahogany. The rook design has a 2-inch-thick stool top, so it was possible to carve low-relief crenelation around the rim without risking any discomfort for a seated player. The finishing was two coats of flat varnish and two coats of hard wax, to withstand minor battering.

For comfort in handling, handholes are 1½ × 4 inches, made by drilling three 1⅜-inch holes side by side and removing the fillets and rasping. Edges of hand-holes and all exposed edges of the pieces were power-chamfered to a ⅜-inch radius, then thoroughly sanded. Because of the size and bulk of the king, the back board was raised 2 inches above ground level, so a player wouldn't unwittingly set it down on his toes. Templates are helpful for the bishop and knight head shapes.

Checkers were originally to be provided as well. It is simple enough to turn disks 16 inches in diameter into conventional checkers, but how does the player move the traditional king—one man stacked upon another? I checked through a number of latch arrangements and finally discarded the lot to come up with a 4-inch hand-hole crossed by a dowel for a grip. Then the player can reach through the top checker and grip the lower one.

In designing the set, I had visualized play similar to that in Stuttgart, with the players moving freely and informally about the board, sitting on the rooks between plays, standing on the pawns on occasion for a better view. But I reckoned without Radio City and international champions. The set has been used only in exhibition games, with the players seated on elevated platforms like those for tennis judges, and "stewards" to move the pieces for them. This made it necessary to skeletonize the kings and queens and to enlarge "window" openings in the rooks to reduce weight.

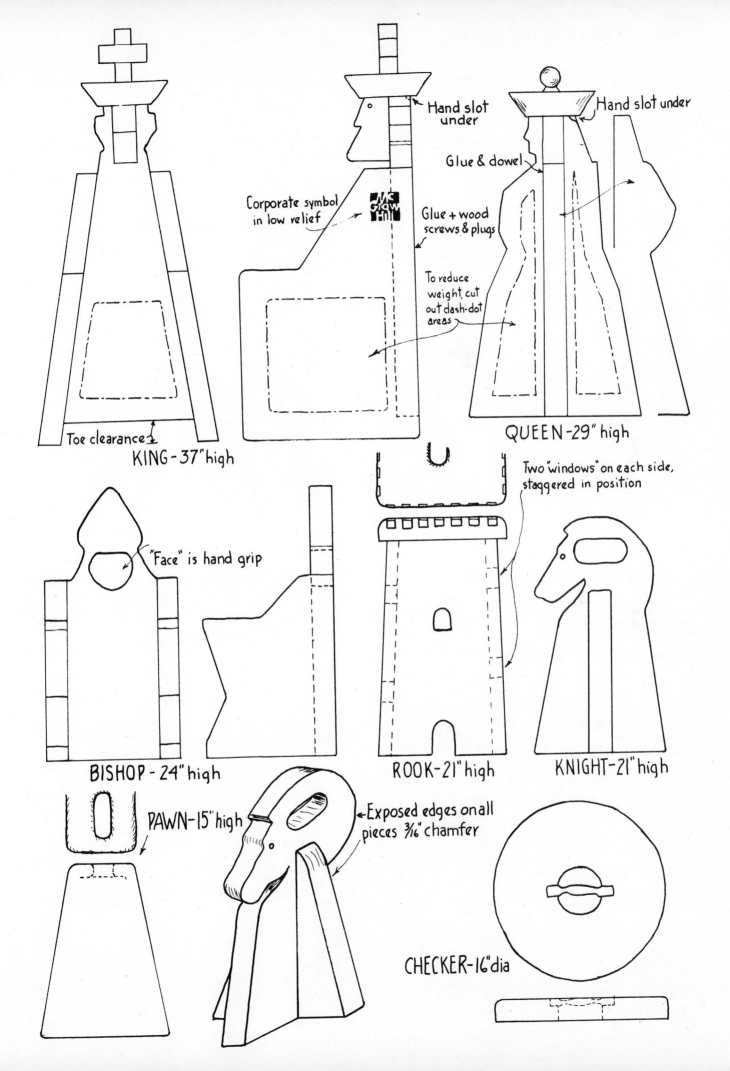

Hand slot under

Corporate symbol in low relief

Glue & dowel

Glue + wood screws & plugs

Hand slot under

To reduce weight, cut out dash-dot areas

Toe clearance

KING - 37" high

QUEEN - 29" high

Two "windows" on each side, staggered in position

"Face" is hand grip

BISHOP - 24" high

ROOK - 21" high

KNIGHT - 21" high

PAWN - 15" high

Exposed edges on all pieces 3/16" chamfer

CHECKER - 16" dia

✳ Try a Mayan Motif Panel:

Powerful and Different Designs from Central America

The Mayan civilization, which flourished in what is now Guatemala and southern Mexico a thousand years ago, is being remembered in carvings—but in Honduras and El Salvador, which were both fringe areas rather than the center for this highly creative and productive people. Honduras, in particular, using its native mahogany, actually produces largely carvings with the Maya motif in "factories";

one producer at least has a series of full-color sheets illustrating standard carvings available for export in quantity. Paradoxically, neither Mexico nor Guatemala seem to be part of the revival, although the designs are so powerful and popular that Nicaragua and Costa Rica have attempted copies. Yet Guatemalan carvers produce such nonindigenous pieces as an Antarctic penguin (page 20) and the snoozing

Left—Most original Maya woodcarving has long since rotted away. Here, however, is a large panel in the National Museum, Guatemala City, showing the inspiration for modern pieces. Bottom left—This panel is well designed and executed, but the figure has two right hands! Trace the standardized face contours on other heads. Below—Simplified facial contours characterize this pair of silhouette panels.

Below—Silhouette head, elaborate compared with the circular one at left center, or the stylized portrait at center. Bottom center—Bold heads are stained then sanded to achieve lighter areas. Bottom right—Guatemalan version of a snoozing New England fisherman.

← All lines chamfered

6¼"dia.

MAYA HEAD -Honduras

Entire surface textured
👁 horizontal gouge cut

Background
gouge-grooved

9"high - MAYA HEADS -Mahogany-Honduras - 9¾"×12" (¾"thick)

MAYA PRIEST -Honduras-Mahogany- ¾×12¼×22"

MAYA PANEL -Honduras-Mahog. 30"long
Background vertical gouge cuts

MAYA HEADS - Honduras - in pairs
Mahogany - Design V-grooved

MAYA WARRIOR
Honduras - in pairs

SNOOZING FISHER
Guatemala

← Original 9"high
Top & bottom
V-grooved

⁵/₈"

fisherman (shown in this group), who would appear to be straight off the New England coast.

So much concentration on the Mayan motif has produced what appears to be a standardized face; each carver, however, makes his own subtle changes. The back-sloping forehead (produced by binding baby heads) and prominent nose, plus all the elaborate headdresses and decorated robes, necklaces, earplugs and the like are included, yet some carvers disregard the buck teeth and pendulous lower lip that others feature. All seem to combine the glyphs or picture-writing symbols with the figures, as the original Mayas did on their stelae and wall panels, and the effect is a very strong, although stylized, kind of work which may appeal to you.

Most exceptional among the carvings I saw were the pieces in the Tourist Information Office in Tegucigalpa, the capital of Honduras. Desk tops and fronts, table tops, chairs, cabinets and other pieces of furniture were covered with bold relief carving, some of which I was able to photograph and reproduce here. (At the time, all I had was color film,

These panels, all but the center head and the door, are on furniture in the Tourist Information Office, Tegucigalpa, Honduras. They are bold and strong, and represent some of the best execution of the Mayan motif. The central head is from Nicaragua, and like the two heads at bottom right in the sketches on the facing page (from the tops of 2½-foot carved souvenir salad sets), lacks the finesse and quality of the Honduran work. Note that relief is fairly deep and strongly accented by background staining, also that backgrounds are textured to avoid monotony. All are mahogany.

Background scallop-gouged

Figure at far left reversed here→

MAYA-MOTIF DESK FRONT—Honduras—Mahogany. 2' high

MAYA-MOTIF CHAIR BACK—Honduras—Mahogany—app. 18"↕

Tooled leather or wood

Background scallop-gouged

MAYA HEADS
(Made in pairs)
Nicaragua-Mahog.

MAYA-MOTIF DOOR—Honduras—Teak—App. 7'↕
Note: Glyph designs on right repeated on left side

107

which had to be converted to black and white, with some loss of margins and definition.)

Almost all of this work is in low relief panels, some conventional rectangles or circles, but many bold silhouettes. Mayan heads and glyphs are also used to decorate giant salad sets—some 3 feet long—that are obviously just for tourists. It is interesting to study the variations from panel to panel, showing individual whims and the desire to escape from boredom that besets carvers like those producing cuckoo clock faces in Germany, for example. Also, a number of variations in finishing have been developed. One pair of heads that is very striking and dramatic is obviously carved deeply and stained dark, then surface-sanded to produce highlights which are retained by finishing with a colorless varnish. Another head, quite blocky and simple in design, is completely surface-textured with horizontal gouge grooves. An in-the-round female figure has the entire surface gouge-scalloped, and her child has gouge lines reminiscent of a lifer's uniform. Most of the figures have darker color in recesses, with lighter color and higher polish on upper surfaces.

Table tops entirely covered with designs—often including a practically life-sized Maya chief or priest—can be purchased for a few hundred dollars; a full-sized door, in Honduran teak, for $160. Pieces illustrated in the second panel range from as little as $2 to about $6 for the largest. (The fisherman, even in higher-lifestyle Guatemala, costs under $2.) Incidentally, study the large warrior in the second panel for a moment; note that he has two right hands—not only amateurs make mistakes!

There are simple Indian figures in the round in Honduras and El Salvador, but they are much less common than panels. And there are other motifs, like the ubiquitous Don Quixote; but most of the carvers are devoted to the Maya and his dramatic doings. As a result, the quality of the design and execution is unusually high, because repetition inevitably helps in such matters.

Nicaragua, while cheek-by-jowl with Honduras, El Salvador and Costa Rica, produces very little in terms of outstanding wood carvings. Pieces available are bold but crude and tend to repeat the Don Quixote and Maya motifs of nearby countries—without, however, an equivalent ability at detail, design and technique. Available work tends to be almost childlike in execution, with rough finish. Four examples are pictured; they may appeal to you as quick studies or slap-dash demonstration pieces.

As a group, Mayan motif pieces are quite unusual, and provide an entire field of design that is quite foreign to what one sees in American shops and exhibits. This is rather surprising when one remembers that Mayan country is nearer than Europe, Mayan history is so strong—and prices at point of origin are so low.

These are not Mayan inspired, but they come from the same area. The two in-the-round figures at left are from Honduras, on display at the Tourist Information Office in Tegucigalpa. The stylizing of the mother and child is interesting, the texturing less so. The kneeling figure has a general face shape, but no features, and body contours are quite simple. The other three figures, each about 17 in. high, are from Nicaragua and seem to be caricatures of a Don, Don Quixote, and Sancho Panza.

Panels Can Be Challenging

"Hey Diddle Diddle" suggested itself as a subject for a rhomboid panel left over from my king-sized chess set (page 101). In this instance, I followed proper procedure: I laid out the entire panel and bosted the background to $1/2$ in. for the sky and $3/8$ in. for the mountains, as at top left. The figures were drawn entirely from imagination. I realized when I had finished that the cow and dog were both in natural poses—and the cat had one human foreleg, the moon had the storied face, and the dish and spoon quite human, if spindly, appendages and faces. Thus my carving was half formal, half caricature. (I would distinguish caricature from cartooning. Caricature is ridicule, deliberate exaggeration or distortion of the subject's distinctive features or peculiarities to produce a comic or grotesque effect; cartooning is lampooning or making something laughable, a pictorial joke.) Also, the entire scene was most unlikely, either formally or in caricature. So I made a matching panel with the scene as

it probably occurred. The cow is attempting a polevault (inspired by a *New Yorker* cartoon). The moon is making a most ungentlemanly gesture. The dog is barking at the cat, who is threatening him with the fiddle, while the spoon is luring the dish into making a pass. Now I have a cartoon, with everything but the dog caricatured.

Contrast these panels with the formal coat-of-arms at the right, or with the shoes below: They're much more fun, more of a challenge, and they get a better audience reaction! The shoes are in effect low relief panels wrapped around their bases. I carved one face with a Mexican scene, then drilled holes through to lighten the shoes, and designed the scene on the other side to fit the holes (much easier than relying on the drill to come out where it is expected). Ordinary fencing staples are driven in to hold the leather lacing thongs. The shoes have been quite a sensation for formal wear, although the scenes are caricatured—another paradox.

Actual size of top left panel is $1 \times 10 \times 12^{1/4}$ in., in mahogany; of its mate $1 \times 12^{1/4} \times 12^{1/4}$ in., in primavera (blond mahogany), tinted with brown stains in several tones. The coat of arms is mahogany, about $1 \times 12 \times 19$ in., and the shoes are ladies' size $7^{1/2}$, in birch, 4 in. high at rear. Coat of arms and shoes are tinted with oil pigments, wiped to show grain, then varnished and waxed, as are the upper panels.

✳ Indians, Idols and Images:

Each Culture Has Its Traditional Carved Figures

Wooden mascots have been considered lucky and essential aboard ship ever since the first dugout. One tale has it that primitive ships venturing into the Mediterranean sacrificed a maiden to propitiate the male spirit of the sea—and put her head on a pole at the prow to prove it. This eventually became the more permanent female figurehead, who was the only female aboard ship considered lucky. By the time of the Phoenicians, figureheads were common. The Phoenicians preferred horses, the Egyptians fearsome monsters, the Vikings dragons and snakes, the Polynesians gods and fishes and ornate designs including humans. But the Chinese and Japanese didn't use them, and they developed the easier custom of painted eyes at the bow, which the Portuguese still use. Captain Cook remarked that he found carved lion heads as figureheads on Maori ceremonial canoes in the 1770s,

although New Zealand had never had lions and Cook was supposed to have been the first white visitor there. Did some explorer precede him; did some intrepid Maori navigate to Asia and back, bringing the design; or were the Maori's origins Asian?

The English became obsessed with figureheads, which four hundred years ago were on every vessel of any size. But the competition became so great that prow figures grew oversized, leading to difficulties in steering and handling and even causing an occasional sinking by the bow when a new ship was launched! Some naval vessels had figureheads that could be taken apart and stored when battle loomed. So, two hundred years ago, the Admiralty banned wooden images aboard ship but apparently never enforced the ban, for figureheads were in demand on all kinds of ships until the iron ship came in the 1850s—and ship carvers turned to cigar-store Indians and store signs to stay employed.

There were figureheads representing the great (or notorious): Cornwallis (12 feet tall and weighing 1 ton), Wellington (4 tons!), Gladstone, Gordon, even Churchill recently (this carving has ears, a rarity in such designs),

Typical cigar-store Indians: Left—Two views of a metal Indian at Old Smithville, N.J. Copies in metal permitted addition of free-standing details with less fear of breakage. Center—A squaw in pine, 30 in. high, by Fred Latimer. It is polychromed and gilded, and is now in the collection of E. Thomas Cain. Right—Rough-cut and completed Indian in redwood 18 in. high on an 8-in. base, by the author. It was carved crosswise of the block, partly to avoid a knot at the knees in back, as well as to allow greater width at the shoulders and wood for the hands.

Florence Nightingale, Nannie the Witch, and so on. There are museums on our East Coast and in various parts of England crowded with them, and others are even worshiped here and there. There is the black angel in a church in Yorkshire, the Black Christ in Porto Bello, Panama, and the Atalanta in the museum at La Spezia, Italy, which reportedly "caused" the suicides of three men—a ship captain, a museum attendant and a German officer who took her temporarily in World War II.

Man probably made images almost as soon as he developed sharp-edged tools; they have been familiar all through the centuries and all over the world. Even the most remote people carved them, with whatever skill they may have had. The tiki of the Polynesian, the idol of the Melanesian, the totem pole of our own northwest Indians, the ship figurehead and the cigar-store Indian are all blood brothers, made in many instances by men with no formal training but often a great deal of skill and experience, as well as more imagination than their fellows.

Your local library probably has books showing examples of storefront figures, circus wagons, carousel figures and ship figureheads, even totem poles. They are involved in every show of folk art, as are signs and household tools and furniture. But some of the foreign forms are hard to find in anything except scientific monographs or, strangely enough, travel literature. The Easter Island figures and the New Guinea ones are examples, as well as the Maori and Polynesian ones. What I have tried to provide here is just a sampling of a very large and diversified field.

Perhaps of greatest current interest is the cigar-store Indian—who was often not an Indian at all and not in front of a cigar store. Tobacco was "discovered" by Columbus, after one of his men learned about it from the Indians, brought to Spain in 1558 and introduced to the French court of Henri II by Jean Nicot, his ambassador to Lisbon. Nicot, in turn, brought some to the queen, Catherine de Medici. ("Tobacco" was the Indians' name for the tube in which they smoked the leaf, and nicotine comes from *Nicotiana*, the scientific name of the plant, after Nicot.) All this was around 1560. Sir John Hawkins brought the leaves to England in 1564, when Sir Walter Raleigh was only about twelve years old. So much for *his* story!

In any case, by the late sixteenth century, the cigar-store Indian was a common figure before English shops. Of course, he might be a black man instead, because there was much confusion about color originally, and he usually had tobacco leaves carved as a headdress and kilt, to replace the feathers the carver had seen on sketches of Indians brought to Eng-

Left—My Indian, before tinting, showed grain lines too prominently. Center—Easter Island head, somewhat elongated to fit the basswood trunk in which it was carved. Right—My tiki, in cherry, after a Bora Bora design. Tattoos and eyes did not really stand out until tinting (second view). Bottom—We have our

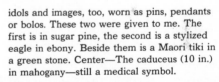

idols and images, too, worn as pins, pendants or bolos. These two were given to me. The first is in sugar pine, the second is a stylized eagle in ebony. Beside them is a Maori tiki in a green stone. Center—The caduceus (10 in.) in mahogany—still a medical symbol.

111

land as captives. By the eighteenth century, a great variety of figures was common, sheaves of tobacco leaves, pipes, even snuff; cavaliers; girls; various animals; and whatever else a carver's or shopkeeper's fertile mind might suggest. They were usually oak or elm, with separate arms and other appendages in most cases, coated with tar or asphaltum to resist the weather, then painted in bright colors. And each time they were repainted, the design was probably changed slightly.

In the early nineteenth century, cigar-store Indians were common in the United States. Some indeed were little more than plank silhouettes with the faces carved in low relief; that made them easier to get in and out of shop doors, because an Indian left out all night might well be removed by some prankster. However, the plank type of Indian also made a convenient addition to the frequent bonfires, so not many survive. The advent of steel ships in the 1850s was accelerated by the battle between the ironclads early in the Civil War, so a great many carvers of ship figureheads and counters suddenly found themselves with time to make Indians and even store signs, and for customers far from the seashore towns where they had always lived. Even so, the continuing demand was so great that these figures were reproduced in metal, either by casting a shell or by forming metal over a mold. And, as always, surface decorations and appendages became more and more elaborate. A number of companies had catalogs offering metal Indians at prices around $50 or $60 and offered to make special figures for relatively little more. But by the beginning of this century, most of the figures were gone; I remember seeing an occasional one during my early childhood, but by the thirties, the Indian was in limbo, not to reemerge until he began to be preserved by the museums.

In sharp contrast to the big good-luck charm called a figurehead and the commercial flavor of the cigar-store Indian are the subjects of most of my sketches. They are similar in being to human figures and in being made of wood (except for the Maori tikis, some of which are miniatures in soft stone), but are essentially devotional. Like the African who strove to express himself in wood, the Easter Islanders, the Maori, our Northwestern Indians, the Polynesians and the primitive savages of New Guinea used wood as a readily available material for idols, images and spirit homes. (So did the Egyptians and early Europeans, the Chinese and the Japanese, as a matter of fact.) Much of their carving was distorted human shapes, but they also carved animals, birds, sea creatures and imaginary monsters.

Easter Islanders, for example, believe they migrated there under leadership of a chief called Hotu Matua, so they make figures of him and his wife—the actual ancestors of some of the inhabitants. They show him sometimes with a weak chin and sometimes with a strong one; they carve him as a two-faced god who, like the Greek Janus, sees both the past and the future. And on an island remote from many species of birds and animals, they carved the albatross and other seabirds, and figures that are half man, half bird. But the figure that is most associated with them is the Moais—which carved in heroic size in stones is the symbol of the island in travel books.

For my Moais, I chose a basswood trunk with a limb crotch that, inverted, became a very large nose and necessitated some elongation of the head—and an unintended caricature of General Charles de Gaulle. The piece is about $4^{1}/_{2}$ inches in diameter by 2 feet high and is set on a redwood base for stability. Some of the inner bark was left on to avoid dead whiteness, and the finish is simple spray varnish and wax. A figure like this can be made with carpenter's chisels, followed by a little judicious knife work in shaping the nose and ear lobes and makes an excellent doorstop or standing figure at the turn of a stair.

My tiki, after a Bora Bora (near Tahiti) one that I saw, was whacked out of a 5-inch wild cherry log; thus it follows the tradition that such figures be made from local wood and be somewhat crude in form. In Polynesia, the fern tree is a popular wood, as is the butt of a palm, and some tikis are carved right on the tree stump, and with axes and large knives rather than more conventional tools. Such a figure is often painted to accent the eyes and tattoo marks, but most of those which find their way to this country to stand before a Trader Vic's are of fern tree and unpainted, partly because of the extremely rough and stringy surface of the wood. Mine is in the garden at the end of a short stone path, so it's well varnished with marine varnish to reduce the checking and dry rot that attacks fruitwoods in our area.

My cigar-store Indian, a male version of the standard figure sketched at bottom right in this group, illustrates how poses can be changed slightly to suit circumstances. I worked in a $5^{1}/_{4}$-inch square piece of redwood about 26 inches long. (The wood was appropriate for the subject but unexpectedly difficult to carve, since it was the whitish sort that has

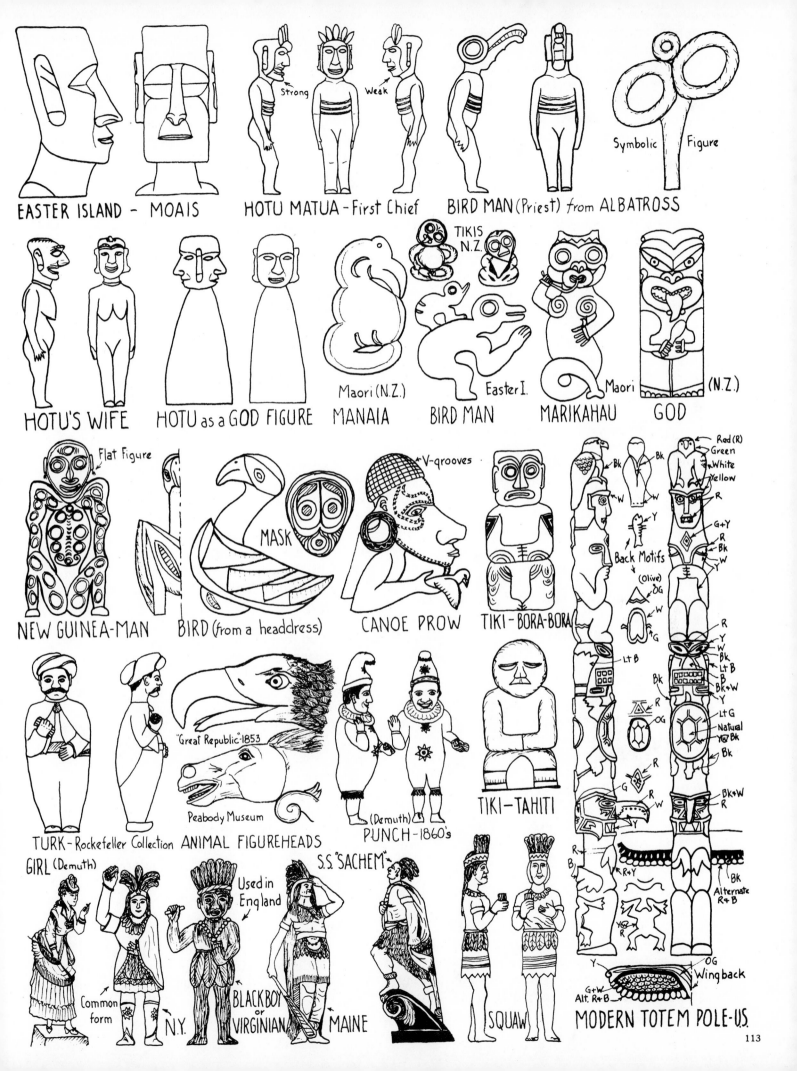

EASTER ISLAND – MOAIS

HOTU MATUA – First Chief

Strong

Weak

BIRD MAN (Priest) from ALBATROSS

Symbolic Figure

HOTU'S WIFE

HOTU as a GOD FIGURE

Maori (N.Z.)
MANAIA

TIKIS N.Z.

Easter I.
BIRD MAN

Maori
MARIKAHAU

(N.Z.)
GOD

Flat Figure

NEW GUINEA-MAN

MASK

BIRD (from a headdress)

V-grooves

CANOE PROW

TIKI – BORA-BORA

Bk   Bk

W   W

Y

Back Motifs

(Olive) OG

W

G

Lt B

Red (R)
Green
White
Yellow

R

G+Y
R
Bk
W
Y

R
Y
W
Bk
Lt B
B
Bk+W
Y
Lt G
Natural
Y & Bk
Bk

Bk+W
R

"Great Republic"-1853

Peabody Museum

TURK – Rockefeller Collection   ANIMAL FIGUREHEADS

(Demuth)
PUNCH-1860's

TIKI – TAHITI

R+Y
R
W

Y

R+
B

GIRL (Demuth)

Used in England

S.S. "SACHEM"

Common form   N.Y.

BLACKBOY or VIRGINIAN   MAINE

SQUAW

Bk
Alternate
R & B

Y   OG
Wingback
G+W
Alt. R&B

MODERN TOTEM POLE-U.S.

113

distinct summer and winter growths, the winter growth hard and resinous, the summer growth soft and spongy, so even razor-sharp chisels rapidly lose their edge and alternate between slicing off the winter growth and breaking out chunks of the summer growth between.) The Indian was positioned crosswise of the chunk, which makes for some difficulties in layout of the design and in initial cutting, but permits a larger figure in a given block and also provides wood for arms and hands if they are held in close. (Most wooden Indians had attached forearms and other appurtenances, and modern ones are often built up of planks because proper sizes of wood are not available. Also, pine or fir is the usual material, although some carvers use cedar and other woods if they are locally available.)

This figure is much more elaborate than the tiki or moais, of course, and I chose to make it more complex by detailing the headband and hair, the fringe at the bottom of the kilt, and the hands and feet. Such details are often painted on and disappear when the repainter is someone of the barn-painting variety. But this figure is in miniature and will be seen close up. Hair and fringe require a small veiner, plus knife work where the grain is particularly recalcitrant. Details of the headband are easier with a knife because of the grain variation, as are eye, nose and mouth details. Eyes, incidentally, have a drilled pupil and outlined iris, plus eyelids. Feathers of the headdress are also detailed with the knife rather than the veiner, because of grain problems. Because my Indian will spend his life within doors, I did not drill the deep hole down from the crown of the head that was customary so the figure could be given occasional doses of linseed oil and/or turpentine to preserve the wood. (My tiki has a natural core fault that serves.) And most of the basic colors are the German sal-ammoniac stains which can be applied over varnish and will penetrate it, given time. However, if they are applied on varnish, a mistake can be wiped off immediately. Acrylics would give a similar finish—a soft gloss tone—if wiped down so the grain shows through. On the original Indians, oil paints were used and covered the wood completely, so it could have been made of anything. In fact, the shift to iron copies in the latter years wasn't even evident.

On a figure like this, when the wood tends to split and crush, a knife is better for detail than a chisel, in my opinion, because a slight sawing motion can be used to avoid crushing. Lettering on the base was made by cutting away the background around the word "FINE" and making V-cuts around the letters of "CIGARS," with the wall of the V nearest the letters vertical. This was also done with the knife because of the curves in the letters. This unusual combination of lettering types was, incidentally, used by at least one carver of long ago who was less concerned with esthetics than with practicality.

Arm bands and hair band were carved integrally, but the bracelets were carved separately from scraps, then broken and glued around the wrists. If you want the challenge, they can of course be carved integrally, but I'd suggest a more amenable wood. They were given a copper tone by painting with a copper lacquer; our Indians didn't wear gold or silver (except for the southwestern ones, and then only in later years). As a matter of hard fact, Indians have skin colors ranging from white to brown; the "redskin" idea came from our ancestors, who were describing the Indians' favorite color for paint—red.

The totem pole is a great American standard as well, which I have dealt with in earlier books. So I have provided here only two views of a rather elaborate modern miniature, with shapes and colors. Other motifs are like those shown for the spoons (page 41) made by the same tribes—Haidas, Tlingit, Tsimshian, Kwakiutl and Bella Coola, in British Columbia and southeast Alaska. Like the African mwiko (which was a single figure), these poles are basically tribal totems rather than idols. They identified the tribe of the owner—his totem was on top, his wife's on the bottom—and the taller the pole, the more important he was. They were made of cedar with flint adzes, abalone scrapers and sharkskin sandpaper.

The New Guinea figures, like the Polynesian ones, were used in meetinghouses and on headdresses, as well as on canoe prows—wherever the user thought a friendly spirit would help him or terrify his enemies. They are very different from our figures, so may provide some fun and relaxation. Again, they are painted in bright colors, in contrast to the Maori ones, which are a uniform dark red with shell eyes providing "headlights."

We have many good-luck charms, worn as pendants, pins, earrings and belt buckles, or carried on a key ring or loose in a pocket. I have included three as reminders—two bolos and a caduceus. Many other designs, particularly those in the next article, are suitable as well.

✳ Sundials—And How to Carve Them:

Each Must Be Calculated for Place and Time

The sundial is familiar to most moderns only as a garden or wall decoration—charming but rather inaccurate. But it was, for centuries, the best available indicator of time, even when it merely showed the noon hour or the proper time to pause for prayers. There are sundials throughout our written history; poets have sung about them, authors written of them. There's one at Glamis Castle, where Shakespeare placed his play *Macbeth*. There's another at Chartres Cathedral in France. Still others are all over Europe and the near East. Ancient Romans captured some and lugged them home as booty. There are noon markers on walls near church spires using the spire as a gnomon, posts set up in the middle of a circle of rocks, monuments like the one to Henry the Navigator in Lisbon that became giant sundials. Ben Franklin saw one on the general post office in London, so, when he became American postmaster general during the Revolution, it reappeared on our first coinage, with its motto of "Be about Your Business" shortened to a more American "Mind Your Business." There were dials on the dollar (first silver, then bronze, then pewter, as the war progressed), on the copper cent, and on the "Fugio note," which was a third of a dollar. It also appeared on a 6-cent note of the City of New York, printed in 1814.

Further, the sun dial is a true example of simplicity, utility and beauty combined. Its lines and markings must be mathematically exact to serve its purpose, yet it can be extremely decorative in an unobtrusive way. It can be as simple or elaborate as anyone could desire. (Some have been made with 80 dials, showing times, season, tides and such for a number of locations.)

Not so long ago, I didn't know any of this, so when a friend in Maine asked me to design him a dial, I shrugged it off with the comment that enduring bronze ones are commonly available, long-lasting and relatively cheap. But I was intrigued, and suddenly remembered that teak will withstand weather, salt and sun very well. So, three books and four magazine articles later, I knew that sundials should suit their latitude and user. I not only made a sundial for him, but two others, of different designs, for my daughters. I also discovered that a small pewter dial I had bought in Williamsburg was designed for 36 degrees north latitude (Williamsburg is 37°15′) and hence was not very accurate in New York, and my larger bronze one is designed for 41 degrees—near enough right in these days of Daylight Saving and confusion about time anyhow.

My dials were made of 1-inch teak about a foot square and so should stand the weather well with minimum attention. Teak just isn't seriously affected by sun, rain or bugs, and with occasional oiling will even retain its color. Besides, it's pure joy to carve. I had a piece of 1/8-inch Monel metal (an alloy of nickel hardened with copper) that will hold its silvery color despite the weather and is stiff enough to

Sun motifs are the decorative elements on this circular form dial. Upper left is an Amerindian design, upper right the sun from the center of the Aztec calendar stone, lower right the Norse god Freyr riding a boar, and lower left the Greek god Helios driving four horses. Motifs are carved in low relief, with the ground sloping from the dial to the edges. Motto is executed, as are dial lines, with a veiner. Gnomon is 1/8-inch Monel metal set in a 1/4-in.-deep slot. Wood is teak, about 12 × 12 in. by 1 in. thick, finished with teak finish.

resist small children's affectionate beatings, and that became two angular gnomons, while the third is a brass rod $1/8$ inch in diameter. Just for reassurance, the dials were backed with $5/8$-inch aluminum T-bar, glued and screwed in place with zinc-coated screws. (Brass screws in this case make an excellent battery, so there is rapid corrosion. Besides, two of the dials are set in concrete, both for accuracy and for security, and the salts in concrete would intensify galvanic action.)

There are a number of shapes of dials besides the familiar circular ones, and several ways to design one. I made one with a circular face and carvings in the four corners, another that is square, with minimum carving, and a third that is set at an angle to the horizontal, to illustrate three types. You can make any of the three rather easily, and suit the decorations to your own preference, although I've provided some designs for examples. Just keep the details simple to reduce the spaces where water can collect and freeze in winter, because the freezing may cause expansion that will break off details, unless the dial is set at an angle so it can drain.

Let's start with a simple sundial of an unusual form. It is called equatorial, because the dial itself is tilted to be parallel with the equator. As a result, the dial face can be circular, with regular 15-degree divisions for the hours (360 degrees circumference divided by 24 hours gives 15 degrees per hour), and the gnomon or style is like a miniature North Pole, aligned with the axis of the Earth. Pick out a board to suit your purposes; the dial itself will be a semicircle, so the minimum shape would be twice as long as it is wide. I selected a board 12 inches wide by 13 inches long, which provided space for a 12-inch semicircle, with decoration and a motto below (see photo). Draw a baseline about a half-inch from one long edge, and on it scribe a semicircle. The center of this circle is the site of the gnomon, and the semicircle can be divided into 15-degree segments with a protractor, or by subdividing it into twelve parts with a compass or dividers. The central division line will become 12 o'clock and the intersections of the semicircle and the baseline will be six, with the other hours numbered *clockwise*. If you want to subdivide for quarter hours, divide each 15-degree segment into four parts (3.75 degrees each). Radiating lines are drawn from the central point through each hour point and on out to as near the edge of the board as you wish to go. This completes the dial itself—but you can add any decoration or motto you wish, and where you wish, as long as it doesn't obscure too much of an hour line. I put the motto across the bottom, and six Zuni and Navajo designs, copied from Indian jewelry, in spaces around the board. (It could be an edge design, or a border just as readily, or one or two large design units in the bottom corners.)

Because the dial will be exposed to the weather all year long, I decided to keep the carving shallow, so most of it was done with a veiner. All the lines and numbers were carved this way, using a $1/16$-inch veiner and a very light mallet. The only problem is to maintain a constant line depth and width, which is usually easiest by achieving depth in two steps, taking a shallow cut originally to establish direction and a second to adjust depth and width. A V-tool can also be used and is easier to keep sharp but is harder to control in cutting.

Right—Three methods of calculating a sundial.

Left—Simple square dial with Italian motto meaning: "The iron bell may wrongly tell; I err not, if the sun shine well." It is 1 × 12 × 12-in. teak, with dial lines and design executed with a veiner. Decorations are cartoons of the sun—rising, at high noon and setting. The $1/8$-in. Monel metal gnomon is set into a slot $1/4$ in. deep, also carries a cartoon of the sun-face profile. Note latitude and identification along lower edge. Finish is teak oil.

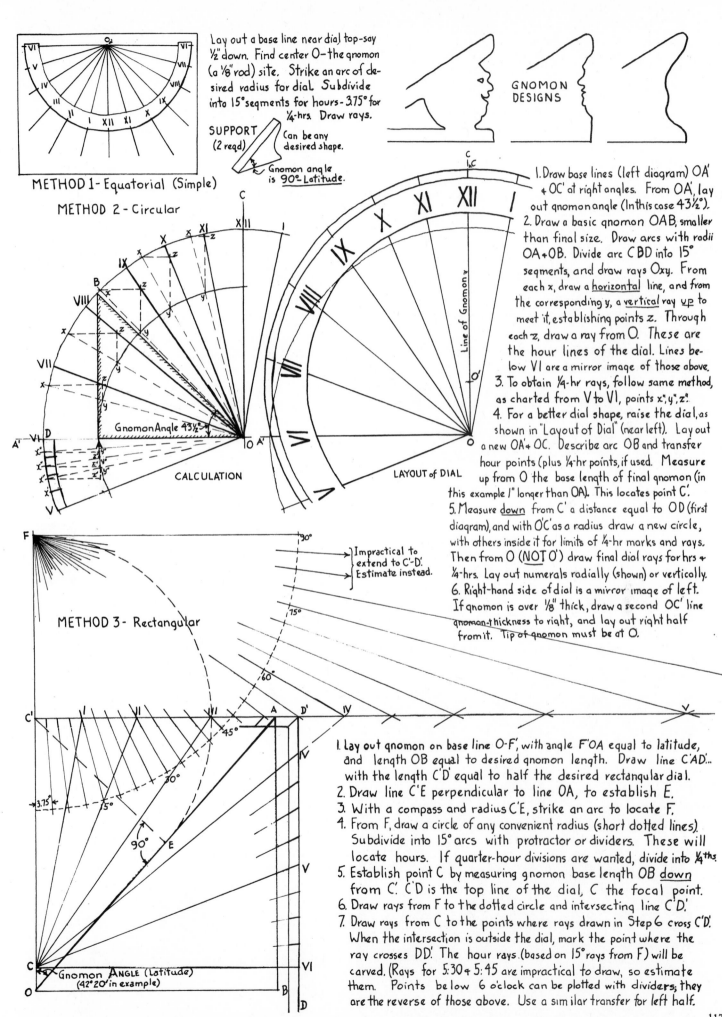

METHOD 1- Equatorial (Simple)

METHOD 2 - Circular

Lay out a base line near dial top-say ½" down. Find center O—the gnomon (a ⅛" rod) site. Strike an arc of desired radius for dial. Subdivide into 15° segments for hours- 3.75° for ¼-hrs. Draw rays.

SUPPORT (2 reqd)

Can be any desired shape.

Gnomon angle is 90°- Latitude.

GNOMON DESIGNS

CALCULATION

Gnomon Angle 43½°

LAYOUT of DIAL

Line of Gnomon

1. Draw base lines (left diagram) OA' & OC' at right angles. From OA', lay out gnomon angle (In this case 43½°).
2. Draw a basic gnomon OAB, smaller than final size. Draw arcs with radii OA+OB. Divide arc CBD into 15° segments, and draw rays Oxy. From each x, draw a _horizontal_ line, and from the corresponding y, a _vertical_ ray _up_ to meet it, establishing points z. Through each z, draw a ray from O. These are the hour lines of the dial. Lines below VI are a mirror image of those above.
3. To obtain ¼-hr rays, follow same method, as charted from V to VI, points x", y", z".
4. For a better dial shape, raise the dial, as shown in "Layout of Dial" (near left). Lay out a new OA'& OC. Describe arc OB and transfer hour points (plus ¼-hr points, if used. Measure up from O the base length of final gnomon (in this example 1" longer than OA). This locates point C'.
5. Measure _down_ from C' a distance equal to OD (first diagram), and with O'C' as a radius draw a new circle, with others inside it for limits of ¼-hr marks and rays. Then from O (NOT O') draw final dial rays for hrs & ¼-hrs. Lay out numerals radially (shown) or vertically.
6. Right-hand side of dial is a mirror image of left. If gnomon is over ⅛" thick, draw a second OC' line gnomon-thickness to right, and lay out right half from it. Tip of gnomon must be at O.

METHOD 3- Rectangular

Impractical to extend to C'-D'. Estimate instead.

90°

Gnomon ANGLE (Latitude) (42°20' in example)

1. Lay out gnomon on base line O-F', with angle F'OA equal to latitude, and length OB equal to desired gnomon length. Draw line C'AD'... with the length C'D' equal to half the desired rectangular dial.
2. Draw line C'E perpendicular to line OA, to establish E.
3. With a compass and radius C'E, strike an arc to locate F.
4. From F, draw a circle of any convenient radius (short dotted lines). Subdivide into 15° arcs with protractor or dividers. These will locate hours. If quarter-hour divisions are wanted, divide into ¼ths.
5. Establish point C by measuring gnomon base length OB _down_ from C'. C'D is the top line of the dial, C the focal point.
6. Draw rays from F to the dotted circle and intersecting line C'D'.
7. Draw rays from C to the points where rays drawn in Step 6 cross C'D'. When the intersection is outside the dial, mark the point where the ray crosses DD'. The hour rays (based on 15° rays from F) will be carved. (Rays for 5:30 & 5:45 are impractical to draw, so estimate them. Points below 6 o'clock can be plotted with dividers; they are the reverse of those above. Use a similar transfer for left half.

Traditional dials had Roman numerals rather than Arabic, and these are still the easier to carve to uniform height and proper shape. If the motto is relatively short, it is easiest to lay out and carve in capital letters. Block letters can be carved with the veiner as well, eliminating many of the problems of carving raised or wide incised lettering.

Because the Indian pins on which the designs are based are essentially flat, and have geometric patterns, I could make them as flat carvings with the patterns indicated by veiner lines and some surfaces cross-hatched to represent color differences of the stones of the originals. The outer shape, however, was established by setting in (vertical cutting) along the outline with a $1/8$-inch firmer and suitable small gouges, then fairing out from a depth of $1/8$ inch so the design stands clear—trenched in the old Egyptian manner.

The gnomon for this dial can be a dowel rod, or preferably a smaller diameter rod (so the shadow is narrower). I used $1/8$-inch brass, glued into a hole and topped with a safety cap that is also an Indian design. These are identified in the sketches. The brass rod and holly ornament are varnished to reduce corrosion of the one and dirtying of the other.

All that remains now is to raise the dial to the proper angle. This can be done in a variety of ways. The simplest is to provide two wedg-

es, as I did. An elaborate device, particularly suitable if the user is likely to move a considerable distance north or south and so needs an adjustable dial, is to piano-hinge a second board of the same size along the bottom and put two brass window-adjusting fittings on the ends. Thus the angle can be set as required.

To figure the proper angle, look up your latitude in an atlas (New York City is about $40^1/2$ degrees north, for example), and subtract this from 90 degrees. This gives the proper angle for the wedges, or the face angle of the dial.

I finished the dial with an oil finish like that used on ship decks; any marine outfitter has one brand or another (mine was Watco Oil Finish). This gives a surface sheen and fills the pores with a plastic, yet is not a surface coat like varnish, which tends to build up, scale and the like, as well as having too much gloss. The surface can be reoiled as necessary or, if teak, can simply be allowed to weather to its natural pleasant gray. It will not erode, rot or encourage insects, as most domestic woods do.

This dial must be set on a level surface, absolutely horizontal, and oriented so the gnomon points true north (not magnetic north). It can be set slightly off true north to compensate for constant longitudinal errors, if any. International time is based on one-hour change for each 15 degrees of longitude east or west of Greenwich, England. Thus, Philadelphia, on the seventy-fifth meridian, is five hours later than Greenwich, and is the theoretical center of the Eastern Time Zone of the United States. New York City, however, is at 74 degrees west, or 1 degree east of the standard meridian, so the sun reaches there four minutes before it does Philadelphia. (Portland, Maine, is 4°45' east, so is 19 minutes earlier than EST in apparent sun time.) This is a constant error, so a sundial can be turned slightly clockwise to compensate for it. If the difference were plus, the rotation would have to be counterclockwise. (San Francisco, for example, is $2^1/2$ degrees west of the one-hundred-twentieth Meridian, so sun time is ten minutes later than standard time.) To figure your longitudinal correction, look up your longitude and the standard time meridian that applies in an atlas.

LIGHT RULES ME; THE SHADOW, THEE

Left—This dial is designed to set at an angle with the horizontal (see text), so has equal divisions. Design motifs are taken from Zuni and Navajo sources, depicting the sun and various other elements. It is 1-in. teak, 12 × 13 in., and set on teak angled supports. This dial, like the other two, has aluminum angle for back bracing and to provide a method of attachment.

Spring Summer Autumn Winter

SYMBOLS *for the* SEASONS

EGYPTIAN SEASONS

Morning Noon Evening

WILD-ROSE ELEMENTS — A Possible Scroll Design

16 17

WASHINGTON FAMILY
This English coat of arms, from
a sundial, may be a source of
our Stars and Stripes.

EMBLEM of RICHARD III
(Note Tudor rose at left)

EURUS (East) *Vase spilling rain*

LIPS (Southeast) *Ship frame*

APELIOTES (Southwest) *Fruits*

ZEPHYRUS (West) *Flowers*

FOUR of the WINDS from TEMPLE of the WINDS

HELIOS - Greek God of the Sun
from a Trojan fresco fragment

FREYR – Norse God of the Sun

EAGLE(?) SACRED PARROT FIRE BIRD SUN GOD THUNDER BIRD SUN GOD

DEER DANCER SNAKE DANCER HOOP DANCER RATTLE DANCER PARROT DANCER RAINBOW GOD KACHINA

— AMERINDIAN SYBOLS *for the* SUN —

AZTEC SUN GOD MOON FACE

32 Selected Sundial Mottoes

Watch, for ye know not the hour

Thou—simple, silent and sublime—
But shows thy shadowy sign from Heaven.
                        —Bernard Barton

Light rules me; the shadow, thee

Time takes all but memories

Time is fleeting; art is long

Every man may be master of his time

I count none but the sunny hours

I am a Shade; a Shadow too arte thou;

I mark the Time; saye Gossip, dost thou so?
                        —Henry A. Dobson

There's nothing as precious as time

Be true as the dial to the sun

May all your hours be as sunny as those I count

Haste, traveler, the sun is sinking now;
He shall return again, but never thou

Carpe Diem   (Seize the moment)

Nulla fluit cuius non meminisse juvet
(Let no hour pass that is not a delight to remember

Redibo, tu nunquam
(I shall return, thou never)

Umbra sumus—tamen his sevum componitur umbris
(We are a shadow, yet time is made up of such shadows)

For the night cometh

Come! Light! Visit me!

Life is a passing shadow
                —Talmud

Horas non numero nisi juventas
(I count only the youthful hours)

Puo fallare la campana il ferro
Ma resplende il sole Io non erro
(The iron bell may wrongly tell:
I err not, if the sun shine well)

Lux et umbra vicissim, sed semper amor
(Light and shadow by turns, but always love)

Tempus fugit
(Time flies)

Sic transit gloria mundi
(So passes the glory of the world)

Cosi la vita (Such is life)

C'est l'heure de bien faire
(This is the hour to do good)

Il est plus tard que vous croyez
(It is later than you think)

The hour passeth

Tempus ad lucem ducit veritatem
(Time brings truth to light)

While Phoebus on me shines
Then view my shades and lines

The learned line showeth the city's hour

More familiar dials are not tilted like this one, but have the dial horizontal or vertical. There are also types which have a ring dial with a central rod for gnomon or are pillars with an arm at the top as a gnomon; some have adjustable gnomons to match the date and so on. But let's keep it simple.

The familiar present-day sundial is a circle or square set horizontally and has a triangular gnomon. Many are inaccurate, because they are made in one latitude and used in another. Others have thick gnomons, so the edge casting a shadow adds on minutes in the day. Two methods of laying out horizontal dials are sketched. Either can be used for a rectangular or a circular dial simply by drawing the desired shape outside the calculated "fan" and extending the rays to meet it. Ray angles, gnomon upper edge and orientation of the dial are the key elements—you can do almost anything you want to do with the rest of it.

There's another way, still, of making a dial that is very easy. Simply make a proper gnomon and set it on a sheet of paper. Pick a sunny day and set the whole thing up where you want it, and draw in the shadows each hour as determined by your watch. You should, however, take into account the equation of time for the day you selected—and remember about longitude and Daylight Saving. Drawing the dial automatically corrects for longitude error, if your watch is dependable, and insures that the dial will be right at least once a year.

Design of the typical dial starts with design of the gnomon. Decide how long you want it to be. (The dial will probably end up almost twice as big.) Look up your latitude in an atlas and draw that angle from the baseline. If the gnomon is to be metal, you'll want to add some on the bottom to go in a slot, or to be bent over to a right angle for fastening. The area inside the triangle can have any decoration your heart desires—as long as you don't disturb the angle or the top edge, which, in theory, is aligned with the axis of the Earth when the dial is oriented.

Because the instructions for graphing the dial are complex and step-by-step, I have lettered them next to the adjacent diagram. Note that the angles near 12 o'clock are smaller than those near six; if yours aren't, you've made a mistake.

If you want quarter-hour subdivisions, you can chart them by the same method you used for the hours, or simply estimate them. It is usually inadvisable to extend quarter-hour rays all the way to the center—even hour lines form a blob there. To reduce this effect, carve the rays shallow at the center and deepen them as you go outward. Rays can be carved with veiner or V-tool, unless the wood tends to tear on the countergrain side. Also, it is advisable to carve in at least two passes, so the second can smooth up any wiggles in the first, either in width or depth. Such carving is best controlled by driving the tool with a light mallet, rather than by hand pressure.

Before you carve the rays, however, decide on what decoration you want. Because the sun is down at least ten hours in most latitudes, there's little point in having rays over the lower portion of the dial. So the whole ray pattern can be shifted down on the wood and still leave room for a motto and/or decoration. (A list of thirty-two mottoes is provided here.) Designs can also interrupt some rays, if you prefer, or go around the edge of the dial itself. Mottoes can be simple block lettering, without serifs, and cut with the veiner as the rays are, or made more elaborate. Carving technique for the designs can vary as well, although it is advisable to keep in mind that deep carving will multiply the number of pockets where water can collect and cause possible trouble. (This is one virtue of a sloping dial. Even a droplet on a surface will catch the sun's rays and be converted into a miniature burning glass on occasion.) I elected to carve in shallow bas-relief, mostly with the knife and under $1/8$ inch deep. Apparent depth can be increased by antiquing the surface after carving, with one coat of the finish to prevent end-grain soaking, followed by a coat of a darker stain (like walnut on teak) which is wiped lightly off the surfaces and left to dry in the carved areas. This will happen with weathering anyway, but the carving will look better initially if it is antiqued.

If you want designs other than those I selected, they can be found in books on mythology or Indians, or in popular books on astronomy, for example. Or you can use a coat-of-arms, or a design which relates to the motto you select.

The horizontal dials, like the angled one, should be reinforced with aluminum T-bar or angle, glued and screwed on the back. This also provides a way of locking the dial to the supporting surface in case you're concerned about pilferage and playfulness. The reinforcement can be grouted onto the base or drilled for fastening. Also, carve into one edge the latitude for which the dial was designed. Finishing is simply a matter of applying one or two more coats of the oil or varnish. If varnish is used, the top coat should be a marine gloss; the less glossy varnishes do not stand up nearly so well in the weather.

If you are more ambitious, or more precise, you can find plans for much more accur-

Equation of Time

This is the difference between *apparent* time—as measured by sundial, for example—and *mean* time, as measured by a clock. The earth rotates on its axis in 23 hours 56 minutes, the extra 4 minutes being occupied in catching up to the sun, which has moved on in its own annual orbit. This 3 minutes 55.91 seconds (actual) is an average; sometimes the sun moves faster, sometimes slower, because of the earth's varying motion in its elliptical orbit. The motion is fastest at the time of the perihelion (January 3), so clock allowance is insufficient and actual noon by the sun becomes later and later, as compared with the standard clock. Also, the ecliptic (the sun's track) is inclined to our equator, so this causes variations as well. Combining these two corrections gives the numbers for the Equation of Time. "Add" means that the sun passes the meridian after mean noon, so the amount shown must be added to dial time to get mean time. Conversely, "sub" means the amount shown must be subtracted from the apparent time on the dial because the sun is ahead of the clock. Time is given in minutes.

Jan.	1 Add	3.5	May	1 Sub.	2.9	Sep.	1 Add	0.1
	6	5.8		6	3.4		6 Sub.	1.5
	11	7.9		11	3.6		11	3.2
	16	9.8		16	3.7		16	5.0
	21	11.3		21	3.5		21	6.8
	26	12.6		26	3.1		26	8.5
Feb.	1	13.4	Jun.	1	2.3	Oct.	1	10.2
	6	14.1		6	1.5		6	11.7
	11	14.3		11	0.6		11	13.1
	16	14.2		16 Add	0.4		16	14.3
	21	13.7		21	1.6		21	15.2
	26	13.0		26	2.6		26	15.9
Mar.	1	12.5	Jul.	1	3.9	Nov.	1	16.4
	6	11.4		6	4.6		6	16.3
	11	10.2		11	5.3		11	16.0
	16	8.8		16	5.9		16	15.2
	21	7.4		21	6.2		21	14.2
	26	5.8		26	6.4		26	12.8
Apr.	1	4.0	Aug.	1	6.3	Dec.	1	11.0
	8	2.6		6	5.8		6	9.0
	11	1.2		11	5.2		11	6.9
	16 Sub.	0.1		16	4.3		16	4.5
	21	1.2		21	3.2		21	2.0
	26	2.1		26	1.9		26 Add	0.4

ate—and complicated—sundials, but they tend not to be as attractive or familiar to most people. Plans have appeared for such dials occasionally in magazines like *Sky and Telescope* and *Popular Science Monthly*. Some incorporate adjustable dials and gnomons, curved lines to accommodate the Equation of Time; some show seasons and other phenomena, or time at other points around the world. For any of these, however, you must start by knowing the date, and some must be adjusted every few days, so metal will stand the wear better—meaning your carving will be a pattern.

Vertical sundials can also be placed on garage doors, walls, or a pillar. It is easiest to set up the gnomon (angle in this case is 90 degrees *minus* the latitude) in place, and establish the hour rays as their shadows are projected by the sun, preferably on a day when the Equation of Time has minimal effect: April 16, June 16, Sept. 1, or Dec. 25.

✳ How Much Detail Is Necessary?

Animals, Faces and a Temple Provide Examples

Any design can be executed simply or with complicated detail—and anywhere in between. An accomplished carver can do amazing things to a poor blank, and a poor carver can ruin the best. These pieces are a series of cases in point. They can be simple, or as complex as you want them.

Consider the climbing bear and monkey at lower right in the sketches. These animals utilize an old principle, namely that opposed and slanted holes will cramp a cord, so that, when coupled with a whiffletree, the parallel cords can be pulled alternately—the same motion as hand-milking a cow—and cause the animal to climb the ropes. When one cord is pulled, the animal will slide his paw up the other loosely held cord. The only necessity is to have a rigid arm design so the cords can be kept separated by a distance roughly equal to the length of the whiffletree. Holes through the forepaws are at an angle to the vertical, as sketched, and allow the cord to slide freely through them. The cord is usually 1/8-inch cotton like that used in venetian blinds, and length of the cords can be whatever the user wants; a carver friend produced a monkey that climbed a flagpole to release the furled admiral's pennant at his yacht club! Releasing the strain on the cords allows the animal to slide back down, and it can be stopped at any point simply by putting a little stress on the cords.

The basic silhouette can be sawed from

Far left—Monkey and bear climb equally well, but contrast sharply in detail. Above—Aleut Salute requires snow-block detailing to suggest igloo entrances, but only the vital noses for facial features. Detailing the ruff is optional, but would detract from the noses. Left—American centaur has much hair detail in fetlocks, and enlarged leg joints for emphasis—but no decorations on armor.

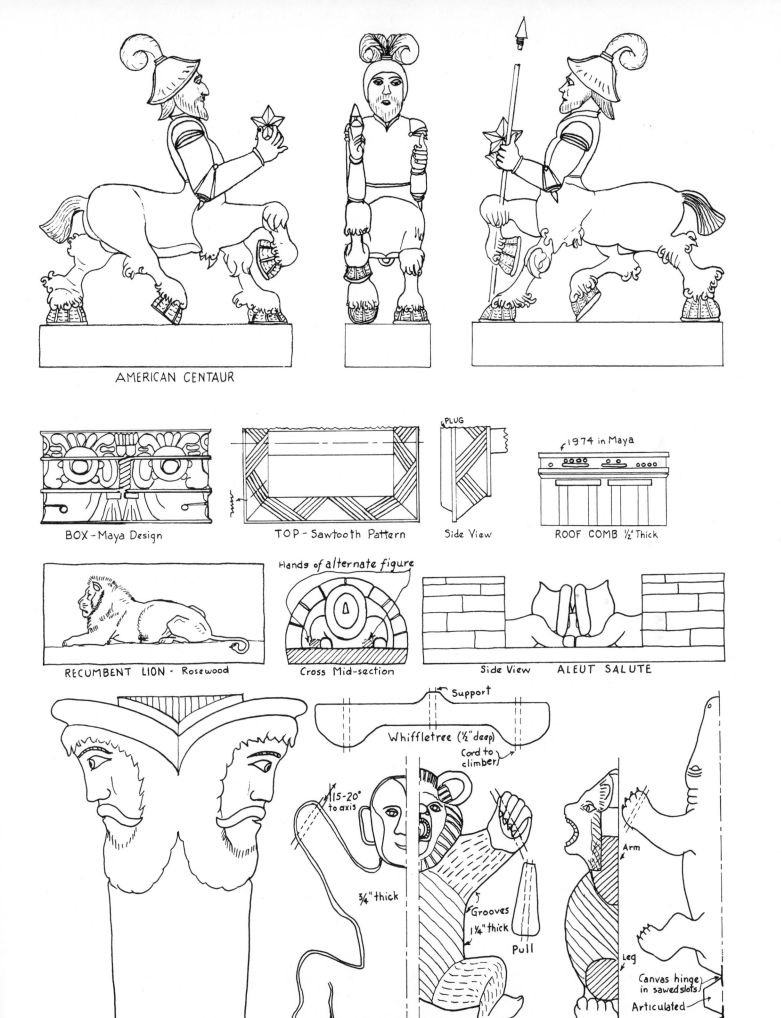

AMERICAN CENTAUR

BOX - Maya Design

TOP - Sawtooth Pattern

PLUG

Side View

1974 in Maya

ROOF COMB ½" Thick

RECUMBENT LION - Rosewood

Hands of alternate figure

Cross Mid-section

Side View   ALEUT SALUTE

JANUS (¼ size)

15-20° to axis

¾" thick

Support

Whiffletree (½" deep)

Cord to climber

Grooves

1¼" thick

Pull

MONKEY & BEAR CORD CLIMBERS

Arm

Leg

Canvas hinge in sawed slots

Articulated

ALLIGATOR

1/2-inch, 3/4-inch or 1-inch wood, depending upon the degree of modeling intended. Carving can be merely chamfering and V-grooves, as in the walnut monkey shown; fairly high relief, as in the bear; or even in-the-round—in which case the lower legs can project forward. It is also possible to make articulated figures like an alligator by making the tail in diamond-shaped sections split and glued to canvas hinges or strung on a cord like beads but separated slightly by gluing or knots. There is nothing special to be done in the carving, except to maintain a balanced figure.

The American centaur was primarily an exercise in carving elaborate fetlock designs. The concept was based on the belief of the Plains Indians that the Spaniards on horseback were part of their horses. Strangely, some people who have seen my carving at first see only a rider on horseback; the fact that the horse head is replaced by a human torso comes to them only with a second look!

I used teak for the figure, laminating two 1-inch boards; the human portion of the figure would have been better and less rigid if I'd either reduced the size or added another lamination so the arms could be separated from the body. Also, both arms are at the same height—greater freedom would have been indicated by a slight difference in their position.

The lance is a separate piece, inserted in the hand and tipped with a silver head.

The basic problem in carving hair is to keep it from looking greasy and plastered. This can be done practically in wood by meticulous shaping of strands either in curls or in separate waves, or by detailing only a mane or a ruff or a tailtip, as in the recumbent lion (photo on page 52). It is difficult if not impossible to show the fine distinctions of individual hairs, of course, and unnecessary if a little time and effort are put into the carving. (See Riemenschneider's Holy Magdelena, page 186.) The need is to have a wood which does not have too prominent a grain, so that lines can be cut in long sweeping curves as well as in tight curls without the ever-present danger of splitting.

Another problem involving hair detailing is the Janus figure. This was carved in an ash fork, with a practically complete head on each arm, as shown in old Greek figures of the god. Janus, whom we have heard of primarily as a two-faced and thus somewhat dubious character who gave his name to January, actually

Left—Janus, in ash 16½-in. high (without matching oak pot on top), has stylized hair and beard, but flows into natural base. Center—"Woman with Jar," by S. Bulkowski, has smooth skin but textured and pleated dress. "Peasant Woman," by B. Korelov, in contrast is merely basic shapes, with gouge scallops. Both are Russian. Right—Stag pierced pattern in bone has more detail than my stag in holly below it. Mine is there to accent the "waterfall and scene" created by the water-stained fir ply behind it.

was the keeper of doors and the doors of his temple were thrown open when a Greek city went to war—thus he was a quite heroic figure. In this design, his hair and beard were both a mass of curls, so several sizes of round gouges and a small firmer were the principal tools. Curls were drawn as I went to suit the irregularities of the trunk, and of course the overall shape and faces were almost finished before the curls were begun. In effect, they're low relief on an in-the-round figure. Finish was a dull varnish for sealing, followed by waxing.

My wife, who on occasion finds our home jammed with carvings, decided to put this one to use as a planter, so I added an oak flowerpot headdress in suitable design. The oak was three sections laminated together, which expedited the hollowing, but it was slightly checked so has cracked through on one side since. However, it was lined with heavy plastic, so it's still in use. (The cracking, by the way, was probably a result of internal stresses from the clamping during gluing, rather than from moisture.)

The two Eskimos emerging from their igloos is in white pine, from a piece I found among the cabinetmaker's scraps. The design was made to fit a 2/3-round section of a 3-inch cylinder. Carving the two heads so the noses just touch in the classic Aleut salute was a bit of a problem, requiring a narrow knife with a long point.

Mayan architects had a rather distinctive temple and pyramid design, placing the temple atop a pyramid in most cases and topping it with a high roof "comb." I combined several such designs in the jewel box sketched and pictured, utilizing the cornice element from Tulum, Quintana Roo, Mex., which has a face at each corner with the nose projecting. (A similar design is used on one temple at Tikal, in Guatemala.) The face is very conventionalized and run through by parallel horizontal bands, so it provides plenty of scope, particularly in rosewood! The box top is provided with a roof comb like those at Tikal, Guatemala—really a shallow and tall temple. It is a separate piece, screwed to the one-piece top. The body of the jewel box is one piece, hollowed out, but would save wood if built up; this, however, tends to cause problems in the exact matching of the miter. Much of the carving was done with small chisels, but some details were whittled, and no sanding whatever was done, so the gloss and color of the wood would show through the wax.

Top—Mayan temple jewel box in rosewood relies on detail in design, as does the Spanish colonial chest below it (the latter is in a Tuxtla-Gutierrez, museum). Both will be viewed closely and handled.

Detail is always a matter of debate as well as of skill and time. You will see frequent mentions of it in this book (particularly in subsequent chapters) in connection with such questions as the proper amount of detail in bird feathering, animal-hide texturing, wrinkles in human faces, veins and tendons in animal legs, suggestion of color contrasts, eye irises, and a host of other areas. The skilled sculptor and the abstract artist both tend to avoid detail; the tyro and the meticulous copyist tend to overdo it. The need is to arrive at a happy medium, including only the detail essential to the composition. Thus, a portrait of an Arab stallion without veins and tendons tends to change his personality—just as the head of an aged man or woman without wrinkles defeats its intention. On the other hand, if a design is being carved, the detail of the design must be faithfully executed, or the design becomes blurred and loses force—witness the Mayan temple. The necessity for design detail on occasion will conflict with textural representation also, as for example, in cross-hatching an area to make it look darker if the area already carries a number of lines. Sometimes, one must be sacrificed for the other, but which to sacrifice is a matter of experience and of trial and error.

❋ A Face Can Be Your Fortune:

How to Carve the Features

Poets have sung about the female face for a thousand years—and carvers have made a mess of it for at least as long. The face has been called the mirror of the mind, the billboard of the brain. Obviously, the face of a carved figure is by far the most important single element; it can do more to identify the carving, to convey mood, condition, race and age than any other single element. Yet it is frequently the crudest part of the carving, largely because the carver has not spent the necessary number of hours learning to carve faces, to know the ratios between the various parts, to see how they vary with individuals. This is an interesting phenomenon, considering how much of our time is spent looking at faces, our own as well as others.

Below—Four of six heads on the pulpit in the Stephansdom, Vienna, somewhat unusual in treatment for dignitaries of the church. They are life-sized and were carved in 1510. Clockwise from top left: Augustine, Ambrosius, Hieronymus and Gregory. Center—A modern Polish figure in oak by M. Lednicka Szezyt. Below right—Female figure in French oak by Ossip Zadkine, showing his characteristic "inverted" style. All three are about life size.

Of the features, the most important are the eyes. On a caricature or small formal carving, the eyes are often small slashes, centered with spots of paint, and the nose a small or grotesque hump. That's allowable on caricatures, even expected, but a formal carving is something else again. As a matter of cold fact, faces are difficult: They can, and perhaps should, take as much time to carve as the rest of the figure. Most of my early heads had a Slavic look regardless of who they were supposed to be, simply because I was afraid to take off the needed chips to make a thinner visage around the cheekbones and temples. After carving heads of all kinds, ages and races, in all kinds of poses, I have finally gotten the nerve and skill enough to make a passable face. I still enviously and grimly admire carvers who do portrait heads, and do them well, particularly of children, who have almost no lines or sharp features and whose identity is frequently signaled by a fleeting expression, hard to capture

Above left—"The Carol Singers," by K. Tchorek, Poland. Note the three different mouth openings and eye positions. Center—A Madonna from Oberammergau; note the slightly Oriental eyes, the full face and strong eyebrow-to-nose lines; compare the eyes of the Mother with those of Child. Right—Two more faces from the Stephansdom, Vienna. Note details of the Christ in agony. Above—Details from a choir stall by Giuliani in the Collegiate Church of the Holy Cross, Baden, Germany. Giuliani was a self-taught sculptor, originally a choirboy.

in wood—or in paint, either, for that matter—unless one has a particular gift.

I said "do them well" in the preceding paragraph for a reason. Too many otherwise good carvings are marred by clumsy work on the head. Too many carvers think that a thin, long face, with prominent nose and a wart on one side, is a good portrait of Lincoln. Or that a full-faced youthful figure, with a shock of hair and seated in a rocker, is a portrait of John Kennedy. Most of these are not portraits, but caricatures, relying on an easily caricatured face to get by.

Faces are highly individual, and must be studied and proportioned at least as carefully as the arms and legs, or the pose of the body. In this panel I have repeated some of the sketches in *Whittling and Woodcarving* and *Design and Figure Carving* of forty years ago; they're still applicable and help to comprise a coherent panel for teaching this particular subject. Further to repeat, here are the basic characteristics of the head: It is oval in shape or, more properly, like an inverted egg. The eyes are in the middle, and each is one fifth the width of the head at its widest part. The eyes are just under an eye width apart. The face is the lower three quarters of the head, with the nose a quarter of the head height, or a third of the face height and centered on the face. The mouth is $1\frac{1}{2}$ eyes wide, and a third of the distance from nose tip to chin. Ears are as long as the nose, in line with it, and just back of the center of the head.

These proportions are only for reference, of course. Jimmy Durante has a large and outstanding nose. Lincoln had a longer than normal nose. Various movie stars have oversize eyes, "heavies" have larger than normal brows, "villains" have hair low on their fore-

Ethnic faces—I made an off-hand suggestion for a "very different" catalog cover in full color and was asked to carve it. Sketches of distinctive child faces were extremely difficult for me. The children had to be between eight and sixteen, two of each sex, and definitely identifiable by race. A number of changes were made from the rough sketch (far right) to the final, then in the carving itself, which is about 15 × 22 in. (double the catalog size). Primavera (blond mahogany) 1 in. thick was used. This permitted staining the background to mahogany, the Chinese boy yellow, the Negro boy a very dark brown, and the Indian girl a coppery red, with their hair black. A little white pigment was rubbed into the white girl's face and her hair is a bright red. Note hair-texturing variations and natural-wood-color background behind faces.

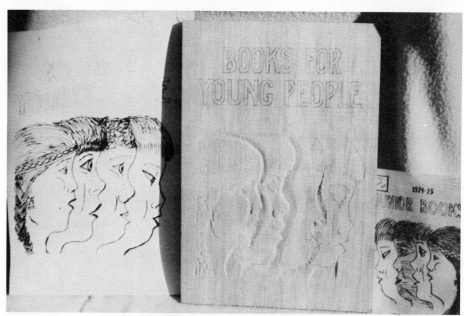

heads, widows have peaks. Those variations are what make an individual distinguishable from the herd. But it's easier to make a portrait—even a caricature—when you have memorized the basics.

For a face which is just a face, not an individual, there are a number of simplifications and conventions. I've tried to sketch a number of them here. The simplest nose, familiar on caricatures and tiny carvings, is simply an elongated pyramid, but on formal carvings of any size it is of proper shape complete with nostrils. It should also reflect the racial and family characteristics of the individual, the high-bridged, thin nose of the Indian, the bulging nose of the boxer, the hooked nose of the Semite, the Roman nose of the patrician, the flattened and wide nose of the Central African, or the tip-tilted small and flat nose of the Chinese. Children's noses are short and more inclined to pertness than those of adults. Women tend to have smaller, more delicate noses than men. Older people get larger and more bulbous noses or more pinched ones. Families tend to have a characteristic nose shape and eye spacing; note how many caricaturists have their own distinguishing noses and eyes on every one of their caricatures.

Ear shape and position are likewise important. Clark Gable's ears were quite distinctive; so are the Devil's. Ears are normally as long as

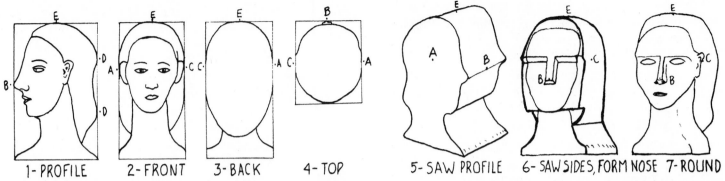

1- PROFILE   2- FRONT   3- BACK   4- TOP   5- SAW PROFILE   6- SAW SIDES, FORM NOSE 7- ROUND

To carve a head from a 1½:1⅞:3-unit block: Lay out as in steps 1 to 4, having outlines touch surfaces of block at A,B,C,D,E. Saw front & back, as in 5. Do not touch high points. Cut away wood at each side of nose. Saw sides of head, as in 6. Locate eyes, mouth, ears, hairline & round.

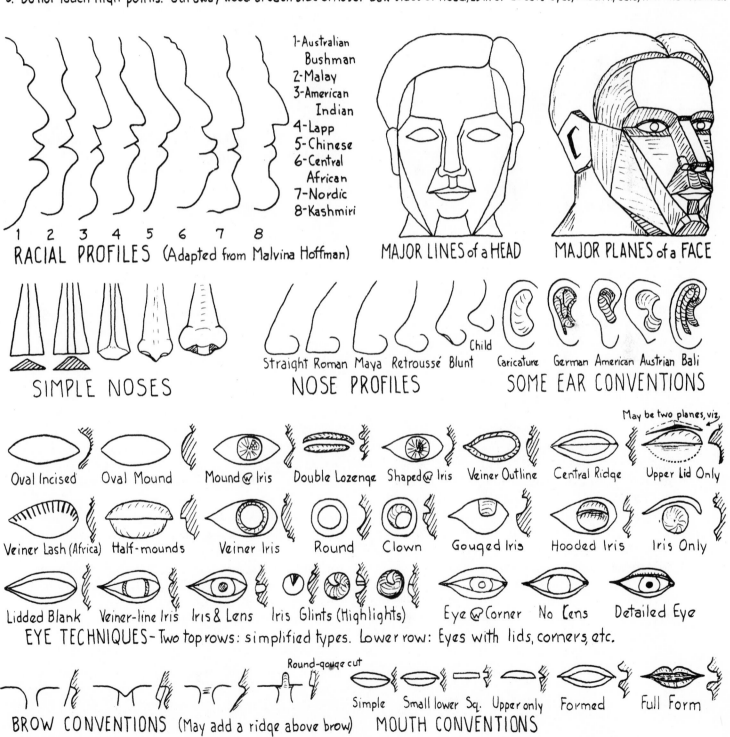

1- Australian
   Bushman
2- Malay
3- American
   Indian
4- Lapp
5- Chinese
6- Central
   African
7- Nordic
8- Kashmiri

1 2 3 4 5 6 7 8
RACIAL PROFILES (Adapted from Malvina Hoffman)   MAJOR LINES of a HEAD   MAJOR PLANES of a FACE

SIMPLE NOSES   Straight Roman Maya Retroussé Blunt   Child   Caricature German American Austrian Bali

NOSE PROFILES   SOME EAR CONVENTIONS

May be two planes, viz.

Oval Incised Oval Mound Mound w. Iris Double Lozenge Shaped w. Iris Veiner Outline Central Ridge Upper Lid Only

Veiner Lash (Africa) Half-mounds Veiner Iris Round Clown Gouged Iris Hooded Iris Iris Only

Lidded Blank Veiner-line Iris Iris & Lens Iris Glints (Highlights) Eye w. Corner No Lens Detailed Eye

EYE TECHNIQUES— Two top rows: simplified types. Lower row: Eyes with lids, corners, etc.

Round-gouge cut

BROW CONVENTIONS (May add a ridge above brow)   Simple Small lower Sq. Upper only Formed Full Form

MOUTH CONVENTIONS

the nose, in line with it, and slightly behind the center of the head when viewed from the side. The usual ear has a personal series of convolutions, so sculptors normally simplify both ear shape and internal structure. I have sketched several examples, taken from carvings of various countries.

Most distinctive of the features is the eye. Because it is basically a pointed oval, and the iris is a matter of color alone, Greek sculptors made a faithful shape—and a sightless eye. It is necessary to define the iris in some way if the eye is to appear sighted, and every sculptor seems to develop his own convention for it. The simplest depiction is a circular incision on a mound-shaped oval. (This convention—as well as the others—can of course be used on carefully formed eyes complete with lids and corners.) Or the eye oval can simply be outlined with a veiner, to make the entire shape evident. There are other variants, like making the eye a pair of lozenges, or showing only the upper lid, possibly bringing it to a peak to simulate the slightly raised iris behind it, as is done in some Guatemalan carvings (page 139). The Kenyans on occasion carve a careful eyeball, then add upper lashes rather than an iris. Carvers in other areas represent the iris with a gouge cut, either up to the top lid or down to the lower, or even provide an eyebrow and an iris alone, with no eye shape at all. Providing lids is of course an added problem and may tend to make the eyes look hooded and sleepy. It's largely a matter of choice: what you prefer and can best execute. It is possible to do a very detailed and anatomically correct eyeball and lids, then to simulate an iris and cut it out so the eye has a glint—a section of the iris remaining to reflect light while the areas immediately around it have been cut away. I've sketched three examples of this; I prefer the hooked shapes to the straight (and optically more correct) triangle.

Brows can also be interpreted in many ways. Most of us have a very slight brow ridge that looks much thicker because of the eyebrows themselves. And our eyebrows stop before the nose bridge, which is a gentle slope. But it is possible to accentuate any peculiarity here by carrying the brow line across, bringing it to a point, or even cutting it back with a gouge. To frame the eyes properly, some experimenting with eyebrow shape is helpful. But it's rather hard to do; when you've formed an eyebrow, there's no way to change it unless you re-do the nose, and possibly the entire face.

The mouth also offers many opportunities—and many pitfalls—for the carver. The "kiss-shaped" mouth of the valentine and the TV ad is regrettably uncommon; most of us have thinner or thicker, and less well shaped, lips. The black races often have thicker lips, which tends to push the mouth out on the profile. Oldsters tend to lose lip shape, or at least blur it with wrinkles or sink it with loss of teeth, so the rosebud mouth of the suckling child rarely lasts in the adult—unless done with lip rouge. The Egyptians had an interesting device: They put a narrow bead as an outline all around the lips. It accents mouth shape and adds distinction, as well as showing the carver's skill.

Whether or not to show teeth and tongue is always a question. Doll makers often show both. A wide grin obviously exposes the inner elements of the mouth. But it is normal to show the mouth closed, or only slightly open, thus avoiding the problem of carving teeth and making them look real rather than "store-bought." It is also a nicety to be certain of the profile relationship of the lips and the mouth. A lovely female Nordic face tends to have the upper lip protrude slightly over the lower, with the nose tip, lips and chin point forming a receding line. But full lips on the African change this, and a thin upper lip on the Nordic male is quite common—witness my profile taken from Malvina Hoffman's ethnic studies.

This discussion has dealt with facial detail rather than head shape, which is also important and identifying. The carver's problem is complicated by the fact that the hair, on head or chin, must be allowed for in the blank, so the head will not be a likeness until hair lines, hair shape and any beard or moustache shape are detailed. I have provided sketches showing the basic lines of the head, the major planes and the way to block a head out of the particularly proportioned block. These sketches can't be laid out on a carving—except for the points of contact in the female head sketched—but they can help if you have them firmly fixed in your mind's eye.

✳ A Comparison of Faces and Figures

Commercial Examples Show Skill

Faces are very revealing, not only on people but also on carvings. They can be simply the usual assemblage of features, frozen in a stony stare or a perpetual grin, as they are on so many caricatures, or they can express a momentary feeling or idea. Whether or not the face adds to the story or quality of a body is a function of the carver's skill. A famous artist once said that the way to learn to do faces is to do a thousand faces—in other words, they take a great deal of study and practice.

The panel is a series of examples of varied foreign techniques, all taken from foreign carvings bought in the United States. The African girl I found at a flea market in western New York State, the two Ecuadorean figures in a country store in southern Indiana, the Don Quixotes in a New York shop and the Bavarian man in Chicago. Thus they're all commercial carvings, and similar ones are available to you if you search them out. Because they are commercial, the faces are probably the prod-

uct of the more skilled carvers in foreign "factories" and are hence good examples of technique—and examples by carvers who have undoubtedly done their thousand faces. At least I thought so; the faces were the major factor in my decision to purchase in each case. I have added one American carving which also has a very good face—quizzical, sleepy, but not fearful at "The Noise in the Night."

The African girl's face is primitive and unformed, yet is very definitely that of a woman and of a black. The carver used the hair, nose and lips to achieve identification. The Don Quixote faces are, by comparison, precisely formed and stylized. Both have the identifying moustache and beard, the long ascetic face and doleful eyes (done by down-turning the outer corners) to accentuate his sadness. Also, both are tall, thin figures, rigid, with the banded armor on the thighs (greaves); they're the Don without a doubt. But look at the variations: The shorter figure has a book instead of the usual weapons, a brimmed hat, different shoulder protection. And techniques

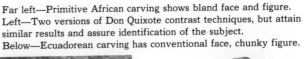

Far left—Primitive African carving shows bland face and figure.
Left—Two versions of Don Quixote contrast techniques, but attain similar results and assure identification of the subject.
Below—Ecuadorean carving has conventional face, chunky figure.

in producing a similar face are quite different. The smaller figure accents the eyes by deep-cut hollows above and below, and makes the whole face an elongated triangle with over-long nose. The larger figure has a largely stylized face also, but it is accented by bold gouge channeling strategically placed.

The two Ecuadorean faces offer a similar contrast. The chunky figure has a conventional face, with sharp vees from nose-to-mouth corners and spaced gouged S-shapes to denote the beard. It is an interesting face and impels one to smile, but is not a personalized face as much as a caricature. The bust, however, has a completely modeled face, with subtle stylizing of the moustache and brows. The ends of the moustache are turned down in solid ridges to accent the recessed mouth. The brows are a single line straight across, interrupted only by a vertical gouge cut over the nose. The face is devoid of wrinkles, yet seems intense and brooding.

As would be expected, the Bavarian man has the most detailed face of all. It is meticulously shaped, particularly the moustache and visible hair, but the face planes have a face texture as well, left by a finishing flat gouge. Also, it is tinted, but *not* painted, so the grain of the wood shows through. It is indisputably a wood carving, but there is nothing wooden about the expression. It is a moving and powerful face; you feel that it is a portrait of a living person, done by a skilled friend. Oberammergau is famous for turning out thousands of faces with agonized and devout expressions, the result of several centuries of making religious carvings, but also produces many of normal people—witness this one.

Left—"The Noise in the Night" is a simple carving, but has excellent facial expression. Below right—Ecuadorean bust has unusual beard stylizing, is much simpler in design and execution than the Oberammergau bust (below left).

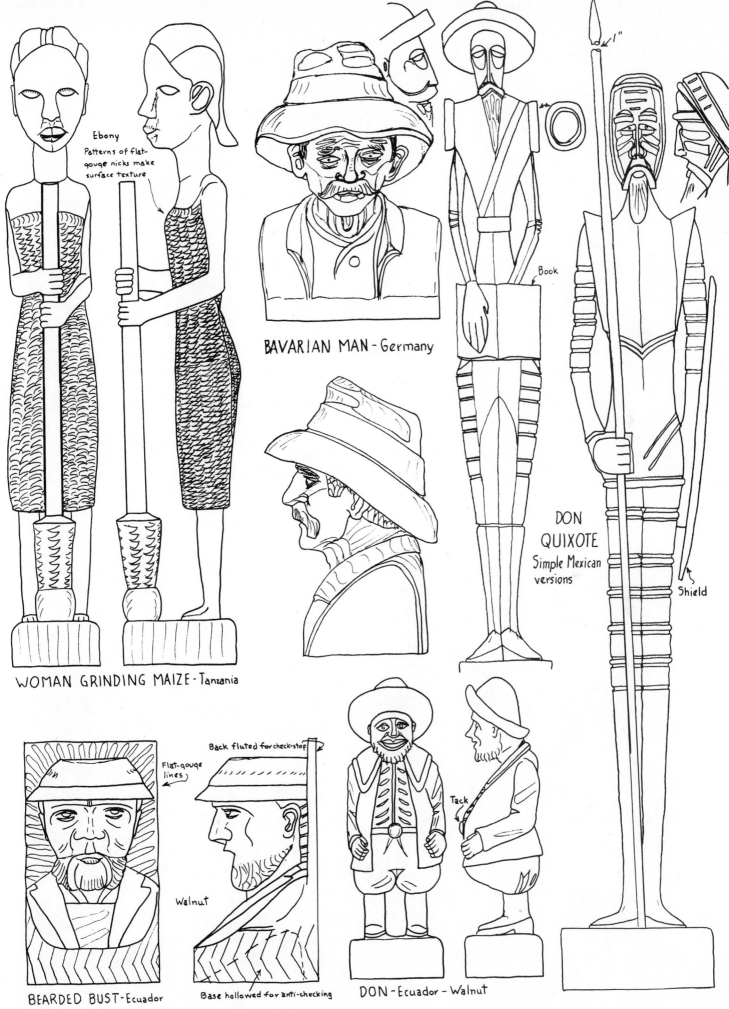

Ebony
Patterns of flat-gouge nicks make surface texture

WOMAN GRINDING MAIZE - Tanzania

BAVARIAN MAN - Germany

DON QUIXOTE
Simple Mexican versions

Book

Shield

1"

BEARDED BUST - Ecuador

Flat-gouge lines

Back fluted for check-stop

Walnut

Base hollowed for anti-checking

Tack

DON - Ecuador - Walnut

✳ Stylizing Can Strengthen Figures:

Some Widely Varied Examples Make the Point

One of the most sophisticated designs I have seen in several years I encountered in Costa Rica—the figure of a pregnant woman by a native artist, R. Cueva. It is carved from a block of cocobola $1^3/_4 \times 4 \times {}^1/_2$ in. and is distinguished by simplicity in shape and lack of detail, as well as by excellent line and sympathetic understanding. While pregnancy is often called the high spot in a woman's life, most figures depicting this condition leave something to be desired.

Not so, however, in this case. The outline of the figure is smooth and softly flowing, and the inevitable thick midriff bulge is softened by pierced carving which at the same time depicts the fetus and helps to create a design. There is no detailing; the arms, legs and face are suggested. Lines of one part of the figure flow smoothly into another.

Also unusual was a series of carvings of Guatemalan natives in costume, produced as a series of uniformly framed plaques. Guatemalan Indians, descended from the Maya, have until quite recently worn distinctive tribal dress. It was, as recently as 1965, possible to distinguish the tribe or town of a man or woman encountered along a road simply by the clothes. Both costume design and basic colors were readily separable because they were the products of local foot looms and seamstresses. Now, as in so many other countries, increasing numbers of people, particularly the men, are donning nondescript mass-produced garments.

Thus, this particular series of carvings has in it some history or at least nostalgia. The carver used mahogany as his material; it is plentiful and easy to work. Also, its natural color is not too far off the basic skin tone of his subjects. It accepts oil colors well and provides an excellent finish.

These figures are about 12 inches tall (in the case of a standing figure), and there may have been as many as twenty in the series. I show three of the most colorful here. The basic technique was to saw out a silhouette, different for each costume, of a man or woman, from $1^1/_4$- or $1^1/_2$-inch wood. Carving is an unusual combination of in-the-round and relief; heads and near arms (to the viewer) being carved

Far left—"Pregnant Woman," by R. Cueva, Costa Rica. Left—Don Quixote, original carver unknown, Central America. Below and right—Three of a series of panels by R. Gasparico, Guatemala, showing, from left to right, a Solala man, a Palin woman, and a Chichicastenango man. Originals in color.

in-the-round, while bodies and rear arms and legs are foreshortened laterally. This does not mean that the entire head is shown, but that the visible portion is fully in-the-round. This permits the outer half of the head, plus a bit, to be carved in proper proportion, with the nose carved free. Also, the near arm and leg may be fully free of the background and properly rounded. This gives the body a great deal of veritability and life, as well as providing interesting shadow effects with lateral lighting.

Major lines of costumes are carved, but none of the decorative detail. Through carving alone one would be hard pressed to simulate the colorfulness of the typical Guatemalan costume; these Indians, like the Finns, are not afraid to use bright tones in immediate conjunction. So the carver concentrated on producing a good figure, with major shadow-creating outlines, then sanded and painted his work in full colors with oils. However, he left the natural color of the wood for skin tones and occasional other elements. Then he mounted the piece on a white-enameled background, with natural-mahogany shaped frames. Several such panels will dominate a room because of their color and size.

Don Quixote is a favorite subject of Central American and Mexican carvers as well as of the Spanish. This particular design is, however, more stylized than most (see pages 98, 108 and 131) and is quite effective as a standing sculpture as much as 5 feet high. The design is much more detailed than the Costa Rican woman—and probably not nearly as good art—but is comparable in its extreme stylizing. It can be made flat-backed, as drawn, or fully in-the-round. However, it should *not* be contoured or brought to normal proportions; its narrowness and scalloped arms and legs are essential to its effectiveness, as are the severely styled face and feet. The right hand can carry a sword (held vertically) or a lance, as sketched; in normal versions, it is made separately and inserted so thinner wood can be used for the body and carving is less onerous.

Figures like these are primarily decorative in concept and execution; they are not expected to be exactly in proportion or "to the life." The Guatemalan figures are more lifelike than the other two, but are somewhat idealized and required less design skill. They help to illustrate that stylizing can be accomplished at any level of carving skill. Also, in the case of commercial carvers, it tremendously reduces the carving time and simplifies the work because a smaller selection of tools is required. The scallops on Don Quixote, for example, are all done with the same gouge, and lines between are simple V-tool cuts. Also, the shield is applied later, so carving of the armor is not hampered by it. Note also that the eyeballs and chin crease are simply veiner lines, as are the forehead crease, the shield decoration, and the foot trim. The base also has simple gouge scallops.

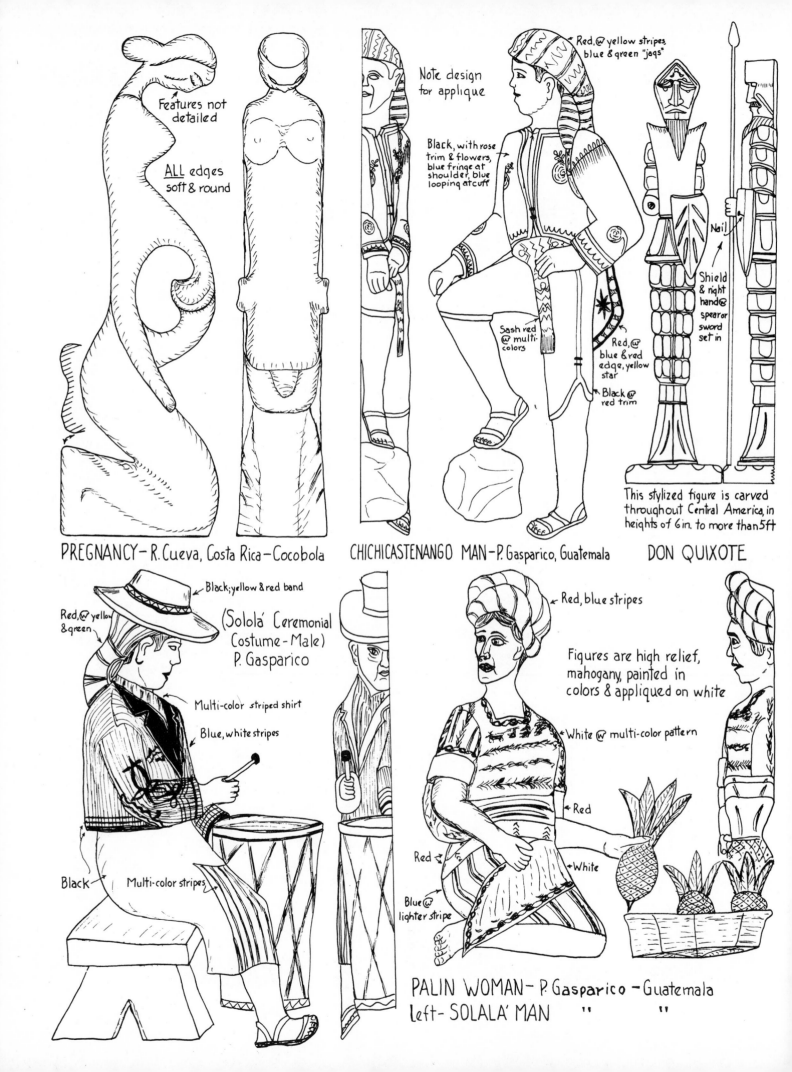

Features not detailed

ALL edges soft & round

PREGNANCY—R.Cueva, Costa Rica—Cocobola

Note design for applique

Red, w yellow stripes, blue & green "jaqs"

Black, with rose trim & flowers, blue fringe at shoulder, blue looping at cuff

Sash red w multi-colors

Red, w blue & red edge, yellow star

Black @ red trim

CHICHICASTENANGO MAN—P. Gasparico, Guatemala

Nail

Shield & right hand @ spear or sword set in

This stylized figure is carved throughout Central America, in heights of 6 in. to more than 5 ft

DON QUIXOTE

Black; yellow & red band

Red, w yellow & green

(Solola Ceremonial Costume—Male) P. Gasparico

Multi-color striped shirt

Blue, white stripes

Black

Multi-color stripes

Red, blue stripes

Figures are high relief, mahogany, painted in colors & appliqued on white

White w multi-color pattern

Red

Red

White

Blue @ lighter stripe

PALIN WOMAN—P. Gasparico—Guatemala
Left—SOLALA MAN   "   "

✳ Stylizing—Old and New:

A Study in Nonportraiture

Two extremes of stylizing are exhibited by modern "Tribute to Johann Sebastian Bach," by Ossip Zadkine (right) and the traditional treatment of the twelve apostles by Tilman Riemenschneider, the great German master (below). The apostles are now in the Bavarian National Museum, Munich, and were carved about 1531. No one can say how the apostles looked, so they are identified by the objects they hold, often symbolizing the manner of death. Symbols date back to the fourth century or earlier, and are typical of the rich symbolism utilized in all liturgical art. Below, left to right—Judas (money in hand), Matthew (halberd or spear), Peter (keys of the Kingdom), Philip (tall cross), Bartholomew (book and flaying knife—he was skinned alive), Andrew (X cross—he was spread-eagled). Bottom, left to right—Paul (holding oars), Simon Zelotes (book and saw—beheaded), John the Evangelist (chalice—it contained poison which did not harm him; he's also shown on occasion with a cauldron, because he was boiled in oil), James the Lesser (fuller's bat—he was beaten to death), Thomas (carpenter's square), James the Greater (pilgrim's garb, often shown in addition to a shell). Note also the stylized robe arrangements and variety of poses. Apostle photos from Hirmer Fotoarchiv Munchen.

✳ Selected Figures from Central America:

Native Designs Show Strength—And a Difference

Many primitive carvers do surpassingly powerful work, probably because they are uninhibited by rules or competition, and are seeking to express something they see. Carvings on the next pages are the cream (in my opinion) of hundreds I saw during two months in Central America, plus a head from Fiji and a caballero from Mexico. These all have strength and power; the others didn't. Costs by our standards were, of course, ridiculous: Ten dollars for the mask (a mask in mahogany is about $30), $3.50 or so apiece for the figures, $20 for the Honduran cart, $5 for the santos, $2 for the five buttons, only 75 cents for the Madonna pendant.

In studying the group, I am impressed by the accuracy of detail conveyed by planes and lines, the common use of veiner or V-tool for details and decoration, the excellent faces and expressions, the naturalness of poses, the lack of rigidity and stiffness, the unsophisticated finish in most instances.

I am conscious, also, that some of the better selections are the result of encouragement and help. For example, the four Guatemalan figures in the first panel are all from the Malin Cooperative in the mountains of Central Guatemala, established about ten years ago by priests. They brought the native Indians back to their Mayan heritage of craftsmanship.

Far left and left corner—These are accurate Indian portraits by Indians, particularly the woodcutter, who has a very powerful face. Second left—Mask (life-sized) of Tecu-Uman, folk hero who fought the Spaniards. Note the incisive face and the veiner trim. He is also shown with two quetzals (birds), one on each side of the headdress. Left—The Madonna pendant is simple, fast to make and very effective. Below—Miniature masks (actual size) intended for use as jacket buttons.

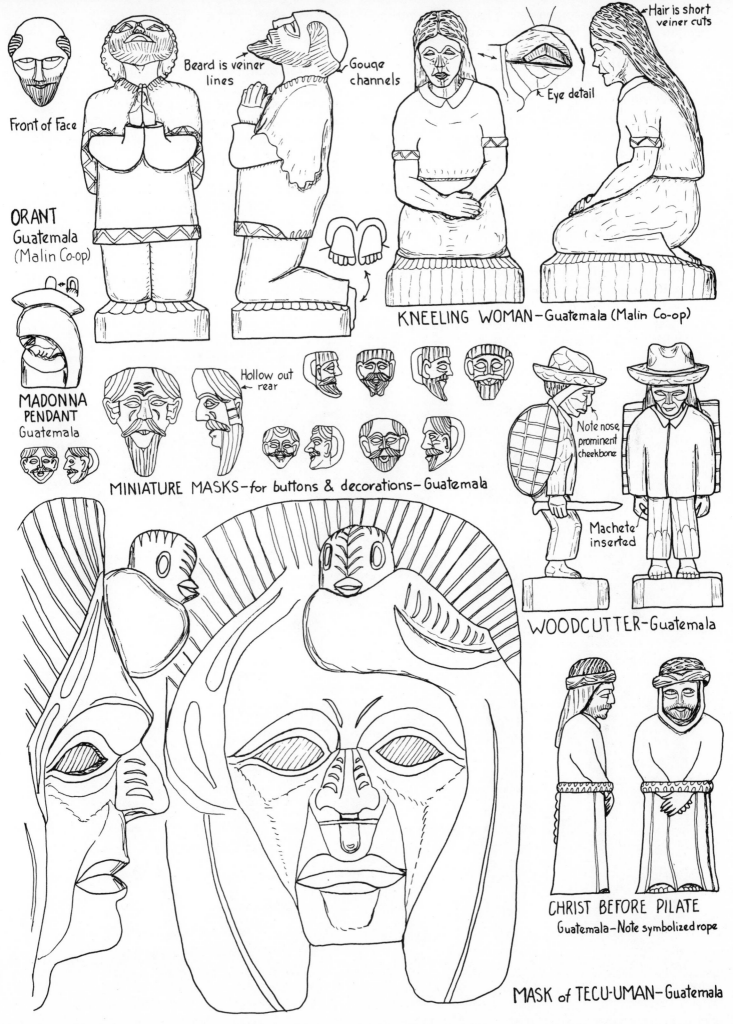

Front of Face

Beard is veiner lines

Gouge channels

Hair is short veiner cuts

Eye detail

ORANT
Guatemala
(Malin Co-op)

MADONNA PENDANT
Guatemala

KNEELING WOMAN—Guatemala (Malin Co-op)

Hollow out rear

MINIATURE MASKS—for buttons & decorations—Guatemala

Note nose, prominent cheekbone

Machete inserted

WOODCUTTER—Guatemala

CHRIST BEFORE PILATE
Guatemala—Note symbolized rope

MASK of TECU·UMAN—Guatemala

(This is not as unusual as it sounds. Spratling, an American, brought silversmithing back to Tasco, Mexico, perhaps forty years ago. It—and the adjacent silver mines—had long been moribund.) It is difficult to appreciate how much ability lies fallow for want of incentive and encouragement—look at the senior Americans who in recent years have undertaken one craft or another to express themselves, and done work far beyond what either they or their teachers thought they were capable of doing. Much of it is very creditable, strong and original work, work of which they can be proud.

There is little to say about the details of producing duplicates of these pieces. Most are self-explanatory. I have drawn front and side views and provided detail that seemed significant. And I checked the selections themselves with local and American artists who happened to be there, as I was, to get inspiration from these fine native artists.

There are exceptions, of course. The buttons, for example, are the work of a trained former carver of masks for Indian dances who has opened a shop in Chichicastenango, Guatemala, high in the mountains. Few fine masks are made anymore; most are hacked out to be hawked to tourists by street vendors. The dances that required them are now rarely done, and even tourists buy few—they buy few gaudy machetes and sheaths made in El Salvador and brought to Chichi because so many tourists congregate there. Anyway, the mask maker began these buttons as a sort of memorial to his art; they were to go on a jacket

Below left—Native head from Fiji is also stylized in hair and shoulders. Far left and below—Honduran figures of a farm woman and an Indian. The latter has arrows, quiver and bow separately carved and added. Bottom—Honduran farmer on his way home with cut wood. Note the use of a "rock" to avoid breakage in carving legs, oversize head, stiff pose.

Below—Monk, finished in dull black, is also stylized, as is the Madonna and Child next to him. He is, however, all angles, while she is all curves.

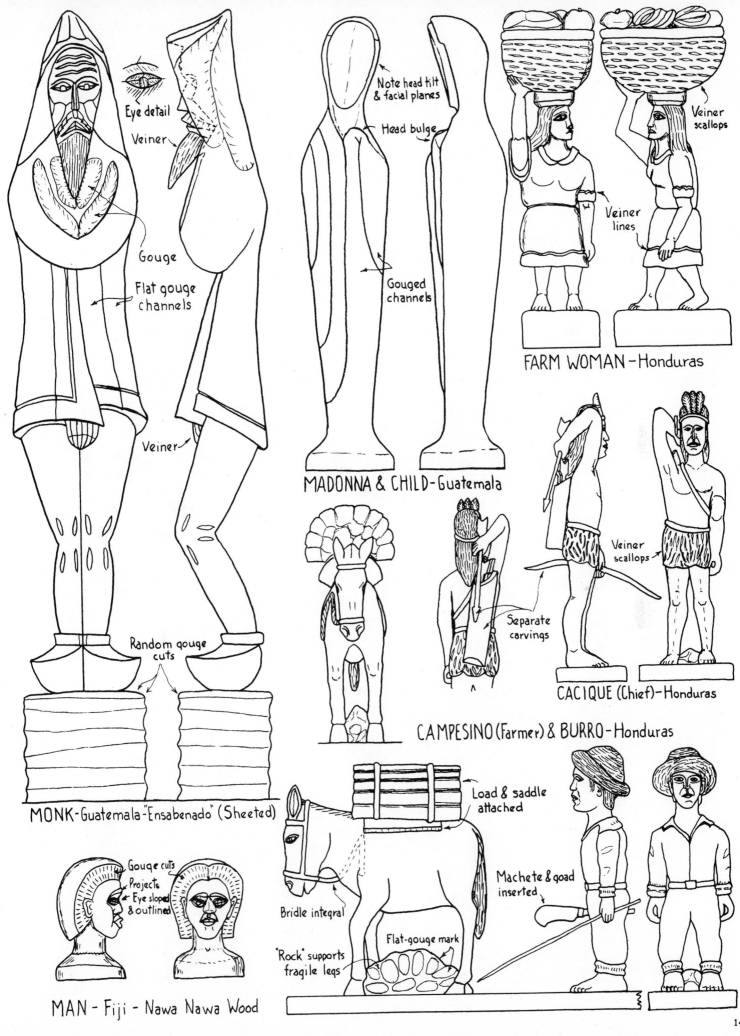

Eye detail

Veiner

Gouge

Flat gouge channels

Veiner

Random gouge cuts

MONK-Guatemala-"Ensabenado" (Sheeted)

Note head tilt & facial planes

Head bulge

Gouged channels

MADONNA & CHILD-Guatemala

Separate carvings

FARM WOMAN-Honduras

Veiner scallops

Veiner lines

Veiner scallops

CACIQUE (Chief)-Honduras

CAMPESINO (Farmer) & BURRO-Honduras

Gouge cuts
Projects
Eye sloped & outlined

MAN-Fiji-Nawa Nawa Wood

Bridle integral

'Rock' supports fragile legs

Flat-gouge mark

Load & saddle attached

Machete & goad inserted

which he has never gotten around to having made. So he sold the buttons to a fellow woodcarver, partly because I singled out the pipes (page 57) in an obscure corner of his shop. The buttons are surprising in their detail and expression. The wood should have been much harder, however, to stand shank strain and abrasion in use.

There is a wide variety in the sophistication of the figures. The Madonna pendant in the first panel and the Madonna and Child of the second panel are modern and show something beyond native craft and design. (The Madonna may be blanked on a lathe.) So does the bent-kneed monk, the caballero, the Costa Rican banana cart. But the Honduran figures and the Guatemalan santo are very simple and untutored; I believe the carver made what he saw as well as he could make it. The Fiji head and the banana loader are obviously made by skilled carvers, but they retain primitive strength and "differentness."

All of these carvings except the Madonna and Child are made in soft wood, like our pine. The Madonna is in a hard and figured wood, and polished to a high gloss. Some are stained or tinted; the monk and the santo are stained flat black, as is the Mexican caballero—a rather unusual finishing treatment but one that makes the figures stand out against almost any background. While the Madonna has only face planes, the others have detailed faces.

Below left—Caballero from Mexico, with slightly stylized arms and legs. Next to him is a more realistic Costa Rican figure of a banana loader; forearms are disproportionately long. Bottom left—Foreshortened figure of a saint, probably adapted from a formal carving. Head is quite flat, upper arms too short. Forearms can be placed in three positions: sideways (expostulating); palms down (blessing); palms up (begging). Below right—A Sicilian cart in miniature, probably the lineal ancestor of the Costa Rican cart (bottom), because of immigration. Few full-sized ones of the latter are now made, but many miniatures. This one has dark-brown stain on some areas, like the wheels and cart body, and the design is cut in with a veiner and small firmer after staining and before final varnishing.

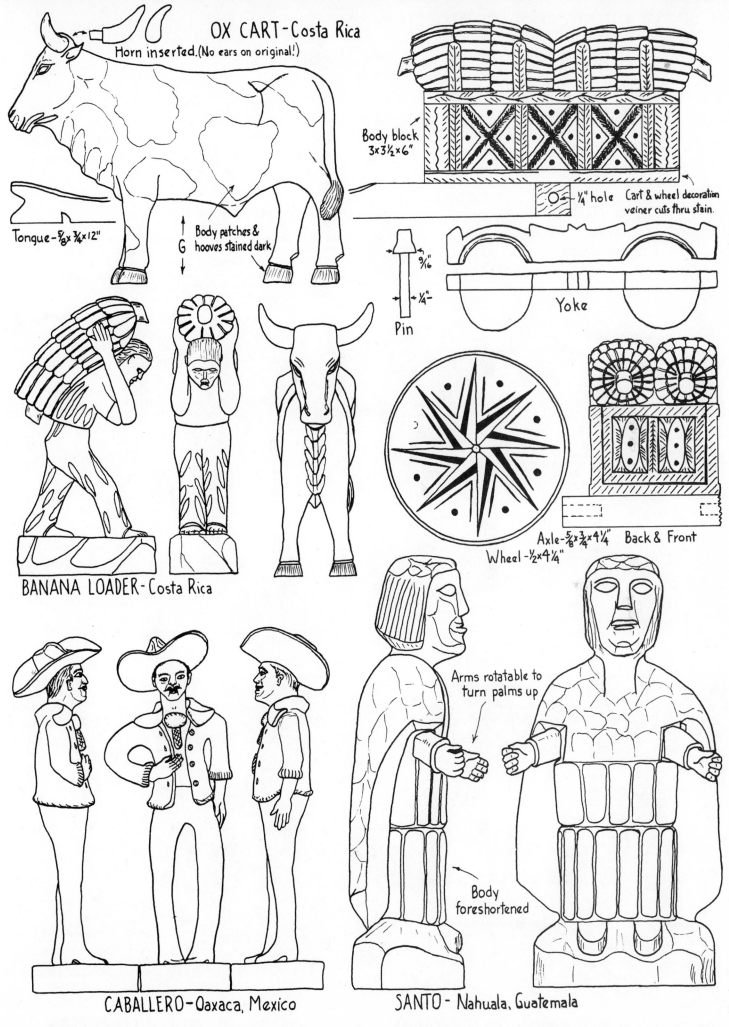

OX CART-Costa Rica

Horn inserted.(No ears on original!)

Tongue-⁵⁄₈ x ¾ x 12"

Body patches & hooves stained dark

G

Body block 3 x 3½ x 6"

¼" hole   Cart & wheel decoration veiner cuts thru stain.

Pin   ⁹⁄₁₆   ¼"

Yoke

BANANA LOADER-Costa Rica

Axle-⁵⁄₈ x ¾ x 4¼"   Back & Front

Wheel -½ x 4¼"

Arms rotatable to turn palms up

Body foreshortened

CABALLERO-Oaxaca, Mexico

SANTO - Nahuala, Guatemala

✳ An Introduction to African Figures:

Few Fetishes, More Figures, as Tourism Takes Its Toll

While African art is very diverse, it is also very "different" to our western eyes, and many Americans simply do not like any of it. It is unlike the art with which we have become familiar in our homes and textbooks, in our art courses. Yet it is very important to the carver, because it is based largely on wood, it is widely varied, is extremely strong although primitive and has styles of representation that differ totally from what one encounters elsewhere.

African carvings were to be found only in a few museums fifty years ago. After World War I, they began to appear in the United States in greater number in the possession of more adventuresome travelers and for the collections of a limited number of connoisseurs. But

The mask and the Ibedji ancestor figures below are traditional, the others much more modern. Note the foreshortened legs and lengthened arm of the pregnant woman (top center) and the separate neck ring, carved from the solid, of the female head (top right). Her earrings are ivory, inserted. In the pair of busts (lower left), the male has touches of red on headpiece, earrings and chin. The squatting man (bottom center) has an abnormally large head and spindly arms as well as a real expression.

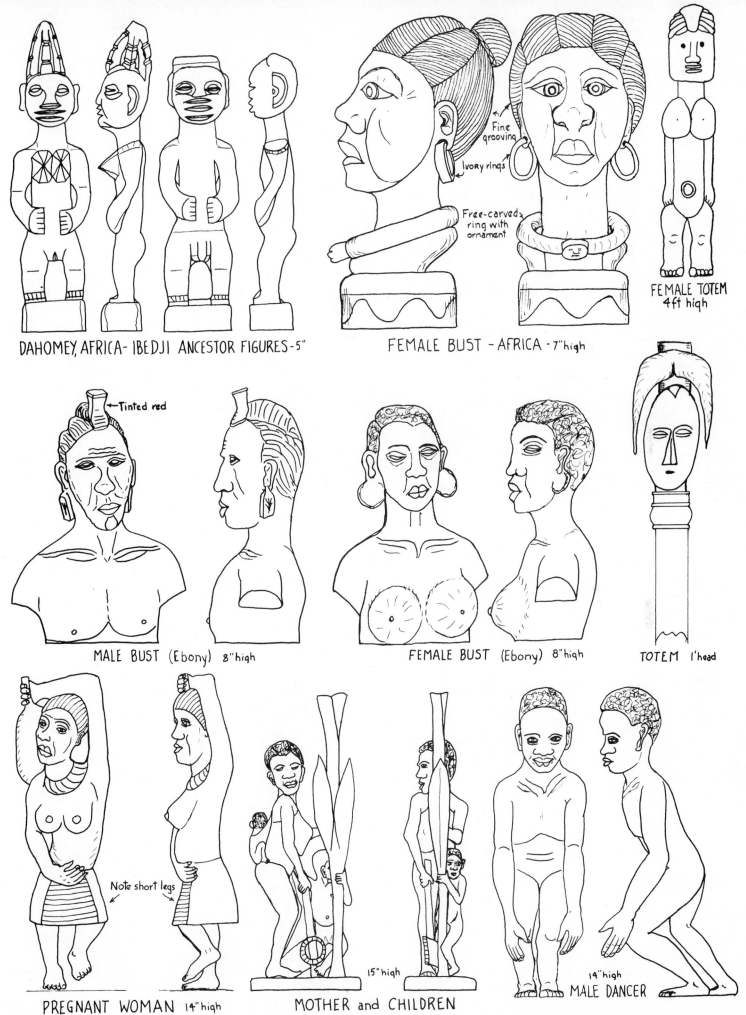

DAHOMEY, AFRICA - IBEDJI ANCESTOR FIGURES - 5"

FEMALE BUST - AFRICA - 7"high

Fine grooving
Ivory rings
Free-carved ring with ornament

FEMALE TOTEM 4ft high

←Tinted red

MALE BUST (Ebony) 8"high

FEMALE BUST (Ebony) 8"high

TOTEM 1'head

Note short legs

PREGNANT WOMAN 14"high

MOTHER and CHILDREN 15"high

MALE DANCER 14"high

145

the tremendous increase in "safari" travelers has resulted in a flood of pieces coming into the country, their adoption as a fad or style by interior decorators and their promotion as an "in" thing.

It should be understood that by "African art" I do not mean the art of all Africa, but from the area south of the Sahara: Egypt,

Morocco and Libya are not sources of important wood carvings these days. We have become most familiar with pieces from the areas

The two left-hand groups may be Makonde, but are possibly attempts at the style by another tribe. The grotesque either utilizes the growth wood for a lighter background, or is painted (probably with shoe polish) to attain this effect. The mask is a double one, with human figures flanking the faces. The nude again contrasts colors sharply, probably with the aid of shoe polish. It is *not* a traditional figure. Note the grotesque faces of the couple, as contrasted with the portrait face of the mother with her children.

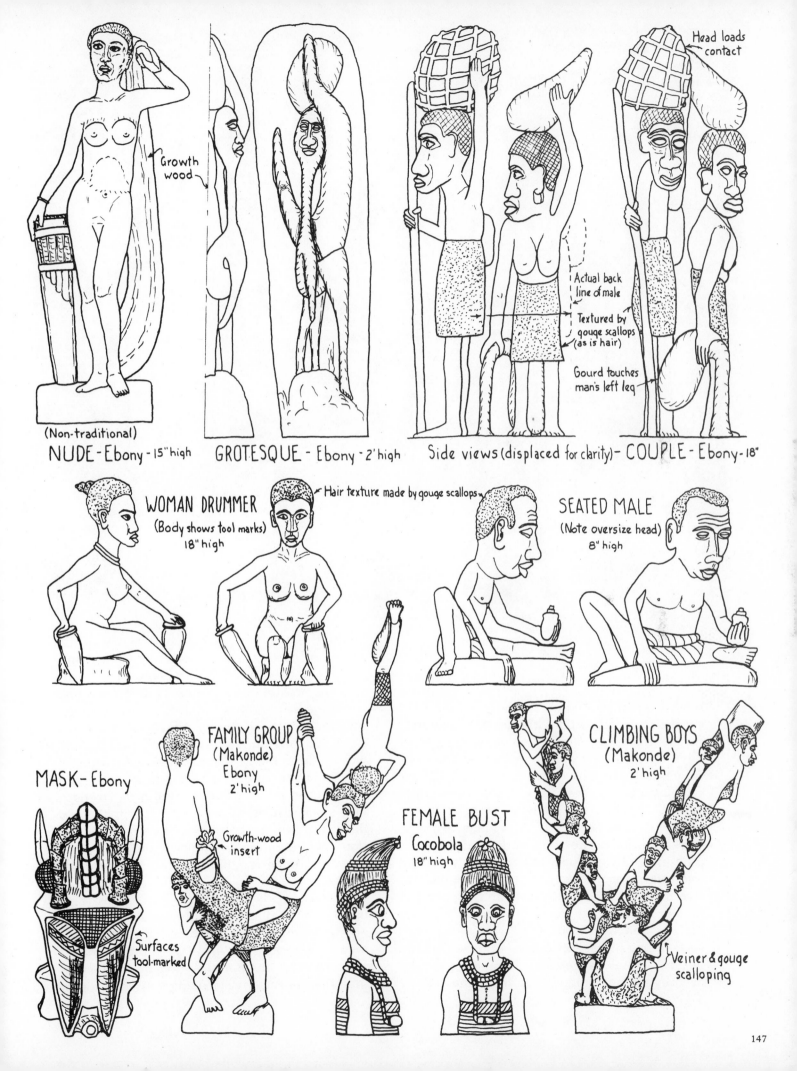

Growth wood

(Non-traditional)
NUDE - Ebony - 15" high

GROTESQUE - Ebony - 2' high

Head loads contact

Actual back line of male

Textured by gouge scallops (as is hair)

Gourd touches man's left leg

Side views (displaced for clarity) - COUPLE - Ebony - 18"

WOMAN DRUMMER
(Body shows tool marks)
18" high

Hair texture made by gouge scallops

SEATED MALE
(Note oversize head)
8" high

MASK - Ebony

FAMILY GROUP
(Makonde)
Ebony
2' high

Growth-wood insert

Surfaces tool-marked

FEMALE BUST
Cocobola
18" high

CLIMBING BOYS
(Makonde)
2' high

Veiner & gouge scalloping

Five Makonde figures (two views of the final one) from the collection of Michael DeNike. Heights of these elongated studies are, in order: 28 in., 28 in., and 23 in. for each of the others. All are black, but some in the collection are not ebony, but a lighter wood blackened with shoe polish.

most frequently visited on the east and west coasts, and very little with that of the interior of the dark continent. Yet wood sculptures have been made by many tribes for hundreds of years in highly developed forms. Styles vary as much as they do in the various countries of Europe, or in those of Asia. These carvings were created by village carvers, working with crude tools and uneducated in our sense of the word, but they are powerful and tell a story. Most pieces were not decorative in intent; they were used in religious and mystic rites. They were fetishes rather than idols or images of gods; they were believed to be dwelling places for spirits—of the earth, the natural forces, ancestors, living people who are revered or singled out for some feat or

because of position. They were fed, talked to, praised, blamed; were part and parcel of the initiation ceremonies into puberty, most important in tribal life for both boys and girls, as well as less-important events like seasonal rites and ceremonial funerals. They were an essential part of family life, rather than a separate religion. In most tribes, propitiation was made to the tree from which the wood was cut, and the cylindrical form of the tree or limb was preserved in order to retain *its* strength and spirit. Most were *not* ebony in the old days; the switch to ebony has come with the flood of money-bearing tourists and their obvious preference for that wood as having more value.

Because of the cylindrical form, arms were usually carved close to the body, with the hands touching the abdomen for reinforcement. However, the arms were often disproportioned, angular, and gave an impression that the muscles were being tensed prior to movement—a very dramatic effect that we seldom get. The figures were also symmetrical and fully developed from all sides. The head might be enlarged and arms and legs foreshortened to create a phallic symbol, just as genitals and navels were often emphasized; fertility is a prime element in tribal life. Facial expression and precise dimensions were considered unimportant; the figure was not intended to be a picture, but the abode of a spirit. Thus the face may have animal characteristics in ears, horns, mouth and nose, and may carry "tattoos" (really symbols)—all for significance rather than realism. This also holds true for clothing, if any, color, headdress and like elements. Almost nothing was done in the way of decoration.

Note that I have used the past tense in this discussion. Much has been changed in recent years because of tourism. Most of the figures pictured here are simply portraits of people, influenced by Western art, training and money. The most visited areas have switched to ebony (or other woods, shoe-polished to look like ebony), smaller pieces—whatever will sell. Wood is still, as it has always been, the principal material for sculpture; only a few communities work ivory, clay, stone, mud, bronze and brass. Human figures are most frequently depicted; animals were until recently placed on cups, bowls and other utilitarian objects and on masks. The seated figure was most uncommon, as was an assembled figure, except for appendages like symbols of other materials. And, in most tribes, the carver was not a tradesman, but a member of a privileged guild connected with the priesthood, if not a part of it.

It is predictable that African woodcarvings will be quite commonplace in the immediate future, particularly those of animals in small sizes, since they are being imported and sold at souvenir prices by the various outdoor jungles set up in the United States. Practically all of these are "factory" products, turned out by the hundreds, but there are occasional better figures among them. A number of those sketched I found in Lion Country, near Los Angeles, which has an unusual shop, operated by a South African, that imports better quality work—at higher prices, of course.

In some respects, the carving of figures similar to these should be instructive to American whittlers, because they preserve the tradition of one-piece work, have a basic simplicity and lack of ornate pretension, and can be produced with relatively few tools. Because many are primitive in design, small errors and disproportion will neither be important nor apparent. They should, however, be made in woods hard enough to take the detail and to provide a good finish. Thus they tend to be projects for chisels rather than the knife alone. Hair is commonly shown with gouge lines, for example, either as lines or scallops. Less well-known figures, like the Makonde, are particularly interesting, with their attenuated forms and swarming groupings. They'll provide plenty of practice in producing figures and faces.

By Way of Comparison

These four American carvings all utilize the form of the wood as African carvings do, and two use the growth wood color contrast as well. The bust at right is by Rick Cain, the one below and the nude with it are by Michael DeNike, both at the 1974 New Jersey Show of the NWCA, and the nude at lower right is by George Clark, at the Claremeont, California show of the NWCA the same year. The latter figure is in California ironwood, an extremely hard wood, and utilizes the total shape of the fragment. Rick Cain has carved his bust to follow the bend of the wood as well. Michael DeNike's figures have an African "feel" to go with their dark color—note the hair of the nude in particular. The nudes are about 2 ft. tall (so sculptures are taller) and the top bust about 1 ft.

✳ Small Figures from the Alps:

From Switzerland and Germany

Like many other members of the Whittlers' Wanderjahr 1973 trip to Europe, I bought carvings—in Holland, Switzerland, Germany. I bought perhaps a dozen human figures, all small, and as many animals, also small (see page 66). They ranged from the traditional to the modern in both design and technique. Most of the pieces were of linden (basswood), some tinted, some not, but I did get two small angels in pear, a Pied Piper and grape pickers in lime.

Human figures sketched and pictured here include the two Magi and the Christus from the shop of Hans Huggler-Wyss in Brienz, Switzerland, most of the others from various shops in Oberammergau, Germany. Most are familiar subjects, although the angel duet,

Christus and woodcarver are new to me. Incidentally, while the Christ child appears in nativity scenes from many countries, the adult Christ is almost never pictured except as an element for church installation. The woodcarver is only the second piece I have ever seen in the round, of a woodcarver plying his art, the other being a familiar squatting figure from China—executed in clay! Simplest of the figures is probably the dwarf musician, a caricature, with the expected oversize nose,

Far left—Two Magi from Brienz (the third is a kneeling elderly figure). Below center—Also from Brienz, this Christus is unusual; details of face and hands are not carved. Lower left—Traditional Oberammergau crucifixion scene, made of chips in a turned case. Watchman and dwarf musician are newer designs. Below another cased miniature, a galleon carved about 1963 by Alex van Elst of Unterammergau for his wife. Angel duet, in oak, is quite modern, has simple flowing lines, no defined features.

eyes largely hollows between prominent brow and cheeks, and beard so crude it looks like a fake. Yet the figure has a certain power that a tyro doesn't obtain.

The night watchman is a more active pose and very detailed despite its small size. It is one piece, except for the staff, and has a well-detailed face and clothing creases. Even the fingers are defined. Disproportion here could ruin the figure, because it is not a caricature. The two Magi are not as simple as they appear to be either, because their faces and hands are well-defined, as are the folds of their robes, which looks heavy and rich. Some of the effect is obtained by transparent coloring, done probably with the German sal-ammoniac-based stains (thinned acrylics will do it, too). Scepters are separately carved and set into holes in the hands, except for the bottom knobs, which are carved integrally. Colors are: wine for the robe, blue for the cape and crown top on the bearded Magus, black for the box and scepter, gold trim. Magus No. 2 has a light-blue tunic, black hose, yellow robe, red head cloth and blue cap top, again trimmed with gold.

The Christus is less well defined than the Magi. Hands and face are shaped, but fingers, eyes, nose and mouth are not detailed. The face is a rounded surface peaking at the nose, with hollows for eyes and mouth areas. The robe is also simple planes, and no attempt is made to show decoration on it or to define the hair. Coloring is simple also, flesh for the face and hands, dark brown for the hair, light tan for the robe. This is another example of the recent trend toward impressionistic figures, which attain their effect through masses and basic shapes rather than through detail. This is hard to achieve, but worth the practice.

The two small angels are similarly simple in contour, although faces and fingers are defined. They are much more rounded than the earlier Oberammergau angels, and have integral, chubby hands rather than the long, separated fingers and variety of hand poses that took so much time and skill—and proved so fragile that export packages had to include spares. (The carver whose "factory" made the earlier angels told me that they took too long, hence had to be priced too high for successful marketing—inflation again!)

These angels have an overall finish of low-gloss medium-brown stain, probably the combination sal-ammoniac finish now being used in most Oberammergau shops and not obtainable in the United States. It is somewhat similar to our oil stains containing wax, but is available in a variety of colors, not just various wood tones. It is a one-coat finish, sealing the surface, providing a desired tint, and brushable to a low gloss. It comes in about twenty tints from transparent through yellow to red and brown and black, so a darker color can be applied

Right—Pied Piper is a well-detailed figure from Oberammergau, dressed in Bavarian (rather than North German) costume. He is in lime, to permit detail, and tinted. Rats are largely head and body shape, with forelegs suggested. (This figure is the basis for my larger "Pied Piper of Mittenwald, page 157.) Far right—Two views of a standing woodcarver, one of the few I've seen. He is about twice the height of the picture, and well detailed. This piece is simply stained to give an antique effect. Note precise positioning of hands and tools. The carver is making a low relief deer in the upright log—and concentrating on the job.

over a lighter one, then wiped lightly for an "antique" effect. It was designed primarily for oak—the sal ammoniac reacted with the tannin—but is much more widely used these days, particularly on linden. (The commercial name is Wachsmetallsalz-Beize, made by Albert Clouth Lackfabrik, Offenbach-am-Main, West Germany. Many years ago, by the way, the most carefully guarded secrets in Oberammergau were those having to do with finishing. Development of a competing craft area in the Tyrol followed revelation of these secrets.)

The angel duet in oak is deceptively simple—rather like a lengthened napkin ring—with clean, flowing lines and almost no definition of detail. It looks as if it could be made of ⅛-inch pie dough, but creates a very recognizable picture on a wall. There are no hands (which should appeal to many carvers), no body definition beyond the line of flow of the robes, no detailing or feathering of the long, narrow wings. The heads are almost like stuffed wigs—a long-bob coiffure over faces no more detailed than that of the Christus. Contrasting sharply with this duet are the grape pickers, basically correctly proportioned statuettes (except that the grapes and bunches are big enough to grace a travel folder). Figures are traditional in treatment, but poses very dynamic. All features are detailed; the boy

even has carved toes. Shadow effects are so good that tinting is unnecessary.

The Pied Piper is a difficult piece, partly because of size and pose, but also because of the slender pipe and the hand positions. The mouth is pursed over the pipe, the head is tilted and thrust forward, the legs are long, slender, and carefully shaped to emphasize his lightness of feet and his tenseness. This one can be tinted or not, but mine is clad in grayed-green hose, a weathered-brown cape, a grayed-green hat with black band and brown feather, and pink shirt. The rats are largely heads and forequarters, to avoid the necessity of carving legs I suppose, although front legs are suggested. He should be easier to carve in a somewhat larger size. Most difficult of the pieces is the woodcarver, who must have hands and tools in a natural position, as well as a piece being carved. The carver's head is cocked in an attitude of proper concentration, the wrinkles come in proper places and the body seems to be tense with effort.

I believe that most of these figures are still made one at a time, partly because of size, partly because of complexity, but many larger Oberammergau figures nowadays are sawed-out blanks which are roughed wet on a multi-spindle profiler. The hand carving is merely removal of the final ⅛ inch of wood and surface effects like insertion of features and wrinkles. Costs are rising there as elsewhere, and old-time carvers deplore the accommodations that have had to be made for the tourist trade, sadly pointing out that the figures look more and more like the plastic copies of some now available.

Below—Pied Piper in ivory; note more traditional costume. Shown about actual size. With it is one of several sizes of swan, also in ivory, the emblem of Neuschwannstein castle. Below right—These grape pickers, in lime, are traditional German figures. Grapes are slightly oversize to make them stand out; children have winsome faces characteristic of Bavarian carving.

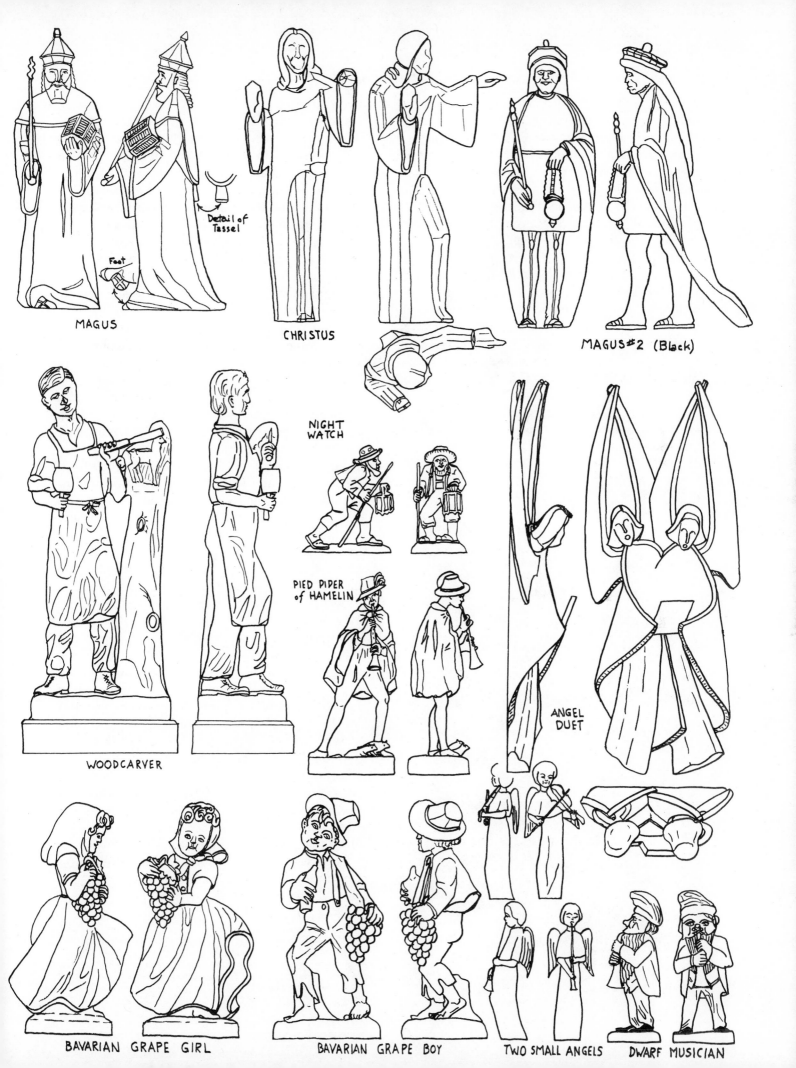

MAGUS

Detail of Tassel

Foot

CHRISTUS

MAGUS#2 (Black)

WOODCARVER

NIGHT WATCH

PIED PIPER of HAMELIN

ANGEL DUET

BAVARIAN GRAPE GIRL

BAVARIAN GRAPE BOY

TWO SMALL ANGELS

DWARF MUSICIAN

✳ Carvings Inspired by Folk Tales:

Three Answers to "Where Do You Get Ideas?"

A frequent question is, "Where do you get ideas for your carvings?" The answer is "Everywhere"—which is not very helpful. Newspapers, magazines, book illustrations, paintings: all these are possible sources. Another is folk songs and stories, because they provide slightly romantic and different-from-life situations and personalities. These were the origins for such pieces as Janus (page 124), the Pied Piper of Mittenwald (page 157) and "The Descent from Ararat" (page 72). I have seen a number of panels, usually tinted, translating the title pages or a familiar illustration from children's books into low relief. But here are three rather simple in-the-round examples, all derived from familiar folk sources and all multiple figures—at least in a sense.

The first is from Edward Lear's familiar nonsense poem: "The Owl and the Pussy-cat

went to sea/In a beautiful pea-green boat,/ They took some honey, and plenty of money, /Wrapped up in a five-pound note. . . ." I was thinking of the jingle one day, and trying to remember the next line, when the idea of the "pea-green boat" as a pea pod, with its passengers as peas, struck me. It was immediately obvious that the money wrapped in a five-pound note could be the sail—made as we made sails when I was a child by spitting a piece of stiff paper on a stick for our shingle boats.

I had a mahogany butt $4^3/_8 \times 10^1/_2 \times 6^1/_2$ inches long, so I sketched a rough design on it and started to shape the piece, which is really quite simple. Only a side view is necessary, unless you want the verisimilitude of a sideward-curving boat to more nearly match the shape of a pea pod. Such a boat would only sail in circles, I'm afraid, but it adds a little more nonsense to the poem. The owl, as captain, sits in the bow. I visualized him as slightly conventionalized, with large eyes and the usual fixed stare created by the feathers around the eyes. Further, I made his head a smaller ball atop the larger "pea" of the body. The cat was designed similarly, but while the captain faces sternly forward, the cat has allowed her attention to wander to one side. Also, she wears a bow to accentuate her femininity. (The owl might well have worn a captain's hat, I suppose, to accentuate his command and his masculinity, but I didn't think of it in time.) Both animals have drilled holes as eyes, to give them darkness and depth. The third pea became a conventional pottery honey pot, to which I added the word "Honey" and a questing bee on top. The five-pound note is also conventionalized, because I neither had one for reference nor did our limited references picture one—and besides this story happened a long time ago, when the pound was bigger.

The sea around the boat is also quite conventional: rolling waves, with a split bow wave. I had placed the sail at an angle and cut

"The Owl and the Pussycat" in mahogany. The "pea-green boat" becomes a pea pod, the figures the peas, with top additions. The honey is also a pea-shaped pot, and the "five-pound note" becomes the child's version of a sail. The sea is very conventionalized, as are the owl and the note.

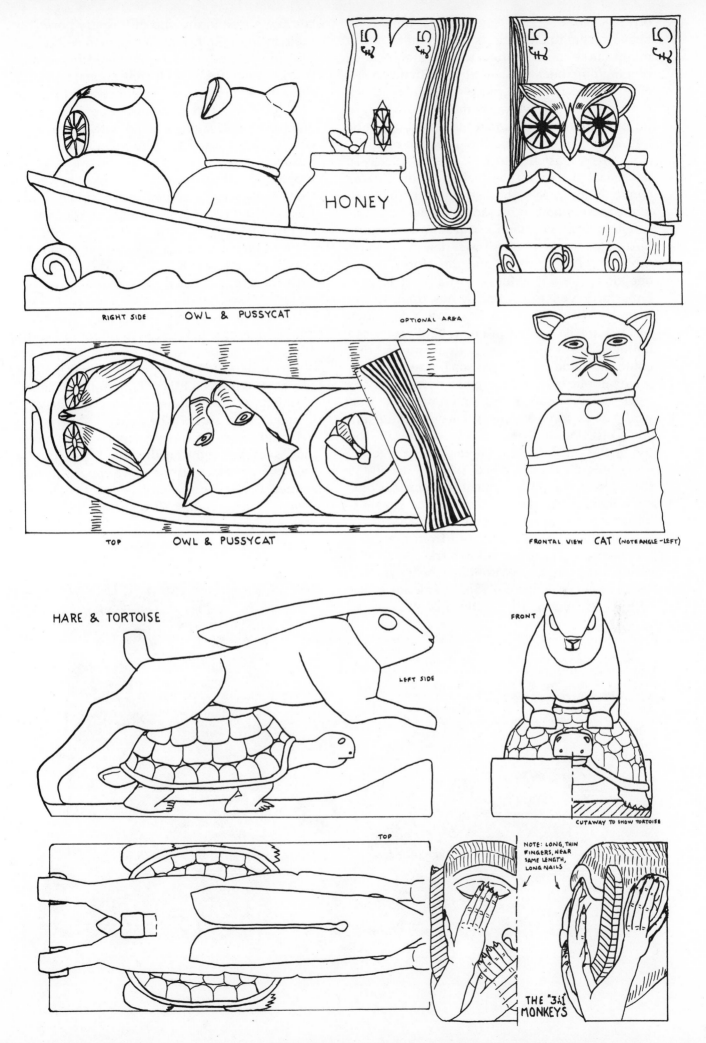

RIGHT SIDE OWL & PUSSYCAT

OPTIONAL AREA

TOP OWL & PUSSYCAT

HONEY

FRONTAL VIEW CAT (NOTE ANGLE - LEFT)

HARE & TORTOISE

LEFT SIDE

FRONT

CUTAWAY TO SHOW TORTOISE

TOP

NOTE: LONG, THIN FINGERS, NEAR SAME LENGTH, LONG NAILS

THE "3" MONKEYS

off the block at the same angle behind it, because I had no elements to add there, but it might have been better to leave the block rectangular, because now it is difficult to decide how to pose the piece for display. Also, the cat faces one way and the sail another, so for one-sided conventional viewing it might be better to turn the cat so she faces the opposite side, or at least forward, as the owl does. In any case, the sculpture makes an interesting conversation piece, and one that is recognized almost immediately by most people.

The second carving, also from a mahogany butt, is of course an illustration of Aesop's fable of "The Tortoise and the Hare." I saw one done by a Japanese artist in soap perhaps forty years ago, and it has stuck in my memory. I made it in a $3^{3}/_{4} \times 5 \times 9^{1}/_{4}$-inch piece with the grain running lengthwise. Both animals are quite blocky and simple, and could be made even more so. I'm not certain, for example that the carapace pattern on the turtle is necessary—and, if eliminated, that would save some nuisance carving. After all, what else looks like a turtle, either from the top or the side? The hare's ears are exaggerated in length for purposes of adding "speed" to the design, and the turtle's neck is outstretched for the same reason. These exaggerations add verve and motion for me.

The third design is adapted from the three monkeys originally carved in a frieze around a stable at a Japanese temple (see page 81), "See no evil; hear no evil; speak no evil." (While in the original, the monkeys were completely separate and differently posed animals in low relief, they were soon seated side by side in the round to make the familiar tourist piece.) A sketch that appeared in *The New York Times* one day suggested to me the idea that the three monkeys be still further combined into a single head with three sets of hands. The scale for the hands had to be reduced a little in order to show any of the monkey's face. Also, animal books showed me that a monkey's hands have much longer fingers than human ones, with all four fingers almost the same length and tipped with long pointed nails. I had a piece of apple wood, well seasoned, that was $4 \times 5^{3}/_{4} \times 5^{1}/_{2}$ inches high, with the grain vertical. This was adequate for most of the head—except the back—so I mounted the finished head in a walnut back panel and base. (I think it might be better without the back, which makes the assembly look like a bookend, even though I sloped the back panel slightly.) The monkey head is somewhat conventionalized, particularly the fringe of hair around the face.

I made each of these carvings from single-view sketches right on the wood, the first two being side views and the piece rough-sawed to shape. Tools were veiner, small firmers and gouges, with a mallet. Finish was flat varnish and wax.

Below—"The Tortoise and the Hare," from Aesop, via a soap carving, in mahogany. The soap carving was shown in my first book, this picture in the third, with no details, so herewith is the pattern. Holes between animals are drilled, then shaped. Right—"The Three Monkeys" converted to a single head with three sets of forearms and hands. In apple wood, mounted on walnut.

✳ The Pied Piper of Mittenwald:

Panels in Tandem, How They Grew

A sandwich ivory carving I found in Ehrbach, Germany (page 66), intrigued me so much that I wanted to try one—in wood. It is essentially three thin pierced panels (far easier to carve than one deep one) placed together in a case so they look like one deep carving from the front. All are made to the same perspective and are designed so important elements in the rear panels are not masked by those in front.

Rather than duplicate the deer and forest of the original carving, I decided to make the Pied Piper of Hamelin. This was not a chance decision; I had written and directed this old fairy tale as a play for children in 1966, and had used a stage set representing half the town square. Because our stage was shallow, we had to design with forced perspective, so each wing (or side), only about 6 feet wide, was painted to look like the buildings of half a city block, and the cyclorama backdrop had two-story buildings, with each story only about 5 feet high. The effect was startlingly realistic, even including a fountain playing in center stage.

Further, the story of the Pied Piper is very interesting; it is derived from the Children's Crusade in the year 1212. At that time, children of Middle Europe spontaneously followed leaders—Nicolas in Germany, Stephen in France—who were also children, on a trek south and east, with the avowed intention of rescuing the Holy Land from the Turks. Many died from hunger and plague on the way, many were enslaved or diverted by tribes along the way, and the pathetic remnants were sold into slavery in Turkey by corrupt Venetian shipowners who contracted to deliver them "free" to Asiatic shores. The crusade was an abysmal failure, but it was perpetuated in the German folk tale called "*Der Ratfanger von Hameln*," first set on paper by the Brothers Grimm. This tale is unusual in that it specifically dates and places the occurrences—in Hamelin, Brunswick, on the Weser River, in the year 1284. The Ratcatcher (our Piper) appears twice, several weeks apart, first in "a suit of many-colored cloth", second on June 26 as "a huntsman with a frightening face and a strange red cap." He took 130 children—all those over four years old—

The Pied Piper of Hamelin—in this case, "of Mittenwald" is more accurate—is a three-panel carving 9 × 12¹/₂ × 8³/₄ in. It is assembled of a series of separate elements and finished with stain and varnish.

through the East Gate of the town into oblivion. Two came back: a blind child who could not see where he had been, and a mute who could not tell what he had seen. Robert Browning, in his famous poem, repeated the story, but substituted a lame boy for the other two, reputedly because he wrote the poem for a lame boy. He also added another element from the Children's Crusade—the settlement of some of the children in Transylvania, which was on the route.

I had bought a Piper figure in Oberammergau (page 151), dressed in Bavarian costume, and I liked the Alps as background. Also I had transparencies of Alpine views, including several of the town of Mittenwald, near Oberammergau. So I moved the site from northern to southern Germany, and got a better background. I projected the church and famed Goethe Haus, at the end of the main street, to proper size on a sheet of white paper, and sketched them in, to provide a back panel. Size was selected to suit a ³/₄ × 9 × 12-inch piece of "white mahogany" (primavera or blond limba) that I had. From another transparency, taken at 90 degrees from the first, I

added Alps behind the church. Then, on another sheet of paper, I projected a foreshortened view down the main street, and sketched in building fronts on each side. When the two sketches were placed one over the other, I found that I would have to move the building fronts apart on the middle panel so the church and Goethe Haus could be seen at all, thus widening the street and creating somewhat of a stage set.

I had originally intended to mount the three panels in a tight sandwich in a shadow box and light from the front only, but it was obvious that the carving was going to be too big to rotate easily and the light would be obscured. Also, sky and clouds are difficult to carve naturally, so I decided to make the panels silhouettes, with the tops open. Then the center panel could be two panels—one on each side, and I could "fake" in the edges of two buildings at the sides of my front panel to frame it as well.

I drew the Piper 8 inches high, almost as tall as the church, with attentive rats slightly oversized—$1^{1}/_{2}$ inches long—around his feet and emerging from the buildings at his sides, and added the cobblestones of a street. This was also to be in white mahogany, $^{3}/_{4}$ inch thick. From the sketches, it appeared that the Piper might obscure some of the scene behind him, but a slight movement of the observer's head should clear that up. To help it, I made

the center "wings" of thicker wood—$1^{5}/_{8}$-inch mahogany cut diagonally across the corners so the panels would be thick at their outer edges and thin at the center. This also provided more surface on which to carve the building fronts.

But when I set the roughed-out panels up, they didn't look right so closely spaced. For proper effect, the two wings had to be back about $3^{1}/_{2}$ inches from the front one, and the back panel about 2 inches behind the wings. Thus I needed a "street" or ramp between them, with the apparent base of the church somewhat higher than the street at the Piper's feet. Perspective again.

There were a number of minor problems as well. Windows in the Middle Ages had little panes, so I "mullioned" the larger modern windows with little V-grooves to suggest tiny panes. This had to be done with the knife to prevent splitting out of the little "panes" between, and dark stain in the grooves made the windows stand out lighter—as they do in actuality. Also, scale was too small for much detail around doors and windows, and roof lines and balcony lines had to be adjusted by trial and error. I avoided modern store signs and house numbers and considerably simplified the ornate Baroque decoration of the church. Also, the back of the Piper and rats had to be cut away, so the rats became in-the-round elements. The building corners at the

FRONT PANEL

TOP RAT PANEL "C" (½) SIDE

NO DETAIL

PANEL BLANK

RAT LEVEL

STREET

RAT PANEL "F" (FOUNTAIN DETAIL)

TOP VIEW OF RIGHT CENTER PANEL

TOP RAT PANEL "B" SIDE

TOP VIEW

ALTERNATE TOP (silver)

ACTUAL STEP (3/16")
INCISED VEE LINES ONLY

3" HIGH for FOUNTAIN

BLANK SIZE

FRONT PANEL | RAT PANEL B | RAT PANEL C | RAT PANEL D | RAT PANEL E (MUST FIT) | RAT PANEL F | RAT PANEL G | BACK PANEL

CENTER PANELS

STREET "LEVEL"

ACTUAL DEPTH of BACK PANEL

DIAGRAM of ASSEMBLY (from side)

RIGHT   CENTER PANELS   LEFT

The 3-panel carving is like a stage set, with front and rear panels of ⁷/₈-in. wood and triangular pillars forming the center "panel" that is a foreshortened view of the village main street.

sides of the front panels also had to be made wedge-shaped to match the center wings.

The real job, however, was adding rats. The wing buildings, only about $3^1/2$ to 5 inches behind the Piper, have doors roughly 1 inch high, so rats emerging from them had to be about $^1/8$ inch long—or one twelfth the size of those with the Piper! I scaled rat size down very rapidly by putting them in serried rows—those behind the Piper only 1 inch long (Panel B). Panel C has a front row of $^5/8$-inch rats, a rear row of $^3/8$-inch ones. Panel D has three rows of roughly $^1/4$ inch rats. The sixteen rats in Panel B are detailed and individually posed; the twenty-seven in the first row of Panel C are shaped but mostly in the same pose. The fifty-two rats in the rear row are little more than elongated potatoes with head bumps added, and the 188 on Panel D are just round-ended lumps. Several spots on each panel were left higher so I could carve a sitting rat with his head above the crowd; others were varied slightly by carving them with nose high or low in random order. Rat column width was also tapered at the sides to show a little "street." Rats on Panels E and F are really just a veiner pattern, with street showing at the sides and columns entering the doors at

each side. The $1^7/8$ inch Panel G has a similar veiner pattern leading out to the sides around the fountain. (The fountain, incidentally, is actually against the church wall in Mittenwald; I moved it out to break up the rat column.) All these panels were made from $^5/4$-inch mahogany scraps; thus the road is really a series of bars rather than one block with an angular top. This makes carving of the rats much easier, but creates the need to obscure positive lines where they are glued together later. I found it possible to do some of this by drilling a hole here and there along joints and inserting a standing rat carved on the end of a plug.

Assembly of such a scene must be visual. If you decide to make one of your own, from different "swipes," you may have to adjust height of rear elements to make the scene look right. If you assemble from parts as I did, it is easy to mask the sides with contour-shaped panels, chamfered or fluted on top to make them less conspicuous.

Use of the white mahogany for the major panels made it possible to tone the elements with various stains, thereby getting more depth and realism into the Piper, church and Alps. Also, a darker stain helps to obscure any variation in color of the filler blocks that make up the road, and "antiquing" (dark stain followed by wiping off on surfaces) will bring up window and building details. Such staining should be preceded by varnishing, so there is less variation of color from side to end grain—and so inadvertent errors can be scratched off with a knife tip. When the desired color is obtained, spray varnishing will hold it.

The Mittenwald church has a pole topped by a ball—probably a lightning rod. I preferred a cross, which I filed from flat silver and inserted. I also filed a tiny silver ball for the top of the fountain. These provide accents when they catch the light, just as the gold wedding ring does on Og's head ("Descent from Ararat," page 72), or the real abalone shells on the sea otters (pages 94 and 96). Glass jewels can highlight the necktie or watchfob of a caricature, the holster of a cowboy (page 111). Silver or copper wire highlights carvings of horses (page 91) or dragons; bits of chain or silver plate will highlight accouterments. After all, why does a bird carver use glass eyes? Or an Indian put jade eyes in a carved jaguar? Or a Maori inlay paua shell in eyes of his gods and demons?

Panels from Transparencies:
Projecting to Scale Provides Easy Patterns

Captain Richard W. Graumann of Rolla, Mo., was inspired to try his hand at woodcarving during a four-week stay in Oberammergau. He projected 35mm transparencies to the desired scale to get elements of a scene, as I did for the Pied Piper (see preceding section). He says that it "saves time and is a significant aid for those of us not so talented with a pencil. I have also carved spires and landmarks, in relief, onto small wooden plates. This makes a pleasant wall arrangement."

Captain Graumann did these two elaborate low reliefs on beech wood. At left is a 9 × 24-inch scene in Heidelberg, Germany, with the Alte Brucke (Old Bridge) in front of the Heiligegeist Kirche (Holy Ghost Church). It has the virtue of being purely geometric forms. He sketched the two major elements on sheets of tracing paper, then superimposed one on the other to get the desired composition—which doesn't exist in that relationship in Heidelberg. Note that this panel retains the original wood surface for a border.

The top panel, 16½ × 26 inches, is the cheese market at Alkmeer, Holland. Here three separate tracings were combined, a cheese sled, men carrying a cheese sled, and the images of the houses. Both panels are walnut-stained, then waxed. (I sent Captain Graumann a photo and sketches of the Pied Piper scene, and he reports that his wife immediately decided that he must also make one like it!)

✳ The Whimsies of Winnie Baker:

Silhouette Panels Need No Titles

Winnie (Mrs. John) Baker, Torrance, Calif., began carving at two and a half or three, had her own knife at eight. After her teens, she dropped carving. In 1967, however, she started carving once more and two years later was winning ribbons at fairs and shows around Los Angeles. She now has a considerable collection—mostly blue ribbons.

"Mexican Musicians" (1969), sugar pine, $1^1/_2 \times 20 \times 26$ in. "Toreador" (1968), sugar pine, $1^1/_2 \times 17 \times 23$ in. "Pioneer Man and Woman" (1974), pine $1^3/_4 \times 13 \times 17$ in. "Lobsterman," 1967 redwood, $1^1/_2 \times 18 \times 24$ in. "Pied Piper," (1971) basswood, $1^3/_4 \times 21^1/_4 \times 32^1/_2$ inc. "Sleeping Old Man" (1967), sugar pine, $1^3/_4 \times 16 \times 21$ in. "Little Fisherman" (1973), basswood, $1^3/_4 \times 6 \times 7^1/_2$ in. "Bookworm" (1974), basswood, $2^1/_2 \times 3 \times 10^1/_4$ in. "Old Woman in the Shoe" (1973), basswood, $1^7/_8 \times 27^1/_2 \times 30$ in. "Hobo" (1969) sugar pine, $1^5/_8 \times 20 \times 22$ in.

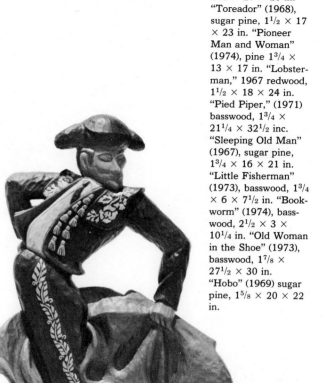

✳ Variety Characterizes Michael DeNike:

He Carves Many Materials

Professional sculptor, woodcarver and teacher Michael DeNike of Wayne, N.J., began as a devoted boy whittler on a Michigan farm. In the early sixties, he gave up his construction business to devote full time to his art, his teaching and, as of 1974, the American Carving School. He has won a number of awards and commissions, including a plaque picturing Albert Payson Terhune. He works in clay, stone, plaster and metal, but prefers wood. These pieces suggest the wide range of his work from tiny birds to massive murals. The 36-in. eagle with broken chain below is in pine, with gold-leafed beak and claws and silver-leafed chain. Under it is a livery sign, 22 × 19½ in. for commercial reproduction, and two sperm whales, both whittled of pine, the upper 7 in. long, the lower 13½ in. On the facing page are more formal sculptures: "Benediction", in cherry, 21 in. high; "Lotus," in black walnut, 41 in. high; and "Rapunzel," in pearwood, 16 in. high. Below them: "New Life," a mahogany relief, 18 × 27 in., and "Young St. Francis," 4 × 6 ft., in black walnut.

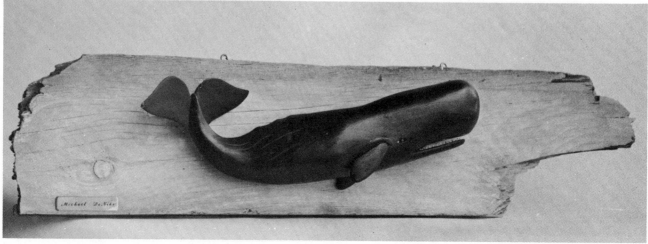

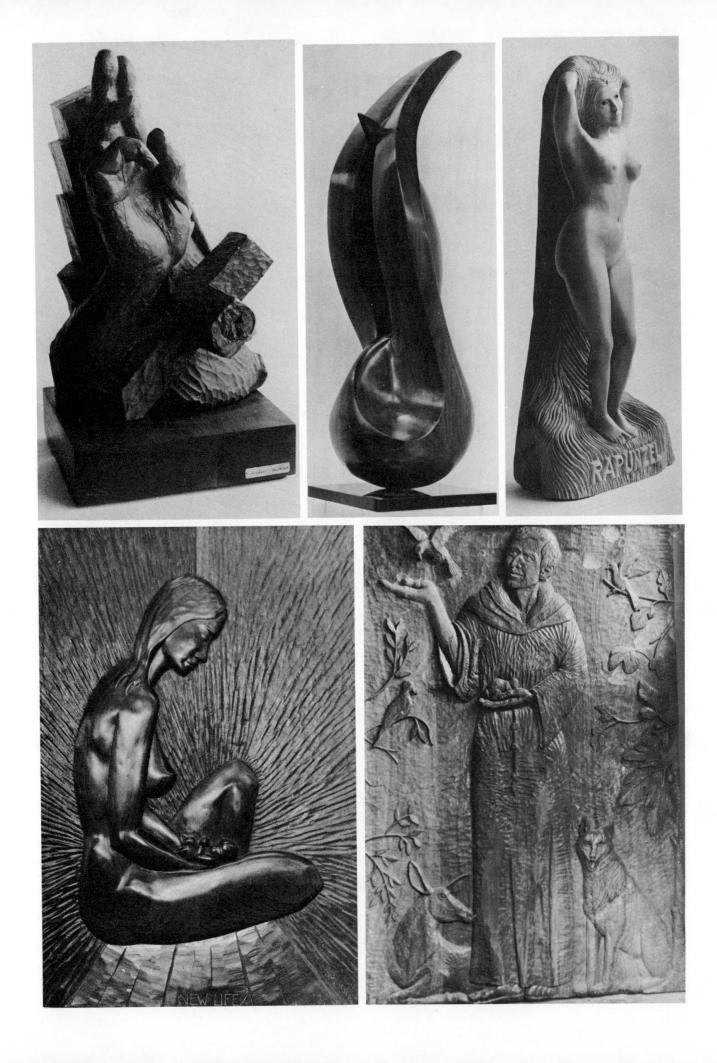

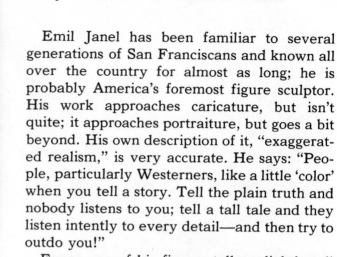

✳ Emil Janel's "Little People":

Why and How He Makes Them

Emil Janel has been familiar to several generations of San Franciscans and known all over the country for almost as long; he is probably America's foremost figure sculptor. His work approaches caricature, but isn't quite; it approaches portraiture, but goes a bit beyond. His own description of it, "exaggerated realism," is very accurate. He says: "People, particularly Westerners, like a little 'color' when you tell a story. Tell the plain truth and nobody listens to you; tell a tall tale and they listen intently to every detail—and then try to outdo you!"

Every one of his figures tells a slightly tall story, and it is always sensitive and a bit whimsical. His figures appear to have laughed a lot, cried a little, worked and played hard, and to want their talk and their music loud and gay. He carves quite ordinary people, almost always male, and almost always lean and lanky as he himself is. Most of his characters are, in fact, reminiscent of him (a very frequent characteristic of caricature, by the way, perhaps because of the necessity for the carver to mime before a mirror to get the expressions he's after).

Born in Orsa, Sweden, over eighty years ago, Emil wanted to be an artist, and was even offered a scholarship in art school, but his father expected him to be a woodsman as he was, so Emil—at thirteen—and his brother went into the forests. His artistic yearnings were expressed in little figures he carved in his spare time and gave to friends. He never considered them as an alternate to his profes-

Top—Emil Janel in a relaxed moment; note his heavily muscled left arm. Center—A 3 × 4-ft. redwood panel of low relief faces. Left—Two life-sized heads flanking a Janel painting. Heads are untinted, in contrast to those in the panel above. Right—A group of 1974 Janel carvings, including three single figures, and two poker games, one with mirrored top view.

sion, even though he began carving at the age of four and beat 250 of Sweden's best artists in Stockholm competition before he was twenty-five. He thought of an artist as a painter—and occasionally he painted landscapes and such himself.

Shortly after he won in Stockholm, he emigrated to Canada with his brother and moved out West because that's where the trees were. He worked for a month in one lumber camp without pay because the foreman knew he couldn't speak English and hence couldn't complain. When he first went to restaurants, his English—and his diet—were limited to "beans." It was a great day when he saw what the phrase "ham and eggs" brought! His carving, a spare-time hobby, caught the eye of a Vancouver gallery owner, who tried to persuade him to leave the woods and work exclusively as an artist. Finally, he did get Emil to emigrate again, suggesting either San Francisco or New Orleans. Emil went to San Francisco because that was closer and earned his ham and eggs for a time by playing the accordion. Then he moved on to Los Angeles, where he met and married his wife, Greta, a Norwegian. After a short time there, and some disappointments with galleries, he moved back to San Francisco, where he has been ever since.

He has carved an enormous number of figures, during the past quarter century, for the Maxwell Galleries. Most are full-length males 12 to 15 inches high; these days they sell for around $500 each. Occasionally he breaks over and produces a bust figure or a group of card players (they sell for as much as $6,000), a chess set, or some other variation just for the fun of it. Some years ago, he acquired a retreat on Russian River north of San Francisco, where he now carves in the summer, and spends his "idle" time carving grotesque figures in the stumps of the trees on his property. His regular pieces are all of alder wood—it holds its color through the years and has a sort of tanned Western look. (He tints his pieces sparingly: They are unmistakably wood.) Much of the wood he cuts himself and carves green, or at least keeps thoroughly soaked while he carves it. All of his figures are older people; he says bluntly: "Only age and experience give character; the young have little to say."

Janel is not a typical woodcarver either in ideas or techniques. He uses a relatively small number of tools and works largely with the wood on his knees. He is left-handed, uses no

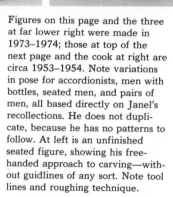

Figures on this page and the three at far lower right were made in 1973–1974; those at top of the next page and the cook at right are circa 1953–1954. Note variations in pose for accordionists, men with bottles, seated men, and pairs of men, all based directly on Janel's recollections. He does not duplicate, because he has no patterns to follow. At left is an unfinished seated figure, showing his freehanded approach to carving—without guidlines of any sort. Note tool lines and roughing technique.

sketches, models, clay workups or even marks on the wood. Everything comes from memory and his "inner eye." He leaves the chisel marks, does not use sandpaper or heavy color.

As an individual, he is shy and retiring, modest, even a bit diffident. So are most of his carvings. He deplores his advancing age and his resulting periodic illnesses because they interfere with his carving—which, it seems, he has never considered work. He enjoys carving, and his figures show it. None is static or stiff; all appear to be men caught at a joyous and busy moment. They have a puckish look, a tolerance and understanding that is rarely expressed in wood or in any medium. Each is, incidentally, made from a single piece of wood, with the exception of occasional accessories, or the accouterments for a poker table (though each player is one with his chair).

His work has been shown in a number of exhibitions and featured in a number of magazines. Here are some typical examples, some dating back to 1950 or earlier, others made as recently as 1974. He had a seventy-piece one-man show at the DeYoung Museum some years ago that drew a record attendance of 10,000 admiring San Franciscans the first day. Yet he lives in a modest San Francisco apartment and seldom appears in public. He takes a limited number of fortunate students, but otherwise spends most of his time producing his little people—for the greater pleasure of us all.

❋ How to Make Your Own Designs:

Modify, Adapt or Innovate—But Try

When Snow White asked why Dopey never talked, one of the other dwarfs answered, "Because he never tried." That's often the reason—and the only reason—why carvers don't make their own designs, or at least vary them to suit their needs. It is faster and surer to follow a design, and it is a quick way to learn; it provides showable products while you drill. But once you've learned facility with the tools and have some knowledge of how various woods react, it's time to cut loose.

There are no shortcuts to design, just as there aren't to learning to carve. Both take a great deal of practice, plus some nerve, natural ability and dumb luck. But if you can carve, you can probably design—even if you can't draw to suit an art teacher. (For most of my life I carved pieces first, then made drawings from them. It was years before I caught myself actually drawing.) Too much ability to draw actually may be a handicap, because drawing goes faster and may become an end in itself, like the collecting and preparation of tools. As my father-in-law used to say, "Too much time is spent in getting ready to start in to begin to commence." Further, the drawing becomes a crutch, or at least a rigid pattern from which the carver is loath to deviate.

The willingness to change as you carve is essential in design. Obviously, lettering, or an overall pattern, or a portrait, allows little scope for deviation. But less rigid designs can be varied as you go to suit the grain or figure of the wood, to avoid a flaw, to compensate for a slip of the tool, or for some other reason. On my recent cigar-store Indian, I moved one leg forward a bit to miss a knot behind the knee. On "Descent from Ararat" (page 72), I de-

signed as I went, suiting my selection of animals to the protuberances, insect holes and other peculiarities of the wood, as well as to its general shape. In many panels, I have capitalized on a figure in the wood, discoloration, or an insect bore or knot, rather than to design without considering them and having to have my design compete with them later. On an in-the-round carving, it is often quite possible to thin a figure or to alter the pose a little to avoid the difficulties of excising, matching and patching a flaw. The important thing is to realize that rarely is any design sacrosanct—you don't even sign your name exactly the same way every time!

A piece is not lost because of one knot or one tool slip. If a remedy isn't immediately visible, stop carving for a while and put the carving where you can look at it frequently. Almost always, a remedy will suggest itself. Flexibility is part and parcel of designing: being willing to strike out in new directions, to take a chance in the hope of achieving something different and distinctive, something that has a flavor for the ages instead of merely the smell of antiquity—like the spoon rack I included with the sketches. That design hasn't been changed in several hundred years, so it is more sentimental than interesting.

Many primitive carvings, as well as mountaineer and backwoods whittling, are strong and good because the maker has a clear idea of what he is doing, an attainable goal—he is picturing what he knows. He doesn't fear failure; unlike the urbanized majority, his childhood curiosity and confidence, his willingness to try something new, haven't been atrophied by fear of offending some real or

 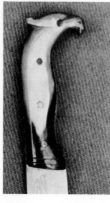

Three poses of eagles as bottle caps in mahogany and a machete handle in horn from Mexico. The caps were whittled in two, four and seven hours, including design, which was adapted from bird books and photographs. The vertical pose has no detail beyond eyes and neck ruff, so goes fast and is strong. The other two poses are more fragile (and take longer) because of projections and leg delineation, also must be handled with more care. Feathering on the spread wings requires an hour alone. The horn head is quite simple and durable, and the crest provides a hook for greater safety in using the tool. Other designs are sketched.

fancied social standard, or of wasting material or time. He's willing to cut loose and spoil a piece or two, so he does his own thing.

This is the essence of design: to have a clear mental picture of what you're trying to make. This surpasses any drawings, because drawn lines have a way of being cut away anyway just when you need them most. The mental image may blur at times; put the piece to one side and work on another until it clears. Many carvers have several projects going simultaneously for just this reason—they get brain fag or plain bored with a particular subject or wood or whatever.

Occasionally, a design idea will hit you from the blue, but this is rare. Ideas usually result from a combination of impulses and recollections, often based on events or happenings over a period of time. I'm not certain that this process can be taught—or even stimulated—although I advise people to clip, photo, note or otherwise collect ideas or things that appeal to them, for later reference, then to review the collection from time to time, so the idea remains in mind, ready for development. I suggest the same thing for odd shapes of wood: Leave them where you'll see them frequently, stumble over them, think about them. That's how my "Stag at Eve" (page 124) came about. But I find that I rarely go to my files except for something specific that I know is there. It seems more natural to select something that really intrigues me from the ideas that are running through my mind at the moment, and to start on it. Often, the start or more thought makes the idea seem less attractive, but some assume solid form.

One simple form of design is adaptation. Take a design or shape and adapt it to your needs: change the shape, the thickness, multiply or reduce the motif, simplify the technique or alter it, converting from in-the-round to bas-relief and vice versa. Consider the four-way head pictured here as an example. The original idea was new; it popped into my head one lazy afternoon in Vermont, and I made the first head from a fireplace scrap. But I realized later that the idea was really a marriage of two things I'd seen, a Celtic plaque in Paris in which one head had added noses where the ears should be (in low relief) and the stylized faces on the cornice corners of a Mayan temple in Tulum, Mexico and one in Tikal, Guatemala (page 125). Still, my first head was a definite innovation; all the larger ones, however, were adaptations.

Six whittled breadboard heads, five traditional in Holland and the sixth taken from an ivy sprig and simplified in veining. Veins are veiner cuts rather than projecting ridges, as they are in nature, simply for convenience in cutting. These are in cherry and 6⅞ in. wide by about 11 in. long, about 1¼ in. wider and longer than the originals, which were in a lighter, less figured wood. Other designs can be developed easily to suit the place of use, and similar head bands can be put on bulletin boards, bedsteads, or picture frame, for example.

Another form of design is the supplementary one, or variant. Consider the breadboards shown here. The owner bought five in Holland, but that's either too many or not enough. So while I was whittling copies of his five, I whittled a sixth for him, combining pine cones and an acorn: His house is an "Acorn" pre-fab on Spruce Lake. When I made my own sixth board, however, I copied the local ivy, because I live on Ivy Way. Later I made a hostess gift with three woodchucks. I've sketched a couple of other designs, and many more are possible, of course. (It is amusing to note that the only wood I could find in Vermont was cherry $6^5/8$ inches wide, so all my new boards are $1^1/4$ inches wider and longer than the originals; both my host and I like wood too well to waste it.)

I did a similar thing with the bottle caps. I sketched a number of designs, then ended up carving a different series entirely—three eagles, probably because of the popularity of eagles these days and the Bicentennial. These caps are designed to take a $3/4$-inch-diameter cork for conventional wine bottles, but can readily be changed to take a screw cap or a larger or smaller cork. Or they can be converted to statuettes, stamps or umbrella or cane handles. Suitable designs can become knife handles. The breadboard designs can be similarly adapted for picture frames, bulletin boards, bed headboards, purse tops.

The important thing to remember in adapting a design is that its particular usage may establish different parameters. A bottle cap may be handled roughly, dropped or twisted, so should have inherent strength and be free of easily broken projections. (This is basic in designing carvings: Avoid projections, particularly across grain, when possible.) Because of this and the time it takes to carve, it should be in a good wood—mahogany (which I used), walnut, cherry, teak. You may want to turn the bases to receive corks, which should precede carving, and this makes some form of holding device advisable, such as a clamp block over the turned portion which can be held in a vise, like a miniature carver's screw. Otherwise, you'll be whittling a rather stubby piece, and, if you're using chisels, you'll have endless trouble. On the other hand, if the end use is as a statuette or handle, you can carve on the end of a longer stick, then cut to length. My basic point is that design modification must also include consideration of production and end use. A heroic-sized piece will stand of itself, but a miniature must be held in some way. The wings on two of the eagles can be broken easily, so can the legs when separated, as well as the bill, so rough carving should be done first and the fragile parts left for finishing. Also, some thought should be given to detail. A big figure can use a lot of it, but a small one doesn't need it, and most whittling projects, for example, are small. The vertical eagle, with legs merely indicated and feathering suggested by the neck ruff, took only two hours and is quite sturdy; he could even be made and sold as a bottle stopper at an almost reasonable price. But the shrieking eagle takes four hours, the wingspread eagle six, plus another hour for wing and tail feathering, so these are statuettes in terms of time and cost.

Many other projects provide endless possibilities for adaptation and variation. Examples include a Noah's Ark, Nativity scene, carousel, circus, parade, Garden of Eden, toy soldiers, chess set. Each is a central idea, with some tradition as to shape and other parameters, but the sky is the limit on possible units.

Another kind of design is interpretive, in which you seek to duplicate in wood what someone else has done in pictures, drawings or words—a line of poetry, a familiar expression, a painting, a nursery rhyme. These are more difficult to do well, particularly if the original is by a competent or well-known artist. But in any case, your own imagination must supply some detail and some proportions because of the third dimension—and there isn't a model to copy. There are a number of such examples in this book: Hey Diddle Diddle (page 109), the Pied Piper (page 157), among others.

Last, there is the all-out new idea, the innovation, which comes out of the blue. Examples are my four-way head and the spacing of the panels in the Pied Piper, or the Owl and Pussycat (page 154). This is the creation of a new idea, whether it be the total design or some element or technique. It is surprisingly infrequent; after all, most sculptors work from models or make subtle alterations of previous sculptures a large part of the time. Don't expect a design breakthrough on every project. One or two in a lifetime is a very real accomplishment for most of us.

Design in these modern times is not what it once was. The primitive used the wood that came to hand, selecting and adapting. His designs were very much influenced by the shape of the wood, the available tools, his limited skill. Now we often start with the design idea and buy or cut the wood to suit. The most readily available form is kiln-dried wood, so shapes are often built up of glued planks. (This also reduces checking.) In a sense, we have removed one limitation, but we have created another: There is less incentive to try something radically new because the wood suggests it. Some carvers even produce arms and legs separately, then test them in several positions before fastening them permanently to the torso.

Another factor in modern design is that we have more varieties and colors of woods avail-

DESIGN SIMPLIFICATION

Optional

KING   JACK

ORIGINAL ESCHER DESIGN

SIMPLIFIED VERSION (EJT)

BOTTLE & DECANTER TOPS, STAMPS

Depress leaf center & vein ribs

6 7/8" wide

IVY

5 5/8" wide

PINE CONE & ACORN

Low-relief or pierced

TWIN STAGS

Design can reverse or continue

FRUIT

FORMAL HANDLE

BROODPLANKEN
Arnhem

Gouge cuts

Round edges

SPOON RACK

Black areas pierced

Gouge crescent

csc

csc

Slotted bar

This area is painted-floral designs

Polychrome & gilt

V-groove

Round edges

Ars Longa
Hindeloopen

173

Development of a design—The first four-way head was 2 × 2 × 4 in. yellow pine firewood, whittled with little facial detail. The second (far left), in 4 × 4 × 8-in. walnut, has more detail, elongated faces, with a 2-in. base added later. A break from formal design was the cocktail table base (center), a walnut stump with the trunk squared but the base left to provide two distorted faces and two (shown) more regular, a result of natural bulges in the trunk, which was a 22-in.-long piece of Ohio "firewood."

Greater detail was achieved, again on a firewood scrap, but this time in a wood like our yellow pine in Mexico. In this elongated design (two views shown), there is a winking eye, and a suggestion of tabards for body, but no shoulders. In the latest design, 6 × 6 × 15 in. in teak, the theme is face cards, combining the King of Spades, Queen of Hearts, Jack of Diamonds and the Joker—two formal male faces, a formal female face, and a caricature. Decorative details identify each figure repeatedly, because the queen's snood and the king's and knave's curled hair of the conventional deck are not possible—no portion of the face beyond the eye is included. Shoulders are suggested for the king and knave, which become a suggestion of a bosom for the queen and a blouse for the joker. The figure is mounted on a circular base with a 4-in. Lazy Susan device, so it can be rotated easily. I found with earlier designs having multiple facets that viewers want to rotate the piece anyway. (For a more complex design, the Lazy Susan can be separate and topped by a mirror surface.)

Having gone about as far as I could with the four-way head, I suddenly remembered the children's cartoon which shows a smiling face when turned one way and a sad face when turned the other way up. The design that grew out of that is a twelve-way head, as at far right top. It is hexagonal in cross-section, with eyes in the middle of each side. Then a face is carved on each corner above and below the eyes, so each eye is a part of four separate faces. There are no eyebrows or foreheads—the cheek of one head becomes the forehead of the face on the opposite end. This design, in white pine, gives plenty of practice in facial variations, and makes a pleasing overall design as well. It *must* be set on a mirror if the top and bottom faces are to be seen simultaneously. This opens a whole new field for variations.

Right: A modification of an Escher design in 1/4-in. mahogany and maple (see page 173). In this instance, the modification was inadvertent, a result of an attempt at memorizing the shape of an Escher postcard sent to a friend. The original design is also sketched. Either may be multiplied or extended to cover a tabletop, for example.

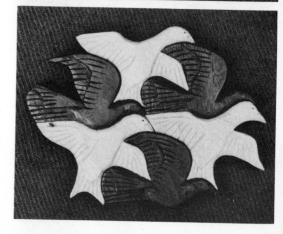

able, better glues, better stains, better tools. I can get teak for less than twice the price of walnut, and the traditionally cheap woods like pine and bass can cost within 15 percent of woods like maple and mahogany. Also, while I may design for 2-inch wood, I find I must settle for $1\frac{7}{8}$-inch or $\frac{3}{4}$-inch laminated—in other words, commercial sizes—unless I want to increase material cost markedly. And I must design to suit the tools I intend to use; there is little point in designing with hollows if my only tool is to be the knife, or to design small detail when all my tools are large.

To all these factors must be added in these enlightened days another—consistency or suitability. Many people understand something of style now, so it is not advisable to mix primitive and precise, caricature and formal, colonial and modern, detailed and undetailed. There is little point in carving a detailed design on a crown set on simulated hair, or to use Maori motifs on a cowboy's shirt, or to mix in-the-round and low relief. These can all be done, but they take some knowledge, experience and nerve, as well reputation. Be yourself in your designs; that's most important.

Below—"The Lithuanian School," a life-sized copy in wood by B. Karalus of a bronze by P. Rimsa pictures home teaching of the Lithuanian tongue after it was forbidden by the Russians in 1864–1904. The faces are particularly good. This is a complex design, requiring assembly of separate parts like the spinning wheel and chair, difficult and not too sturdy. Compare it with the panel behind it at the New York World's Fair of 1939, with its bold simplicity, inverted muscles, tinting, visible joints—a much more modern style. Right—"The Judgment of Paris," a cedar panel 7 in. wide by $9\frac{1}{4}$ in. high, carved in Salzburg, Austria, during the first half of the 16th century and now in the Victoria & Albert Museum, London. It is a very high relief, over-detailed and overly "busy" by modern standards. Some undecorated areas and a less-detailed background would help.

✳ So You've Been Asked to Teach:

Some Hints for the Neophyte Instructor

Teaching classes in whittling and/or wood-carving is becoming increasingly common because of the recent emphasis on crafts, on "going back to the land," and on economy in the face of rampant costs. Adult education classes, community colleges, historical societies, youth groups, high schools, all are seeking anyone with craft skills to assist in meeting the demand. Available facilities—and good teachers—are usually limited.

Often, of course, the people taking the course are dilettantes, in search of some craft expression, no matter what, so a little instruction and production of a satisfactory simple piece or two satisfies their needs. On the negative side, some sincere seekers after knowledge are turned off, and many courses are not completed, simply because the instructor has been unable or unwilling to transmit his own interest and enthusiasm.

The basic difficulty, in my experience, is that the layman simply does not realize that whittling or woodcarving is time-consuming. A common request is for a one-time lecture-demonstration, in which the lecturer is expected to turn out a masterpiece in an hour or so, while covering all the fundamentals of the craft, its history and some of the art aspects as well. A close second is the single-session two-hour "training course" for a group of senior citizens, Boy, Girl, or Cub Scouts or what-have-you. Most of the audience will arrive with borrowed—and dull—knives or tools, and the instructor could well spend the entire period teaching them the fundamentals of sharpening (with the certainty that they will decide whittling is as dull as their knives). Or he can provide tools and pre-cut blanks so class members achieve an objective—and assume thereafter that there is nothing to the craft once the menial work is done.

In either case, the instructor has his problems. If he has the students with dull knives come early so he can sharpen their knives, he's in as much trouble as if he provided the equipment and spoon-fed the class. The answer lies somewhere in between; the instructor should not sugar-coat the craft merely for audience effect, nor should he spend too much time on drill.

Obviously, some time must be devoted initially to understanding the tools and how they are used, or the consumption of bandages will be overly large. It is vital to understand about wood and its grain, the care and handling of the knife and later the other tools, relative hardness of various materials and all the rest. But that can be salted in with demonstration and practice, just as can history and examples. In recent years, I have shortened the initial session by explaining about a knife and its peculiarities, then handling out a two-page sheet (see next section) that repeats what I've said and amplifies and pictures the important elements. This works particularly well when the students are older and have had experience with other tools.

It seems to be advisable to let students begin carving as soon as possible, in contrast to the traditional European idea of a lengthy apprenticeship. But early carving does not mean that instruction can be, or should be, abandoned. It can be interspersed in each session, either as an initial element or when the opportunity offers, depending upon class size. Further, if carving is begun early, the instructor must be much more alert for mistakes and correct every misstep as soon as it occurs.

Sessions can be any length desired, of course, but it is preferable to have at least two hours, or even three, per session. I prefer fewer, but longer, sessions—three hours, if possible—because I find that interested students are really just going well when a two-hour session ends, particularly if some lectures or slides introduce the session. I also prefer Saturday morning to any evening of the week, because students, particularly adults, are fresher, or two sessions a week.

Class size is a matter of much debate. A class of serious students should number no more than eight, a class of dilettantes—who may or may not attend regularly—can number twelve to fifteen. I have worked with single-session groups as large as forty Boy or Girl Scouts and multisession groups of twenty-five in which parents and children worked together. It was my hope in the latter case that the parents would help the children, but some parents had two children along—and two art teachers turned up, each with two promising students in tow. In the second place, children under fifteen have a short attention span. The children's attention at best was divided, and in several cases the elders were not nearly as adept or as quick to learn as the children, so the class was too large for me to give adequate attention to everyone. Fortunately, the series was short—only four two-hour lessons. It is possible, in such cases, to ask a friend who is also a whittler or woodcarver to assist.

In teaching beginners, I prefer four or five three-hour sessions if whittling alone is involved, and double that number if simple woodcarving is also to be included. If you are so fortunate as to have a select group of dedicated students, the number of sessions can easily be doubled, but most modern-day classes will inevitably include dilettantes and experimenters who will rapidly lose interest when they discover that whittling goes slowly and requires real work and patience.

Because students have vastly varying degrees of tactile training and ability, and work with widely varying degrees of confidence and speed, any class will tend to break into groups working on different stages of a project. This leads to mistakes, accidents and spoilage of blanks, unless the instructor keeps it under control. I have found it best to insist on the first few projects that students work step by step with me, and I try to select projects that make this feasible (see photos).

A good first project, for example, is the whammydiddle, which can be made from natural materials and incorporates a number of basic cutting strokes. It can also be produced by beginners in one to one and a half hours, so their interest does not pall, and the opportunity for diversity in speed and confidence is not so apparent. (In general, the speed of able beginners is about a third to a fifth that of a skilled carver—a whammydiddle should take you about fifteen to twenty minutes.) The whammydiddle involves a variety of cutting operations, including two careful ones—cutting the rack teeth and making the propeller. It is, when completed, a unique thing of which the maker can be proud. It also lends itself to step-by-step instruction.

Second and third projects should incorporate similar elements to reinforce what the student has learned and to give him practice. It is also advisable to have elements that are repetitive, so he can finish one or two in class

Books Helpful to the Carver and Teacher

Books helpful to the carver and teacher will depend a great deal upon his personal interests, of course, but I have found these particularly useful. Some are now out of print; some are rare in the United States; but many, or their equivalents, will be available in a good local library. The leading nonlibrary source for these books is Dover Publications, Inc., 180 Varick Street, New York, N.Y. 10014, which has reproduced many older books as inexpensive paperbacks.

Among books available from Dover are:

Primitive Art (totem poles, boxes, etc.), Franz Boas.
African Sculpture, Ladislas Segy.
Decorative Arts of the Southwestern Indians.
Decorative Arts of Sweden, Iona Plath.
American Indian Design and Decoration, Leroy H. Appleton.
Design Motifs of Ancient Mexico, Jorge Enciso.
Pennsylvania Dutch American Folk Art, Henry J. Kauffman.
Medieval American Art, Pal Kelemen
Sun Dials, Albert Waugh
Art Anatomy, William Rimmer.
Art Students Anatomy, Edmond J. Farris.
The Human Figure, John H. Vanderpoel.
An Atlas of Anatomy for Artists, Fritz Schider.
Animal Drawing, Charles R. Knight.
An Atlas of Animal Anatomy for Artists, Ellenberger, Baum and Dettrich.
Alphabets and Ornaments, Ernst Lehner.
Handbook of Ornament, Franz S. Mayer.
Other books which have been helpful include:
Art in Africa, Tibor Bodrogi. McGraw-Hill Book Co.
Grinling Gibbons, David Green. Country Life, Ltd., London, England
Monuments in Cedar, Edward L. Keithhahn. Bonanza Books, N.Y. (being remaindered in 1975).
Trees and Other Wooden Bygones, Edward H. Pinto. G. Bell & Sons, London.
European Folk Art, H. J. Hansen, Editor. McGraw-Hill Book Co.
Haida Myths, Marius Barbeau. National Museum of Canada, Ottawa.
The Woodcarver's Art in Ancient Mexico, Marshall H. Saville. Museum of the American Indian, New York.
Indians of the Pacific Northwest, Ruth Underhill. Sherman Institute, Riverside, California.
Indian Art of the United States, Douglas Y. D'Harnoncourt. Museum of Modern Art, New York
Indian and Eskimo Artifacts of North America, Charles Milles. Bonanza Books,
Eskimo Art, Cottie Burland. Hemlyn Publishers Group, London and New York.
The Sculpture of Negro Africa, Paul S. Wingert. Columbia University Press, N.Y.
The Decorative Arts of the New Zealand Maori, T. Barrow. A. H. and A. W. Reed, Wellington, N.Z.
The Art of Maori Carving , S. M. Mead. A. H. and A. W. Reed, Wellington, N.Z.
The World of Birds, Fisher and Peterson. Crescent Books (Crown Publishers, N.Y.
Natural History of the Birds of Eastern and Central North America, Edward Howe, Houghton Mifflin, Boston.
Masks, Andreas Lommel. McGraw-Hill Book Co.
Artists in Wood, Frederick Fried. Crown Publishers, N.Y. (remaindered in 1975).
American Folk Art, Jean Lipman. Pantheon Books, N.Y. (new edition now).
The Craft of the Japanese Sculptor, Langdon Warner. Japan Society of New York.
Shipcarvers of North America, M. V. Brewington. Barre Publishing Co., Barre, Mass.
The Yankee Whaler, Clifford W. Ashley. Houghton Mifflin, Boston.
American Figureheads and Their Carvers, Pauline A. Pinckney. Kennikat Press, Port Washington, N.Y.

Libraries have directories showing books in print, and often have interchange privileges with state libraries or other larger reference libraries. It is also helpful to have available *Chip Chats*, the bimonthly magazine of the National Wood Carvers Association, 7424 Miami Ave., Cincinnati, Ohio 45243; and the *National Carvers Review*, quarterly of the National Carvers Museum, 14960 Woodcarver Rd. Monument, Colorado 80132. Both publish regular listings of books, tools, materials, finishes, etc. For data on wood, see monthly bulletin of International Wood Collectors Society, Eleanor P. Frost, Editor, 148 Summer St., Lanesboro, Mass., 01237, or publications of U.S. Forest Products Labs., Madison, Wis.

and then work on the others for "homework." Something like a chip-carved panel or a fish weathervane does well for this, and I have also used a name panel successfully. (The latter is quite good in that each student feels he is making something individual and special—his name—while V-grooving the letters is a method common to all.)

There is great variety in the speed with which students learn, of course. The person with a mechanical bent, the person naturally good with tools, the artist in other media, the enthusiast—all these will outpace the rank beginner, the handicapped, or the essentially clumsy persons. The artist, in particular, may indeed outpace the instructor at times, and must be cautioned to wait for his slower contemporaries lest he spoil his workpiece, to his own chagrin. Also, the instructor must cooperate by making basic projects relatively simple, by encouraging and aiding the slower workers (but not to the detriment of the class—he must *not* begin doing the slowpoke's carving *for* him), by providing the fast worker with more

detail to carve (the veins in the fish fins, more elaborate chip-carving designs, and the like), by asking the naturally faster worker to assist in instructing the slower ones, and by assigning the slow workers more homework. If projects require only one session or a bit longer, the disparity in carving speed will be less apparent, and it is also possible to interest the fast worker in an auxiliary (but similar) project he can do while he is waiting for his slower contemporaries to catch up.

Further, some people are naturally timid about really cutting in—either through fear of making a mistake, or "wasting" the wood, or the time spent on the project thus far, or of cutting themselves. They need extra care and encouragement, with some swashbuckling cutting by the instructor from time to time to increase their daring. Others are perfectly willing to play dumb and let the instructor carve most of their project to "help them catch up," to ask a stream of questions or to want special help. They can thus rob the general group of instruction time and slow up the

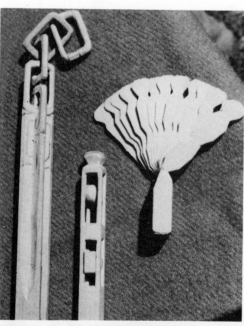

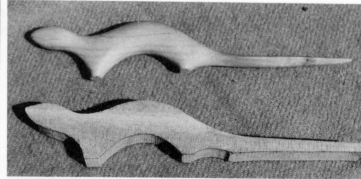

Typical teacher's aids—An initial project using natural materials (willow, apple, cherry, or other straight-grained and pithless twigs) is the whammydiddle (lower right). It is essentially an axle carrying a plug propeller, with notches cut in a line to make a rack. A second stick is used to stroke the rack and cause prop rotation. Above it is a simple otter (courtesy Will Bondhus), made in straight-grained soft wood, which, with a little rounding, becomes a paper knife. At lower left are step-by-step figures of the author's Skipper Sam'l, and above them demonstration pieces for the chain, ball-in-a-cage and fan. At center is a monogram, showing basic V-cuts with a knife.

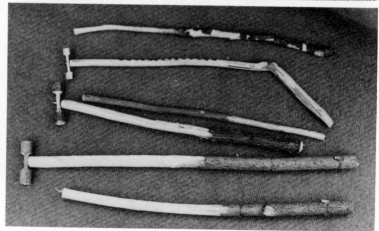

whole process. Following the Biblical injunction about the lost lamb can make difficulty in a woodcarving class!

Teaching woodcarving is more involved than teaching whittling, of course, both because more tools and techniques are involved, and because some form of table or bench and holding device is usually considered necessary. If projects are carefully selected, any sturdy bench or table will do, but as the work progresses in complexity, some form of holding device becomes necessary, requiring tables equipped at least with carpenter's vises and/or holes for woodcarving screws.

For figures and busts, the woodcarver's screw is helpful, however. This suggests use of a manual arts room in a local school, although the usual benches with undercabinets become a nuisance after a time because your knees keep bumping the base. Some teachers have designed their own benches and tables, some of which are somewhat portable, with detachable legs, so they can be moved to different teaching sites. But it is possible—by selecting projects carefully, as I said earlier—to avoid many of these problems. A $^3/_4 \times 4 \times 12$-inch board can be nailed or held with double-sided adhesive tape to a bench, for example, and a small figure blank can be nailed or glued temporarily to a base which in turn can be fastened to the bench. A board as large as $^3/_4 \times 12 \times 12$ inches usually has enough surface that friction will hold it stable under ordinary circumstances.

For woodcarving, it is usually advisable to provide tools, rather than to rely on what the student can bring. I have usually provided standard commercial tools, then sold them to interested students at the end of the course. This procedure requires selection of projects to suit available tools, and the instructor must be willing to undertake the necessary sharpening of new tools, an onerous chore when a large number of tools is involved. For a class of six or seven, I provide a dozen tools: six $^1/_2$-inch firmers (carpenter's chisels are cheaper), a veiner, two $^1/_4$-inch flat gouges, two $^1/_2$-inch half-round gouges, and a $^1/_4$-inch half-round gouge. I add from my own set another dozen or so tools, including the seventh $^1/_2$ inch firmer, a V-tool, some spoon gouges of various sizes and shapes, $^1/_8$ and $^1/_4$-inch firmers, etc., as the projects may require. I have two or three mallets of the proper size, but encourage students to whittle their own from a 2×2-inch slab until they determine which size and weight they want. Some instructors I know have unique methods of providing tools to beginners—several make their own, sometimes from files, old sawblades, or even umbrella stays.

In addition to the formal tools, it is also necessary to provide abrasive stones and slips of various sizes, both for demonstration and for practice, drawing tools such as dividers, triangles and squares—even proportioning dividers, calipers and other such sophisticated equipment on occasion. Common woodworking tools such as chisels, saws and planes may be found necessary—again depending upon projects—as well as a scratch awl, breast drill and bits, carbon paper, riffler files, rasps, sandpaper and any necessary hardware, like brads (to copy designs). Other aids may well include photographs and/or slides of whittling and woodcarving projects, reference books and illustrations, ranging from the ultrasimple to the sophisticated (a little inspiration doesn't hurt), and from traditional folk art to historical museum pieces. If the teacher does not have such material, it can be purchased from museums and art stores, or found in art books and the like. And always an appropriate stock of adhesive bandages.

Incidentally, to cover the cost of materials, we usually charge a $5 fee, which takes care of two or three blanks—such as a dog, a Skipper Sam'l and a nameplate (whammydiddle materials are available for the collecting in most areas), plus a beginner's whittling knife for the whittling course. Such a knife retails for about $1.75. In some cases, we have added a copy of my first—and most basic—book, *Whittling and Woodcarving*, which can be purchased in quantity for something over a dollar.

In teaching a group, particularly a larger one, a blackboard or several large sketches will be helpful to reinforce the demonstration and discussion. I have used both charts and the board; the board has greater flexibility, but it does take time to make the sketches as they are needed, and eventually, some sketches must be erased to make way for others. Some instructors provide mimeographed or offset copies of such sketches to students.

Many teachers will also have individual students or small groups for pay. This is a totally different situation; it should presume that the student has particular interest and that the teacher can then proceed at a pace and in the direction that the particular situation requires.

✳ A Basic Instruction Sheet for the Knife:

Selection, Use and Care

When I learned that my "small class of parents and children" had bulged to twenty-five people a while back, I decided that I needed some sort of take-away teacher's aid, so produced this two-sided sheet of typical knife cuts. It proved so useful and popular that I have used it since, even though classes were smaller. It has proved helpful in assigning "homework"—study of it is in fact "homework"—and has reiterated and put into more permanent form the remarks I make in introducing tyros to the knife as a tool.

I have checked the sheet with a number of people. H. M. Sutter of Portland, Oregon, contributed a specimen sheet he has used for a number of years; it shows three basic knife cuts, the same as those the late Ben Hunt suggested in his whittling book of 1944. Later, in his 1961 edition, Ben dropped the guided cut, which both Mr. Sutter and I feel was a mistake, particularly in instructing beginners.

In my own first book, *Whittling and Woodcarving*, in 1936, I mentioned four "grips" for the knife, corresponding to the pointing, drawing, slicing and thumb-pushing sketches in my current chart. I also wrote of

eight cutting actions or strokes: straight, sweep, stop or outline, chisel, scraping, tip, saw and rocking. These are mostly self-explanatory from the names.

I believe the usual whittler is basically a craftsman; hence he has some skill with tools. Thus he will instinctively use a knife correctly. Women, with their experience at paring fruit and vegetables, are much better trained at the paring cut than are men—the most important single cut in figure carving. (But many expect the wood to act like a vegetable and are a bit surprised at its greater resistance and lesser tractability.) Women in general have greater finger dexterity than men, but men have greater arm control and so do much better with the heavier cuts. (They also usually handle the mallet better than women for this reason, but there are notable exceptions.) In either case, even the tyros among adults seem to learn rapidly how to handle a knife well enough to avoid cutting themselves and to use an appropriate cut in a particular situation. However, so many people are being taught whittling in short courses these days that this condensed instruction manual may be of help to others.

One added note for beginning carvers: It may be advisable to put an adhesive bandage, glove finger or rubber fingertip (from office supply stores) over the ball of the right thumb, and possibly a bandage or glove finger on the middle joint of the right index finger (this one to avoid blisters) for a time. Some beginners have even worn a left glove with considerable success. (If I had, I might have avoided my first whittling scar on my left forefinger, acquired over sixty years ago.)

Many beginners have an instinctive fear of cutting themselves, and some have been taught never to cut toward themselves. Both of these must be countered by sane advice and demonstration, reiterated whenever you note someone holding back from fear. Everybody cuts himself at one time or another; I recently was the first as I began a new class. Students believed I had done it with intent to ease their fears; I only wish it were so! In any case, the use of adhesive bandages will decline rapidly after the first session in which actual finished wood is cut; for some reason, whammydiddle whittling does not seem to lead to cuts.

The Basic Cuts

THUMB CARVING -- Rest the thumb on the block of wood and pull the blade toward the thumb by squeezing the fist. Illustration "B" By keeping the thumb rigid the blade should barely touch the thumb when the cut is complete. In case of doubt place a piece of adhesive tape around the thumb. Since this method offers the greatest control use it whenever possible.

GUIDED CARVING -- This requires a little practice but is not difficult. Place the back of the blade on the tip of the thumb of the opposite hand and push or rotate the blade through the piece of wood. See Illustration "C" This method is necessary when you cant reach to cut by thumb carving.

CHIPPING -- The important things to do in chipping are keep the slant of the blade the same when cutting from both sides and cut the piece of wood entirely free -- dont pop or break it loose. Illustration "D" It is usually easier to make a series of light cuts on the same line.

"B"

"C"

"D"

Excerpted from a notebook-sized sheet issued to Boy Scouts by H. M. Sutter, these are the three basic cuts in carving with the knife. With them alone, a youngster can produce things like neckerchief slides and simple shapes, but I feel that more cuts are necessary for complete versatility.

POINTING CUT
No control - hence danger.
Force from arm muscles

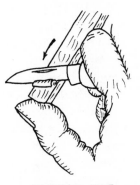

PARING CUT
Good cut control - watch thumb!
Force from hand clenching

Hand may be turned over

DRAW CUT
Poor control - tends to
follow grain. Arm force

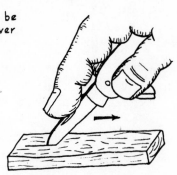

SLICING CUT
Close control - may tend
to follow grain. Arm force

← OR →

THUMB PUSH
Short cuts - greater pressure
Close control - Arm force

ROCKING CUT
Chip carving - good
across grain - Arm force

4th + 3rd fingers
guide on surface

CHAMFER or CURL CUT
Close control - must cut _with_
grain. Arm rotation + force

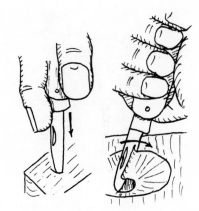

STAB or DRILL CUT
Series of hand pushes.
Danger of blade closing

HOLLOW CUT
Tip cuts concave.
Watch grain!!!

TYPICAL KNIFE CUTS ··· ONE HAND↑ and TWO HANDS↓

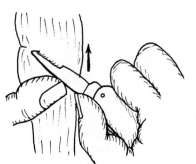

LEFT-THUMB ASSIST
Close control - more force
Short, precise cuts or shaving

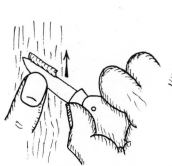

LEFT INDEX-FINGER ASSIST
Shaving cuts. Work must be
clamped or held by left hand

LEFT-INDEX DRAW CUT
Shaving + detailing. Gives
close control with more force

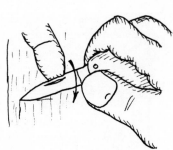

GUILLOTINE CUT
Adds force at blade tip.
Left index finger - or thumb push

The Knife—Select knives to suit your project or location. A pocketknife is more portable, but less safe, than a fixed-blade one. I carry two pocketknives, one regular size, one a penknife, each with two blades, the smaller one pen shape, the larger B-clip (see sketches). Thus I have both small and large blades, wide and narrow, short- or long-pointed. Blades are carbon steel rather than stainless; they hold an edge better and longer, but corrode if not kept oiled. Knife can be $10 or more. For heavy cutting at home, I use a fixed-blade knife with larger handle; it's safer and easier to grip. (A cork over the tip makes it transportable.) For tiny detail, a small disposable-blade knife with pointed blades is useful, but blades are over-thin and the screw chuck has a habit of releasing and letting the blade swivel at inopportune moments. For most work, a 1½ in. blade is long enough. Blade width is important: The wider the blade the larger the surface resting on the wood, stabilizing the blade and giving a straighter cut. The narrower the blade, the less the support and the greater the control needed, but the greater the ease of carving concave surfaces and in limited areas. Beware of knives that do not open and close securely or that allow the blade to wobble sidewise, or that have blister-causing crevices or corkscrews, too many blades or too-rigid finger impressions.

Keep the knife sharp, so excessive force is not required to cut with it, and so the blade cuts cleanly instead of tearing the wood fibers. Good steel, properly sharpened, will hold its edge for a day or two in constant cutting of soft woods, but may need a touchup after an hour or two on hard woods. It's best to carry a small, fine-grained stone in a case for touchup, even a strop (leather, mounted on a wood block and oiled) for a really keen edge for finishing; a good whittler usually has edges he can shave with.

A knife is an edged tool and is therefore worthy of utmost respect. Momentary loss of attention—from fatigue, carelessness, watching TV, conversing—can cause trouble. Never put anything in front of the blade that you don't expect to cut. Beware of sticking the blade tip into the wood tightly; the blade may close on your fingers. Also, keep your hand out of the way when you close a blade. Never open two blades at once. Watch the heel of the blade; a finger that slips forward onto it may get a nasty cut. The "boss" on a folding blade helps avoid this; it also protects the handle from abrasives.

Don't hammer the blade back to drive it in unless the blade is a sloyd made for such treatment. Never sharpen on a wheel, unless you are removing nicks or reshaping; then cool the blade twice as frequently as you think necessary to prevent burning. Don't use the blade to pry, and don't apply sidewise pressure. *Don't* pare fingernails, cut paper or cardboard, fiber tapes, wire, or scrape with a good blade; that takes the edge off faster than whittling. Cutting newly sanded areas is also hard on a honed edge. Last, a little oil on blades, pivots and springs is a help. Pockets and hands are sweaty, and sweat corrodes.

Using the Knife—Adjust chip size to wood and grain and design. Large chips can be cut in soft wood, particularly with the grain, but may tear out the end, cause splits, or "run" with the grain. The harder and grainier the wood, the smaller the chip. Reduce chip size as you approach finishing. Don't try to finish details in an area until you finish adjacent ones; if the knife slips, there's no wood left to correct a gash. *Cut* chips loose; don't try to pry them out. Wedging may break the blade tip, split the wood or cause dents and bruises on adjacent edges used as fulcrums.

In cutting a slot of V-groove, make a center stop-cut first, then angle to it from each side. Cut *with* the grain at all times, if possible; counter–grain angle cutting causes splits unless your knife is razor-sharp. Cutting across grain is always harder and slower than with-grain cutting and is likely to make trouble because of the increased pressure. Therefore, make across-grain cuts before adjacent with-grain ones to avoid splitting and overruns. A pointed blade can be used to drill a hole by rotating it, but it tends to tear across-grain edges and there is danger of breaking the knife tip. If you cut accurately and cleanly, and remove feathers and splinters as you should, sanding should be unnecessary; it blurs sharp outlines and "smears" the surface. Use worn sandpaper lightly, if you must sand.

✳ Pointers on Sharpening and Mallets:

A Roundup of Suggestions

"... and he that cleaveth wood shall be endangered thereby. If the iron be blunt, and he do not whet the edge, then must he put to more strength...." (Ecclesiastes 10: 9 and 10.)

Tool sharpening has always "bugged" carvers, but the recent tricks credited with solving the problem make traditionalists shudder, because they involve buffing or lapping wheels, emery cloth, fluid abrasives, flexible hones and the like. I have been impressed particularly by the number of carvers who hold an edge on knife and/or chisels by buffing or even sanding on old paper, and by specially built power-operated hones, some with emery-charged maple disks with peripheral grooves matching the shapes of various gouges. If you're in a hurry—and who isn't when sharpening is involved?—these devices save considerable time. Here is a roundup from conversation and correspondence:

Bill Higginbotham, Camarillo, California, uses a paddle of $^1/_4$- or $^3/_8$-inch wood, $1^1/_2$ inches wide and 11 inches long, with a $4^1/_2$-inch handle whittled at one end. He faces the rest with $1^1/_2 \times 6$-inch strips of 8- or 9-ounce belt leather or heavy suede, roughening the smooth face of the leather so it will hold to the paddle with contact cement. The handle end of the leather is beveled, then the rough leather surfaces are coated with any of these lubricants: petroleum jelly (Vaseline), lanolin, graphite grease, fine-grinding compound,

My mallets include two heavy cocobola ones (rear row, left) and two lighter maple ones of the conventional "potato-masher" shape. In the front row are the three small mallets sketched on the next page.

lamb fat, or any other greasy substance that will remain pliable. (Lamb fat is less desirable than some of the others because it may become rancid and must be heated so it will soak in.)

One greasy surface is coated with No. 400 Carborundum dust, sprinkled on and spread evenly by stropping with a knife. The opposite face has a similar coating of jeweler's rouge. A small amount of fine machine oil or mineral oil will ease the spreading. (When stropping to spread the dust or rouge, the knife blade is laid flat on the strop and moved heel first to avoid rounding its cutting edge.) To use the strop, hone as a barber strops his razor, first on the Carborundum side, then on the rouge side. Stropping should be fairly frequent to maintain a sharp edge.

Andy Burt, Tucson, Arizona, says he has a complete selection of stones, hones and slips, but has always had trouble sharpening, particularly V-tools. His criterion is, of course, an edge that he can shave with. In the past year or so, he has "stumbled onto" a technique that really works for everything, as long as you can get to both sides of the blade. He starts with a cheap two-grit manufactured stone with medium- and fine-grit sides. He gets the shape of edge he wants, then strops on a leather strop charged with rouge or a fine valve-grinding compound to get rid of the feather edge. He says, "This is quite visual, and usually a few strokes do it." Then he has a *loose* buffing wheel on his bench grinder (*not* a sewn wheel), charged with the white chalk compound used commercially for polishing stainless steel. (He has tried tripoli, rouge and other buffing compounds, but likes the chalk better than any.) Says he: "Buffing the tool away from the cutting edge gives it the most beautiful edge I've ever been able to get—the V-tools in particular. The loose-flapped wheel gets into every cranny of the tool." He tests by taking a cut or two across whatever wood he is carving; if any part of the edge "drags," it's back to the buffing wheel for a few seconds.

Fred Latimer, McGraw, New York, reports: "The Japanese wood-block artists held all chisels on the stone the way we would a gouge—from the side. Place the bevel flat on

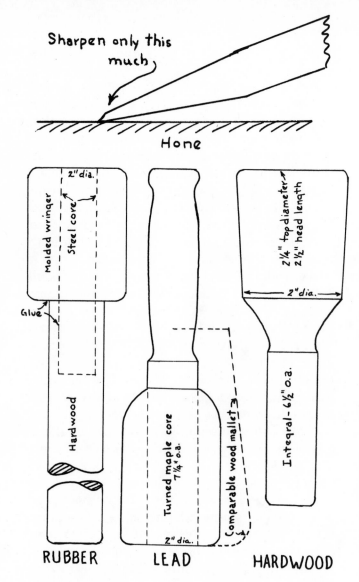

Sharpen only this much

Hone

Molded wringer
Steel core
2" dia.
Hardwood
Glue

RUBBER

Turned maple core
7¼" o.a.
2" dia.

LEAD

Comparable wood mallet

2¼" top diameter
2½" head length
2" dia.
Integral—6½" o.a.

HARDWOOD

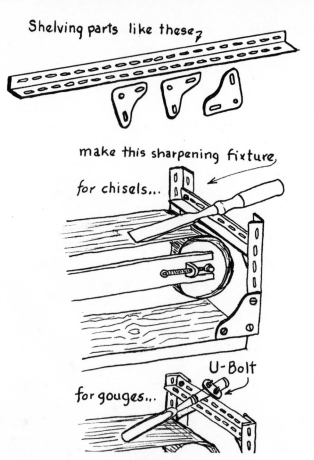

Shelving parts like these

make this sharpening fixture,

for chisels...

for gouges...

U-Bolt

Top left—How J. C. Stanfield gets a tool to hold an edge. Right—Dr. Knapp's fixture for honing is made of shelving parts. Left—Three small mallets, the upper two as heavy as a bulky "potato masher," yet much smaller in diameter, and the third for light and finishing cuts.

the stone and push left to right. The bevel is reshaped or sharpened quicker and to the sharpest possible edge. This works with parting tools as well. For stropping, I use a cloth buffing wheel and jeweler's rouge on an electric drill."

Dr. Bill Knapp, Flint, Michigan, finally bought a belt sander of the type used by lapidaries. He built a "fence" or fixture on the end of the belt (see sketches) from metal-shelving parts bought at Sears. The tool is placed on the belt with the handle resting on the fence, and moved forward or backward to attain the desired bevel. When this is achieved, a file mark is made on the handle where it rests on the fence, so it can be reset the same way for future sharpenings. He gives gouges a steeper angle by adding a rail or resetting the rail higher from the belt. Because the gouge must be rotated, he puts a U-bolt at the file mark to position the tool properly. He does final honing with a buffing wheel and compound.

Writes J. C. Stanfield, Annandale, Virginia: "The basic problem is usually too coarse a stone. I seldom use anything coarser than a barber's hone and an Arkansas stone. A second primary fault is trying to sharpen the entire bevel of the tool rather than just the cutting edge. As a result, the bevel is slightly rounded, and a true edge is never obtained. *Only the final 1/64 or 1/32 inch of the edge need be sharpened* (see sketch). You are usually at the correct angle when the edge picks up a film of oil from the stone as you stroke.

"If the tool is new or nicked, start with a bench grinder and fine wheel. Use slips *only* on the inside of gouges; never a coarser stone, to remove the wire edge from time to time. Next use a razor stone (a barber's hone) for smooth honing, with the slips to take off the wire edge as before. I have a bench grinder with 3¼ × 7-inch spiral-sewn muslin buffing wheel and jeweler's rouge for stropping. On V-tools, the bottom corner must be rounded off slightly, both in grinding and honing, to eliminate the hook that otherwise develops where the two cutting edges join. The slip must also be the correct shape to fit the inner surfaces, and excess pressure on either side

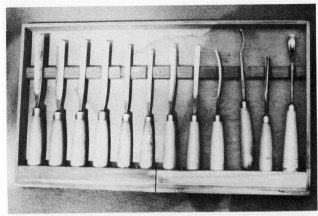

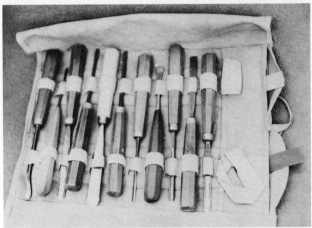

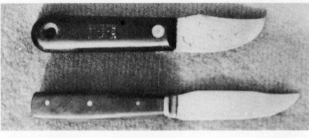

Top—One way to store tools—in drawers by type and size. The cabinet can be provided with drying packets, and tools selected to suit the job. Center—A heavy canvas roll with end pockets for slips makes a convenient carrying device for tools on trips. End flaps protect cutting edges. Above—Two heavy-duty carver's knives ground from putty knives. Handles are comfortable, the steel is good, and the knives are cheap—and shape can be whatever is desired. These were made by J. J. Phillip, Whittier, California, who warns of the danger of burning the steel by too rapid grinding.

must be avoided. Also, to save money, emery cloth can be used to replace the wide variety of stones that I have. By folding it, you can clean out V's; by wrapping it around a finger or doubling it, you can clean out gouges; and by laying it flat on a magazine or similar cushion, you can use it as a flat stone."

At the Columbus (Ohio) Chippers' Show, I was given an abrasive-impregnated rubber strip $3/8 \times 1 \times 6$ inch for honing tools. The giver explained that a swipe or two *away* from the cutting edge at regular intervals makes the usual stropping and honing unnecessary. In the limited time I've had in which to try it, it seems to work. It is available in coarse-, medium- and fine-grained sizes.

William Engel, Fairview Park, Ohio, carries two pocketknives, one a penknife and the other what used to be called a jackknife. The larger knife has three blades, a sheepfoot, a clip and a spey. The first two he has sharpened from one side only, one on one side, the other on the other. The resulting long bevel has a cutting action like that of a drawknife, but it *is* directional. Bill remembers that his carpenter-contractor father liked a long bevel on wood chisels and plane irons, and that he sharpened them with a figure-eight motion on the stone. To maintain even wear on the stone corners, he did some semicircular sharpening on each corner.

Through the years, I have developed that habit of using a light mallet rather than my hand to drive veiners, V-tools and small chisels generally. This gives me better control, more uniform cuts and no overruns or problems with knots or grain in harder woods, particularly when my bursitis is kicking up. Also I have fewer bruises and no heavy callous or lump in my right palm, which some carvers accept as an occupational hazard. The mallet I use is turned from hard wood, with a head roughly 2 inches in diameter by 3 inches long, and weighs 6 ounces. Easier to use than the conventional "potato-masher" mallet of cocobola or lignum vitae, which I use for roughing, is a lead or babbitt head. Chester Card presented me with a turned maple handle with a 2 × 3-inch lead head cast on it. This one weighs about $1^{1}/_{4}$ pounds. It is easier to maneuver than the larger wood one but is tiring if used for long periods.

H. M. Sutter, Portland, Oregon, sent me another kind of mallet devised by a friend: a $2^{3}/_{4}$-inch length of a 2-inch wringer from a washing machine, with the steel shaft set into a 6-inch length of broom handle or $1^{1}/_{8}$-inch dowel. The rubber surface gives bounce and is easy on tools and wrist, while the steel core gives weight and solidity to the blow. It weighs 13 ounces, as compared with 18 for my cocobola one, and takes a little getting used to, since the rubber causes the chisel to cut longer than you expect.

You might want to try some of these variations for yourself. On the other hand, I met a carver not long ago who uses a pneumatic impact hammer with his chisels, which gives him 3,000 blows a minute with, he says, excellent control. That's all of a piece with the chainsaw and dental-drill approach—which mechanizes what for most of us is a hobby. If it's the money you're after, mechanize.

❋ Every One a Masterpiece:

Five Examples of "Technical Acrobatics" from Museums

We all know whittlers who have made chains from matchsticks, pliers from toothpicks. I've been awed by Riemenschneider's and Donatello's carved faces, by Dürer's praying hands, by Gibbons's quaking foliage, by Mestrovic's powerful panels, intrigued by the Chinese nested spheres in ivory, the Balinese fisherman in ebony, the Indian screens in various woods. But these pieces, except for the ship model perhaps, each adds a touch of whimsy to the skill and imagination it takes to produce a masterpiece. They are a fitting group with which to close this book. Far left—Carved about 1895 by Jakob Abplanalp of Brienz, Switzerland, this life-sized rose, plus a butterfly with antennae, is from the same piece of pearwood as the back panel. (The frame is separate.) Abplanalp carved "several" of the roses; one in Grindelwald is supposedly even better than this one. The box below it was carved about 1890 by Andreas Bauman, also of Brienz, from maple and is about 7 in. square. Flowers are Edelweiss and Alpenrosen (a dwarf rhododendron), all carved from the solid. These are what Bauman's grandson (a teacher at the school there) calls "technical acrobatics carvings." Both are in the museum of the Kantonale Schnitzlerschule in Brienz. The model below them is the stern quarter of a French galleass in the Mariners Museum, Newport News, Va.
Left top—The Holy Magdalena, by Tilman Riemenschneider, now in the Bavarian National Museum, Munich (photo: Hirmer Fotoarchiv Munchen). According to legend, she prayed for a covering for her nudity. The figure, about lifesize, is known familiarly as the "hairy Madonna." Beneath it is a point-lace jabot 9 in. long, carved in limewood by Grinling Gibbons, once owned and worn by Horace Walpole, but now in the Victoria and Albert Museum, London. This, again, is a single piece.

[*Italic* numbers (*91*) indicate drawings, or frontal photos of low-relief subjects, that can be copied for patterns.]

Abplantalp, Jakob, carving of, 186
Aeolian harp, *14*
Africa, carvings from, 14, *55*, 60, *61*, 131, 144, *145*, 146, *147*
Alligator, *61* (crocodile); articulated, *123*
Alphorn, *12*
Amerindian designs, *41*, *119*
Angels, *2*, *32*, 150, *153*, 186
Animals, designs for, *58*, 60, *61*, *65*, 66, *67*, 68, *69*, 72, 73, *78*, 88, 94, *95*, *113*, 154, *155*, *171*
Antiquing of wood, 121
Anvil, carved, *25*
Apostles, carved, 137
Articulated toys, *37*
Assemblies, 84, *85*
Austria, carving of, 126, 127, 175
Averso, Joseph, carving by, 79

Baker, Winnie, carvings of, *162*, *163*
Balancing a carving, 48
Bali, carvings from, 68, *69*, 80
Balkan carving, *12*
Barometer, carving for, *92*
Barrettes, for hair, *30*
Bauman, Andreas, carving by, 186
Bear, climbing, 122, *123*
Bells, *3*, *12*
Bilboquet, *21*
Birds, designs for, *2*, *22*, 33, 53, *55*, *65*, 66, *67*, *69*, *71*, 72, 73, 74, 75, 76, *78*, 79, 82, *83*, 88, *89*, *92*, 93, 96, *113*, *171*
Boats, carved, 84, 186
Bola, *24*
Bolo, slides for, *111*
Bone, carving of, 96
Books, for carvers, 177
Boomerang, *20*
Breadboards, *171*, *173*
Butter molds, *5*
Butterfly toy, *13*, 20
Buttons, carved, 138, *139*

Caduceus, carving of, *111*
Cain, Rick, carving of, 149
Candlesticks, carved, *29*
Capiz shell, *4*
Caricatures, by Janel, 166–169
Carriages, silhouettes of, *26*
Carvings, finishing black, 62; for 4-color reproduction, 128; quantity, for cuckoo clocks, 78

Chair, carving of, 106, *107*
Chase, Chas G., carvings by, 74
Checkers, design for, *102*
Chess men, giant, 101-*103*
China, carvings from, 11, *20*, 66, *67*, 87
Chip carving, *8*, *12*
Christus, 138, *139*, 150, *153*
Circus, carved, 96
Clark, George, carving by, 149
Climbing bear, 122, *123*; monkey, 122, *123*
Clist, Edward, carving by, 79
Clocks, cuckoo, 77, *78*
Coach, stage, *28*; Wahington's, *28*
Coat of arms, *109*
Cockhorse, *24*
Cocle indians (Panama), designs of, 57, *58*
Compote dish, *29*
Cookie molds, *5*
Costa Rica, carvings from, 70, *71*, 94, *95*, 134, *136*, 142, *143*
Crocodiles, designs for, *61*
Crow call, *13*
Cuna indians (Panama), designs of, *55*

DeNike, Michael, carvings by, 149, *164*, *165*
Designing, 170
Desk, carvings for, 106-*107*
Detail, how much? 122
Dolls, designs for, *55*
Dolphin, *45*
Door, carved Spanish-Colonial, *43*
Dragon, *20*; komodo, 96
Drums, *13*
Duck, *79*

Eagle, carving of, *78*, *164*, 170, *173*
Ear, human, carving, *129*
Easter Island, carvings of, *113*
Ecuador, carving from, 131, 132, *133*
El Salvador, carving from, 98, *99*
England, carving from, *6*, *38*, 186
Enlarging patterns, 1
Equation of Time, 121
Escher, M.C., designs from, 88, *89*, *173*
Eskimo, carving depicting, 122, *123*
Eye, human, carving of, *129*; in fish, 48

Faces, human, 126–*129*, 131–*133*; racial, *128*, *129*
Fairy tales, carvings from, 154, *155*, 156, *163*

Feather, *34*
Fenner, Donald M., carvings by, *4*
Fetishes, Amerindian, 57, *58*
Figure, human, *85*, 86
Fiji, carving from, 140, *141*
Finishing on carvings, 70, 151
Fireboard, 88, *89*
Fish, carved, *2*, *32*, 84, *85*, *89*; tropical, *46*
Fisherman, *105*
Flute, *22*
Foliage, carved, 82, *83*
Furniture puzzle, *87*

Gazinta, *21*
Germany (West), carvings from, *36*, 66, *67*, 77, *78* 96, 124, 127, 150–*153*, 186
Gibbons, Grinling, carving by, 186
Gnomon, in sundial, 118
Gourds, carved, 96
Grain, allowing for, 46
Grasshopper, *33*
Graumann, Richard M., carvings by, *161*
Guatemala, carvings from, 57, *58*, 68, 104, *105*, 134, 135, *136*, 138, *139*, 140

Hair, how to carve, 124, 149, 186
Hawk, red-shouldered, 75
Head, human, design of, *99*, 104, *105*, 144, *145*
Head, human, 4-way, 174, 175; 12-way, 175
Headrest, African, *55*
Heron, green, 74
Honduras, carvings from, 104, *105*, 106, *107*, 140, *141*
Horn, carving of, 42
Horse, *32*, *171*; fetlock detail, 122; *123*; heads, *19*; Persian, *89*, *91*; winged, *89*, *91*
Human figure, design of, 72, 73, *99*, *113*, 124, 126, 131, 132, *133*, 138, 139, *140*, 144, *145*, 146, *147*, 150, *153*, *162*, *163*, 166–169

Idols, designs for, *58*, 110–*113*
Iguana, *69*
Images, carved, 110, 111, *113*
Improvisations, 97
India, carvings from, *22*
Indian, American, carvings from, *41*; design of cigar-store, 110, 111, 112, *113*; design for weathervane, *33*
Indonesia, carvings from, 66, *67* (see also Bali)

Inserts, of shell, 70
Instruments, musical, *12*
Intalgio carving, 88
Intarsia, *51*, 92
Italy, carvings from, *6*, 41, 87
Ivory, carvings of, 96, 124, 152

Jack-in-the-box, *20*
Janel, Emil, carvings by, 166–169
Janus, design for, *123*
Japan, carvings of, *67*, 81, *83*
Jewelbox, design for, *123*, 186

Karalus, B., carving by, 175
Knife, for chip carving, *8*; how to use, 180
Knots, designs for, *29*, *31*
Kubbe stol (Norwegian), *55*

Liberty, Statue of, *33*
Lithuania, carving of, 175
Llewellyn, Richard, 1
Lougesy, Don W., carvings by, *29*
Love spoons, *38*, 96

Madonna, stylized, 140
Maggioni, Gilbert, carvings by, 75
Magi, *2*, 150, *153*
Makonde carving, 146, *147*, 148
Mallets, use of, 183
Maori designs, *51*, *113*
Masks, *58*, 59, 138, *139*, 144, 146, *147*
Maya motifs, 98, *99*, 104, *105*, 106, *107*
Maya, woodcarving by, 104
McCoy, Grainger, carvings by, 75
Mermaid, *38*, *45*
Mestrovich, Ivan, 1
Mexico, carving from, *3*, *5*, *10*, *12*, *28*, 41, *43*, *69*, 70, 124, 142, *143*
Michaelangelo, Buonarrotti, 1
Miniatures, of people, 94, *95*
Minotaur, 63, *65*
Moais (Easter Island), *113*
Mobile, *17*, *46*; to assemble, 50; types of, 50
Molds, butter, *5*; cookie, *5*
Monk, design for, *140*
Monkey, *71*; rope-climbing, 122, *123*; the three, 81, *83*
Mottoes, for sundials, 120
Mouth, human, carving of, *129*
Multipart carvings, 84, *85*

Netsuke, *67*
New Guinea, carving of, *113*
Nicaragua, carvings from, 106, *107*, 108

Nichols, Laurie, carvings of, *95*, 97
Noah's Ark, 72, 73
Norway, carvings from, 60, *61*, 80
Noses, human, carving of, *129*

Oak, carved leaves, *78*
Ornaments, Christmas, *2*
Otter, sea, 95, 97
Owl, snowy, 74
Oyster, articulated, *25*

Paddle, canoe, *58*, 59
Panama, designs of, *55*, *58*
Panels, carved, 80, 81, 83, 104, *105*, 106, *107*, 134, 135, *136*, *161*, *162*, *163*; pierced, 81, 82, *83*; tandem, 157, *159*
Panels, designed from fairy tales, *109*, *163*
Penguin, 20
Pennsylvania-Dutch carvings, *6*, *8*
Peru, carving from, 41
Philippine Islands, carving from, 80
Pied Piper, 151, 152, *153*, 157, *159*, *163*; in ivory, 67
Pig, *35*
Pipe rack, *8*
Pipes, shepherd's, *12*
Plow, *35*
Poland, carving from, 126, 127
Polynesian figures, 111–*114*
Ponapé, carving from, *69*
Pony, *2*; head of, *19*

Popgun, *17*, *21*
Portugal, carving from, *41*
Prairie schooner, *28*
Propellers, *32*
Properties, for stage use, *25*
Puzzles, wood, *17*, *87*
Pyrography, on bird feathers, 74, 79

Questions people ask, 79
Quixote, Don, 98, *99*, *133*, *136*

Rack, pipe, *8*; spoon, *173*
Reducing patterns, 1
Religious figures, *80*, 150, *153*
Riemenschneider, Tilman, carving of, 186
Ring, napkin, 94, *95*
Rose, one-piece carving, 186
Rosewood, carving of, *52*, 94, 124

Scandinavia, carving from, *6*, 40, *55*
Scoops, small, *29*
Scrimshaw, *96*
Sharpening of tools, 183
Shell inserts, 70, 97
Ship carved model of, 186
Shoes, carved, 109
Sicily, carvings from, *6*, *28*, 142
Signs, *35*, *36*
Silhouette, in carving, 51; of carriages, *26*
Simplicity, in design, importance of, 98
Sky hook, *24*

Snakes, designs for, *61*
Snowmen, *2*
Spain, carving from, 131, *133*
Spools, in carving, *22*
Spoon rack, *173*
Squares, method of, 90
Stars, *2*
Stools, designs for, 54, *55*
Stylizing, 108, 125, 126, 134–*136*, 137, 165
Sundials, 115–121
Sweden, carving from, 96
Switzerland, carving from, *12*, 80, 150, *153*, 186
Swordfish, *33*
Sycamore, carved leaves of, *78*
Symbols, for saints, 137

Tahiti, designs from, *113*
Tanagram puzzle, *17*
Tandem panels, 157–*159*
Tangerman, E. J., carvings by, 5, 8, 9, 10, 14, 16, 18, 19, 20, 22, 25, 26, 32, 38, 46, 51, 52, 63, 64, 72, 73, 77, 80, 84, 86, 87, 88, 91, 93, 96, 97, 101, 109, 110, 111, 115, 116, 118, 122, 124, 125, 128, 154, 156, 157, 170, 171, 175, 179
Teaching, 178; designs for, *178*; books for, 177
Teak, for sundials, 115
Temple, Maya, *123*
Thailand, carvings from, *12*, 94, 95
Thumb piano, 14
Tiki, 110, *113*
Toast tongs, *11*

Tongue depressers, for toys, 12, 18
Tools, 48, 62, 185
Tops, for bottles, 170, *173*
Totem pole, *113*
Toys, *12*, *16*, 122, *125*
Tramp carving, *8*
Trobriand Island carving, 69
Turkey call, *13*
Tyrol, carvings from, *41*

USSR, carvings from, 5, 20, 80, 94, *95*, 124

Vanes, weather, *32*
Viking, head of, *55*
Vinci, Leonardo da, 1

Wales, spoons from, *38*
Weathervanes, *32*
Whales, carving of, 34, *44*, *46*, *164*
Whammydiddle, 178
Wind harp, *15*
Windmill, *32*
Wood, zebra, 52
Woodcarver, carving of, 151, *153*
Woods, protection against rotting, 112
Woods, selection of, 62; variety in carving, *46*;
Woods, special for birds, 76

Yo-yo, *21*

Zadkine, Ossip, carvings by, 126, 137